MW00529232

# Keep On Cookin'

## A Celebration of Life Through Cooking

**All proceeds from this collection of mouthwatering recipes
will be used to develop solutions to homelessness**

By Chef Cardie Mortimer

Design by Maria Maka

Copyright © 2020, Cardie Mortimer

All rights reserved. Any unauthorized reprint or use of this material is prohibited. No recipes in this publication may be reproduced, distributed, or transmitted in any form or by any means, electronic or mechanical, including photocopying or other electronic or mechanical methods, without the prior written permission of the publisher, except in the case of brief quotations embodied in critical reviews and certain other noncommercial uses permitted by copyright law. For permission requests, write to the publisher, addressed "Attention: Permissions Coordinator," at cards4u1012@aol.com.

This work is written from the memories of the author and his perspective and the assistance from co-collaborators. Any references to real people and establishments are used with the permission of the entities involved.

Recipes are written to the author's preference and are to be used as guidelines for the reader. Cardie Mortimer makes every attempt to identify and specify all ingredients in recipes. It is then the reader/ cook's responsibility to know their own needs and be mindful of food sensitivities, allergies, and the potential risk of contamination.

ISBN: 978-0-578-62734-2 (Hardcover)

Title: Keep On Cookin': A Celebration of Life Through Cooking

Author: Cardie Mortimer

Front cover image: Cardie Mortimer

Book design: Maria Maka

Forewords: Melanie Cordell and Norman J. Scherzer

Stock background images courtesy of the free use commercial-use databases, Canva and Pixabay.

Photographs owned by Cardie Mortimer with exceptions on pages 37, 77, 117, 241, 255, 257, and 265.

Pictured on front cover, clockwise from top right: Napoleons with Velouté Sauce (recipe page 217), Grilled Shrimp, Salmon, and Scallop Seafood Salad with Blackberries (recipe page 57), Grilled Cherrystone Clams in Champagne (recipe with alternate image page 37), Oven-Baked Portuguese Citrus and Garlic Shrimp with Yellow Rice (recipe page 203), Marinated, Buttermilk Grilled Chicken Thighs with Garlic, Honey, and Raspberry Puree (recipe page 149), and Slow-Cooked Beef Short Ribs in Tawny Port (recipe page 221).

Printed by Cardie Mortimer in the United States of America.

First print edition 2020

# My Dedication

Many of us share the sentiment that our mothers are the best cooks on the face of the Earth and I wholeheartedly agree! For this reason, I dedicate this cookbook to my mother, Elisabeth Smith Mortimer, who sadly passed away from breast cancer at the tender age of 71 in 1997. In addition to teaching me how to cook, she also taught me how to enjoy and love the life that we have been given. Mom, I am so indebted to you for all of your "true love." You continue to inspire me every day. I hope that I have made you proud along the way and I pray that one day I will be reunited in Heaven with the best cook and mom a son could possibly ask for! You will always and forever be my guardian angel!

From Your Most Loving and Grateful Son,

Cardie

# Table of Contents

# Table of Contents

# Table of Contents

# Table of Contents

**Mains (Continued)**

# Foreword I

I always knew I wanted to make a difference, but as a kid, I wasn't sure what that would look like until my first mission trip to inner city St. Louis. I was twelve years old when my youth group taught vacation Bible school to poor children who were either living on the streets or "doubled up" in tiny apartments. I'll never forget walking in a parade, dressed as a clown, and giving a 5-year-old African American girl with pigtails some candy. My heart exploded with joy when she smiled. We walked together, hand in hand, for the rest of the parade and were best friends from then on.

Over the next four years, I was blessed to participate in three more mission trips, experiences that helped shape who I am today. When I was 16 years old, my parents got divorced. I moved two hours away from my hometown, and I felt like my life was over. I couldn't find a church like "my" church. I had a hard time making new friends and all I wanted to do was remember my life in Panama City. A year went by, and I felt like I had lost all hope. My family was disengaged, my mom worked all the time, and my sister left home soon after we turned 17. My faith and connection to a church gave me a sense of identity. When I couldn't find that same connection in this new city, I was miserable. I met a guy, started partying, and ended up homeless three months before my high school graduation. When my family moved to south Florida, I stayed behind, determined to finish high school. I moved in with my boyfriend's family, sleeping on their couch with my belongings in a suitcase whenever I could. Sometimes I slept outside, worried about my safety and my next meal, wondering how I would get a ride to school and work.

Our experiences in life make us who we are. It's like molding a piece of clay into a coffee mug. There are several steps to get to the final version of that mug. During these hard times, I felt angry, questioning why, yet knowing something better was in store for me. This feeling was in my gut, you know? I moved to Knoxville, Tennessee and began working at a domestic violence shelter. Wow! Was this meant to be, or what? During my tenure, I expanded the emergency shelter from eight beds to 32 beds and added seven transitional housing apartments. In 2010, I became the director of the Tennessee Valley Coalition for the Homeless (TVCH). Boy, was this a huge honor! I was 32 years old and scared to death, thinking strategically about how to end homelessness in a 12-county area. Eight years later, another board member introduced me to Chef Cardie Mortimer after meeting him on a trip they both happened to be taking. Miracles really do happen! Rick Garner, a retired veteran and board member of TVCH, created a Chef Dinner fundraiser to benefit homeless veterans in June 2019.

I hadn't met anyone with a heart as big as mine until I met Chef Cardie. At this moment, I knew we were going to be friends forever. Chef Cardie had been praying about doing something to help people who were homeless, especially homeless veterans. I didn't know, until the fundraiser, that he shares a special connection with the homeless population.

Chef Cardie prepared a four-course, Louisiana Cajun meal. As he prepared the gourmet meal in East Tennessee, mind you, hundreds of miles away from his home in New Jersey, I witnessed him leading a team of cooks and volunteers and praising and thanking everyone for their help. I kept thinking, "Wow, this man has come all this way to give back." I had never met someone willing to spend countless hours planning a meal, ordering shrimp from Louisiana, and handling the logistics of kitchen space and food delivery ahead of his flight, to cook a gourmet meal for 70 people, all to help homeless veterans. That's heart!

When Chef Cardie starting cooking and plating the meal, everyone quickly recognized his passion and talents. Watching him work, you could tell he had worked alongside the best of the best, with chefs like Emeril Lagasse, Paul Prudhomme, Kevin Belton, Sean Roe, and Robert Irvine, just to name a few. The Cajun barbecue shrimp and the jambalaya had just enough spices and flavors to make you believe you're sitting at a table for two in an authentic Louisiana restaurant. I don't know if you're like me, but presentation is everything. I want to see how the food is plated. That lets me know how much the chef cares about the way his food is delivered. Chef Cardie exceeded all of my expectations. As each course was delivered to my seat, all I could do was stare in awe of how the colors of the food matched with the smells of the spices, how each course built upon the next. I couldn't help but dig in. I wanted to lick the plate clean and the only thing that stopped me was how I had to be professional because this fundraiser was for my organization. Just writing this is making my mouth water.

As we ate our dessert, Chef Cardie shared a story about a man named Charlie, who lived on the streets in New York City. Over time, Chef Cardie and Charlie became friends. One day, Cardie was heading to work and saw police near the area where Charlie usually slept. His heart dropped when he realized that Charlie had passed away. He found out that Charlie had frozen to death. This infuriated him, so he made it his life's mission to ensure that no one would freeze on the streets of New York again. He purchased hundreds of mittens, scarfs, and hats and began handing them out. On the night of our fundraiser, Cardie presented TVCH with a check in honor of Charlie. This money will go toward helping people stay warm during the winter months. Charlie's Fund has been established so that TVCH can carry out Chef Cardie's wishes.

If you've picked up this book, then you may be standing where I was twenty years ago, confused, wondering what direction you should take. Maybe you're wrestling with a dream that just won't let you go. Maybe you've dipped your toe into running your own kitchen and now you're ready to dive in headfirst. Maybe you're looking for a way to give back and by purchasing this book, you'll take part in helping someone get off the streets. Maybe you've got the passion and the dream of being a culinary or gourmet chef but only want to cook for family and friends. Well, I've got good news, this cookbook is a steppingstone along your journey to get you to your destination!

As you get ready to take the next step in your culinary journey, I want you to hear something loud and clear: You can do this. You've got this! I can make this promise to you: Chef Cardie has your back. As you read through these pages, you'll be encouraged, motivated, challenged, taught, and ultimately, set loose to make delicious meals. That's what Chef Cardie does, and that's what *Keep on Cookin'* is all about.

My deepest gratitude to Chef Cardie and his team for donating all proceeds of the sale of this book to end homelessness!


Your friend,
Melanie Cordell, CEO
Tennessee Valley Coalition for the Homeless


PS: On September 24, 2019, at 3:30 pm, we officially ended veteran homelessness in 12 counties of East Tennessee!!!!!

# Foreword II

At first I was puzzled when Chef Cardie asked me to write a forward for his new cookbook, "Keep On Cookin." I am hardly a good cook and certainly do not consider myself a cooking critic or gourmet.

But I get the connection.

The mission of the cancer support group that I head, the Life Raft Group, is to give patients with a rare cancer called GIST (Gastrointestinal Stromal Tumor), gifts of quality life and that is what Chef Cardie does with his cooking. Most of us remember when we were not feeling well as kids, our moms bringing us comfort food. I remember mine was hot chocolate pudding served still in the pot with a big spoon. Or chicken noodle soup, which my culture often referred to as "Jewish penicillin." Whatever the dish, it was cooked from the heart and served with love. And it made one feel better.

And that is what Chef Cardie does. He makes people feel better. Drawing from multiple cultures and most importantly, from his heart, he has showered us with countless comfort foods made with the gourmet touch of a master chef. His main secret ingredient is love, the love of a man who wants his readers to be happy.

So, somehow, he has created a connection between my Jewish chicken soup background and his combination of Cajun, Creole, and Southern cooking teased with classic French. And he has created a connection with me that simply made my heart sing.

Enjoy

Norman J. Scherzer
Executive Director, the Life Raft Group

# PREFACE

Happiness is therapy. That is why I am here. That is why I am writing this cookbook.

This cookbook represents the finest of my life's passion contained in my favorite recipes which have evolved to include the tastes from different kitchens as well as my life experiences. They are to be enjoyed by everyone. Whether it is for a casual family dinner, a special occasion, or to serve a hurting friend, these recipes will be very useful. It is not a themed cookbook or one with unique concoctions (and heaven knows it is not for dieters). Instead, these are the recipes for dishes I have reminisced about with roommates in hospitals, meals that remind me of loved ones, entrees provided for people in need, plates which opened the eyes of others, and delectable salads (not just for the dieting loved ones among us). It is an emotional cookbook that reflects me and hopefully helps you find your own zest for life.

"Keep on Cookin'" has been a work in progress for over five years but my yearning to share what I lovingly create was reawakened during my recent culinary travels. They helped me remember that this is not just a hobby, it is what makes me, me. It sounds redundant, but I need to share all of this with you. I thrive off of seeing the smiles of people when they savor my cuisines at a service event or a demonstration. Witnessing someone discover (or rediscover), their love for food is a profound honor and privilege. Relaying our cherished stories to others strengthens memories and develops lifetime bonds. We remember when others provide us with a delicious meal and we remember when we are given the opportunity to make someone else's day with a "slice" of our culinary creations. Food holds the power to unite us and it is therapeutic for everyone involved. It gave me my life back during some very difficult times and I have faith in its ability to do the same for others. I have faith in its ability to reach you.

My parents continually inspired me and the upbringing they provided allowed me to find my proper place in this world. I can speak all I like about my ideals and sharing joy, but my family lived by the idiom, "actions speak louder than words." Therefore, through this cookbook, I present to you a piece of my heart and soul. To better see what words cannot possibly convey, I welcome you to search "Culinary Therapy: Neighborhood Journal" on YouTube.

## Hooray!

My wonderful mother was the first person to encourage me to cook. She enrolled me in Tulane University's summer cooking school in the late 1970's despite it not yet being considered a "career building" pursuit. I continued to attend for three consecutive summers and graduated with a diploma from what is now the prestigious, New Orleans French Culinary Institute. It is my personal quest to replicate the love, the joy, and the comforts my family and culinary teachers instilled in me 40 years ago. I learned about Cajun, Creole, and Southern cooking with a taste of classic French cuisine and now I am sharing it all with you.

While these teachings have been foundational, my cooking style has been influenced by my many different experiences and even other occupations! My first real job was as a grill chef and as a dishwasher at a North Jersey ice cream restaurant in my late teens. I moved on to be a professional actor and producer for many years. I even tried my hand as a business manager in the motion picture industry and finished with a stressful, yet rewarding, 27 years long career as a finance executive for the American Broadcasting Company (Disney), in New York City. During these times, I often moonlighted in restaurants on weekends, at times alongside some of the world's most acclaimed chefs. Anyone who is, or has ever been in those fields understands how demanding they are, but I had to make time for my craft. It has always been and will always be, an outlet and refuge for me.

## The Culinary Therapy Tour (2008-Present)

My personal health scares and physical disabilities have motivated my culinary endeavors to become more philanthropic. Realizing that there were many people who could not easily enjoy quality meals and my cooking demonstrations, I decided to bring such experiences to various organizations. My "Culinary Therapy" tour, my most rewarding venture thus far, has visited and shared the joys of cooking with countless school districts, hospitals, nursing homes, and rehabilitation facilities. To witness the look of sheer delight on the face of an adult with cerebral palsy as he or she discovers the heavenly aromas of fresh herbs placed in their hands is a priceless and humbling event. We can show and share true love and we can overcome any obstacle in our way by helping those less fortunate!

## Cooking From My Heart to Yours

My recipes are intended to go from my heart to yours. I am even sharing some of my "secret ingredients" for my most cherished dishes (eat your heart out, Duke the Dog from that baked beans commercial). I invite the young people out there to try some of my recipes under adult supervision. Maybe it will begin your lifelong love affair with cooking and hospitality like it has with my elder son, Charlie, who has been working and managing in the food and beverage field for years and with whom I could not be prouder. For those older in age, but just as young in heart, you are equally welcome to use my recipes to strengthen (or even begin!), your own cooking prowess. It is my wish that you all enjoy these meals and share them with others.

From the deepest part of my heart, thank you to everyone who has helped me, educated me, nurtured me, and contributed to my career along the way. I am truly indebted to all of you for your great love and your endless support!

6

Planning
Prepping
Preparing
Plating

The
4 P's

# Chef Cardie's Four

# "P's" of Cooking

Before sharing these simple recipes with you, I wish to act as your culinary instructor and explain how I cook and how I would like you to think while you cook. I stress four essentials: **"planning," "prepping," "preparing," and "plating,"** which will contribute to the successful outcome of your dishes. By simply following this "yellow brick road," a lot of work and unnecessary stress will be eliminated from your culinary life.

## Planning

"Brain power" is as important as any other kitchen tool when preparing a meal. Before the work even begins, it is a good idea to pull out a pen and pad or electronic device, read through what the recipe requires, and ask ourselves what this job will entail. "How many people am I cooking for?" "How much food should I buy based on the recipe amounts?" "Will I need to buy more food since Fat Albert and his family will be attending?" "What time will I be serving dinner?" "Realistically, how long will this recipe take me and can I finish the bulk of it before Perpetually-Early Petunia and her seven kids arrive?" "What dishes can be made the day prior or even a few days earlier to eliminate some hassle?" It is amazing how much planning ahead makes a difference. In unison, can everyone please say, "holiday dinner stress?"

## Prepping

Most chefs follow a similar protocol when it comes to their prepping process. Many will call their staff in early each morning to prepare for that evening's dinner service. They will be chopping onions, garlic, celery, and carrots. They will cut their beef and pork loin steaks for grilling, fillet their fish, and countless other undertakings. Did you know that sauces and soups are often created the day prior in order to give the flavors time to blend? Attending to such tasks beforehand makes for a more enjoyable cooking experience because it is a smoother process with less grunt work and therefore, better results!

To ensure that nothing is forgotten, you can try using separate cookie sheets to hold each recipe's ingredients and tools (including bowls). Remember, while it is easy to add items, it is almost impossible to subtract something once it has been added to the mix so re-read your recipes and keep your work area clean and organized.

### Preparing

This is the fun part (unless you are in a restaurant setting creating more than 60 orders in an hour)! For the common cook, the real blood, sweat, and tears have already been shed during the planning, shopping, and prepping stages. Everything is already right in front of you. Thank earlier you for making this so easy!

Continue to keep your recipes at your fingertips and be mindful that not everything cooks at the same exact temperature or in the same amount of time. Garlic cooked for too long will burn. Forty-five minutes to an hour may be needed to properly sauté your caramelized onions. You can cook certain things simultaneously but do not forget about that prime rib of beef in the oven! Whatever you do, do not overcook the damn thing! Yes, I am temperamental when it comes to the food I am making!

Similar to how you wrote things down in the planning stage, it can be helpful to schedule how you will be preparing your items. Having two microwaves or ovens can complicate matters so unless you are a professional and regularly feeding many people, this route is unnecessary. A simple alternative to keeping your food warm is to just drape it with heavy-duty, aluminium foil.

### Plating

Give yourself a round of much deserved applause because you have worked so hard to make a memorable and delicious meal. We have now arrived at the artistic phase! Treat your final presentation as a work of art. It is your artistry and sincerity that immediately transforms a meal from ordinary to gourmet.

However, please hear this loud and clear. Do not get overly crazy about decorating your plate. Keep it clean and let your food speak for itself. Having said this, I recommend to always incorporate color in your presentation. I like to use a pretty white plate with small cherry tomatoes, chopped parsley or green onions, or even diced red and yellow peppers. You could also emulate Emeril Lagasse and sprinkle some "BAM" spice around the plate if you so desire. Make it look as good as it tastes!

Now on to the real fun... my recipes! They come from my heart and are heading to yours so let us "Keep on Cookin'!!"

*Perfection!*

# Appetizers

# Appetizer

This is one of the recipes that will have everyone talking at your next cocktail party. It is a major break from the same old, over-cooked and often dried-out buffalo chicken wings that you see on every restaurant menu in your town. You bake these brined wings in the oven so the chef has time to enjoy a few cold ones before dinner time!

## Brine & Wings Ingredients:

- About 50 meaty chicken wings (5-7 pounds) (winglet portions are discarded or used for making chicken stock at a later time)
- 6 (12 ounce) dark beers (I use Irish Guinness)
- 2 cups chicken stock (p. 89)
- ½ cup Kosher salt
- 2 cups light brown sugar, packed
- 3 tablespoons Emeril's Bayou Blast spice
- 2 tablespoons freshly cracked pepper

## Sauce Ingredients:

- 2 cups fresh parmesan cheese, grated
- 10 fresh garlic cloves, minced finely
- 2 tablespoons Emeril's Bayou Blast spice
- 2 tablespoons any hot sauce (such as Tabasco or Frank's)
- 2 tablespoons Worcestershire sauce
- Juice from 2 large lemons
- ¼ cup drinkable white wine
- 1½ cups olive oil
- Fresh, flat leaf parsley, chopped finely (for garnish)

# 24 Hour Beer-Brined
# Parmesan and Garlic
# Chicken Wings

## Brine & Wings Directions:

♦ Combine the listed ingredients into a 6 quart stock pot. Stir well. Bring mixture to a full boil and then turn off the heat. Remove from the heat and allow the brine to completely cool to room temperature, approximately 30 minutes.

♦ Place the chicken wing portions into a zip-lock storage bag. Two bags of 25 pieces each may be required for this recipe. Pour the brine over the wings until they are completely immersed in the liquid. Seal the bags tightly and place them in the refrigerator for 24 hours.

♦ Preheat oven to 400 degrees Fahrenheit.

♦ Cover a large cookie or baking sheet with aluminium foil and spray with non-stick cooking spray. Line up the chicken wings alongside each other without stacking.

♦ Bake the wings for 50 minutes. Turn them over after the first 25 minutes. Remove the wings from the oven and allow them to cool slightly. Make your sauce.

> *Chef's Note: Do not overcrowd the baking sheet during the cooking process. I cook about 25 wings per batch.*

♦ Preheat oven on the broiler setting.

♦ Submerge the cooled chicken wings in the sauce. Place each wing onto a clean baking sheet covered in aluminum foil and sprayed with non-stick, buttered cooking spray. Broil the wings for 3-4 minutes, or until the cheese has browned completely.

♦ Serve wings on a family-style platter or in a bowl. Garnish with chopped flat leaf parsley.

> *Chef's Note: If you wish to serve your wings with blue cheese dressing, celery, and carrots on the side, please be my guest. However, I think you will find that the dressing you just made works perfectly!*

## Sauce Directions:

♦ Using a wire whisk and large metal bowl, combine all ingredients **except for** the olive oil. Stir well. In a very slow stream, add the olive oil while whisking to form an emulsion.

# Appetizer

This recipe is one of the easiest ones to make in the cookbook but, then again, I hope you do not find any of my dishes too difficult to prepare! The good news about this beautiful appetizer is that there is no cooking involved. None whatsoever. It is about using the freshest of ingredients (especially your smoked salmon and herbs), and the simple assembly itself. It can even be made the day before your big party and left to chill in the refrigerator! One dish down! The only bad news (and it is not too bad), is that good, smoked salmon from Alaska, Norway, or Nova Scotia is fairly expensive. You can find packages of sliced, smoked salmon at your local fish store or certain gourmet supermarkets though. I ask you to use one full, 8 ounce package of salmon for this recipe for a simple reason: when your guests taste this dip, with their cracker in hand, I want them to tell you that they can taste the pieces of smoked salmon from their first bite to the last! You will truly be a culinary folk hero to all of your guests!

## Ingredients:

- 1 (8 ounce) package good smoked salmon, chopped coarsely
- 1 (8 ounce) package cream cheese, thawed to room temperature (see Chef's Note)
- 2 tablespoons lemon juice (about ½ lemon)
- ½ cup sour cream
- ¼ cup real mayonnaise
- ¼ cup red onion (about ½ small red onion), chopped finely
- 3 large garlic cloves, minced finely
- 2 heaping tablespoons prepared horseradish
- 2 tablespoons Old Bay seasoning
- 2 tablespoons Worcestershire sauce
- A few good shakes any hot sauce (such as Tabasco or Frank's)
- 1 tablespoon fresh dill, chopped finely
- 1 tablespoon fresh chives, chopped finely
- Plenty of freshly cracked black pepper, to taste
- Whole fresh flat leaf parsley (for garnish)

# Alaskan
# Smoked Salmon
# Spread

## Directions:

*Chef's Note: To avoid breaking out the heavy "artillery" to mix your cream cheese, you can either microwave it in a mixing bowl for 30 seconds to soften it or you can use 8 ounces of whipped cream cheese instead. Then everything can be blended with a large metal spoon or rubber spatula.*

♦ In a good sized mixing bowl, combine the cream cheese, lemon juice, sour cream, and mayonnaise. Using a handheld electric mixer or large "standing" mixer, on slow speed, combine these ingredients well until a nice, smooth "batter" has been achieved.

♦ Add to the mixture all other listed ingredients **except for** the smoked salmon. On slow speed, mix to combine everything well.

♦ Add the chopped salmon. Do not break apart the fish with the handheld mixer. Instead, using a large rubber spatula, gently fold the salmon pieces into the middle of the mixture while slowly turning the bowl.

♦ Place the mixture into a pretty serving bowl or small Pyrex dish. Garnish with whole pieces of flat leaf parsley. Cover the salmon dip tightly with plastic wrap and refrigerate it for a few hours (overnight is best). Let the dip sit out at room temperature for at least 30 minutes before serving.

♦ You can serve your dip with an array of gourmet crackers (I use rosemary bruschetta), toast points, or slices of toasted naan or pita bread.

# Appetizer

I learned how to make this delicious appetizer while I was a student at culinary school in New Orleans. It being so part of the local culture, learning how to make the dip was an unofficial requirement. They sure do love their Saints and LSU Tigers down there and nearly every bar and restaurant had (and continues to have), a version of this recipe on their menu, especially on football Saturdays or Sundays. I have tons of memories of watching the fans and tourists on Bourbon and Canal Streets while enjoying this tasty dip. Believe me, anything goes in the Big Easy and this is perfect to snack on while watching the show (and of course, the games)! You can serve this marvelous dip with toast points, some mixed gourmet crackers, or even crispy tortilla chips. I have even been known to toast a few pita breads and slice them into bite-sized pieces. I warn you though: there is always a fight to the finish for the last of this incredible dip so make sure to get a taste of it while you still can!

## Ingredients:

- 2 (large) packages fresh baby spinach leaves, stems removed and discarded
- 1 (6½ ounce) jar marinated artichoke hearts, drained and chopped roughly
- 1 heaping tablespoon Kosher salt (for cooking spinach)
- ¼ cup drinkable white wine (for cooking spinach)
- ¼ cup cold water (for cooking spinach)
- 4 tablespoons unsalted butter (½ stick)
- 2 medium Vidalia onions, chopped finely
- 3 tablespoons fresh garlic (about 4 or 5 large cloves), minced
- 2 tablespoons Emeril's Bayou Blast spice
- 4 tablespoons all-purpose flour
- 1 cup milk
- 1 cup heavy cream
- 2 teaspoons fresh lemon juice
- 1 cup mozzarella cheese, cubed into ½ inch pieces
- 1 cup Monterey Jack cheese, cubed into ½ inch pieces
- ½ cup fresh parmesan cheese, grated
- Plenty of freshly cracked black pepper, to taste

# Baby Spinach, Artichoke, and Three Cheese Dip

YIELD: SERVES ABOUT 10

## Directions:

♦ Preheat oven to 350 degrees Fahrenheit. Lightly grease a 9 x 5 inch ovenproof, Pyrex glass baking dish with non-stick cooking spray.

♦ In a small pot or 3 quart Dutch oven, over medium-high heat, add 1 heaping tablespoon of Kosher salt, ¼ cup of wine, and ¼ cup of water and bring to a boil. Add the spinach leaves and cook until wilted, about 4 minutes. Drain the spinach in a colander and allow it to cool for 5 minutes. Using a clean kitchen towel or some dry paper towels, squeeze the spinach to remove most of the excess water. Chop the spinach coarsely and set it aside.

♦ In a medium sized Dutch oven, over medium-high heat, melt the 4 tablespoons of unsalted butter. Add the chopped onions and cook, stirring for 5 minutes, or until they turn translucent. Add the minced garlic and Emeril's Bayou Blast spice and stir for an additional 1 minute.

♦ Add the 4 tablespoons of flour to the pan and, stirring constantly, create a light roux, about 2 minutes. In a steady stream, slowly add the milk and cream, stirring constantly until thick and creamy, about 2 minutes. Add in plenty of freshly cracked black pepper.

*Chef's Note: Many versions of this recipe call for 8 ounces of thawed cream cheese. However, I find this milk and heavy cream roux tastes so much better!*

♦ Add the reserved drained spinach and lemon juice and stir to incorporate well. Add in the cubed mozzarella and Monterey Jack cheeses and chopped artichoke hearts. Remove from the heat and pour the mixture into the prepared Pyrex dish. Top with ½ cup of freshly grated parmesan cheese and bake until everything becomes browned and bubbly, about 12-15 minutes. Do not burn!

♦ Serve the dip hot with your preferred chips or toasted breads on the side.

# Appetizer

Brie cheese is, by far and away, one of my favorite cheeses to eat. When it is baked in puffed pastry, flavored with fruit marmalade and a touch of maple syrup and surrounded with fresh strawberries, kiwis, and blueberries, it is as if you are tasting a piece of heaven. I made the Brie pictured here for a teacher of the year celebration that I catered in Bergen County, New Jersey. I have tremendous respect and total admiration for all of the great work that our teachers do and I wanted to serve food that was extra special. The guests filled up on this appetizer (and my jumbo lump crabmeat dip on page 41), and they hardly had any room left for dinner!

## Ingredients:

- ♦ 1 (large) round President Brie cheese
- ♦ 2 sheets puff pastry, frozen and then thawed to room temperature
- ♦ ½ cup all-purpose flour (for rolling out two pastry doughs)
- ♦ 1 (8 ounce) jar apricot marmalade
- ♦ 2 tablespoons brown sugar
- ♦ ¼ cup real maple syrup (not the commercial one used on pancakes)
- ♦ ¼ cup ice water (for egg wash)
- ♦ 1 large egg, beaten (for egg wash)
- ♦ 1 pint fresh strawberries, sliced
- ♦ 1 pint fresh blueberries
- ♦ 3 kiwis, sliced thinly
- ♦ Optional: crackers of your choice (to serve alongside)

# Baked Apricot Brie in Puff Pastry with Fresh Fruit

## Directions:

- Preheat oven to 350 degrees Fahrenheit.

- With a sharp knife, carefully cut off the top part (or white rind), of the Brie cheese. Leave the rinds on the sides and bottom of the cheese intact.

- On a marble cutting board or large aluminum cookie sheet, use your hands to spread ½ cup of all-purpose flour. Place the thawed pieces of puff pastry on top of the flour and roll them out without tearing the dough. Roll out two pieces large enough to cover the bottom and top of the Brie round.

- In a mixing bowl, combine the apricot marmalade with 2 tablespoons of brown sugar and ¼ cup of real maple syrup. Stir well to blend completely.

- Place the cheese in the center of one of the puff pastries. Using a rubber spatula, spread the marmalade and syrup mixture over the top part of the cheese only. Place the other pastry sheet over the top of the round as well. Using your fingers or the back a fork, lightly crimp or fold the edges of the puff pastries until the cheese is completely sealed. With your fork, gently poke a few small holes in the top of the pastry so the steam can escape.

- Mix the ¼ cup of water with one large egg to form an egg wash. With a pastry brush, "paint" the entire round of the puff pastry with the egg wash.

- Place the Brie in the center of a cookie sheet that has been covered with aluminum foil. Bake in the oven for 30-35 minutes, or until the entire pastry has turned golden brown.

- Remove from the oven and, using a spatula, transfer the cheese round to a serving cutting board or pretty platter. Let the cheese rest and cool for 10 minutes before slicing. Garnish the Brie platter with an assortment of fresh fruit.

> *Chef's Note: I personally believe the puff pastry provides a nice bite on its own, but you can serve crackers or bread alongside the baked Brie if you so desire.*

# Appetizer

I created this recipe for a fabulous cocktail party that I catered many years ago at the Jersey Shore. Tired of wrapping regular frankfurters in puff pastry, I slowly simmered kielbasa in dark Guinness beer and added Pepper Jack cheese and caramelized onions to make these tasty culinary packets. They were served with a spicy French mustard and some sweet duck sauce on the side. These were a genuine hit with the guests on hand and I have been making them ever since!

## Ingredients:

- 3 pounds Polish kielbasa sausage (about 4 large links)
- 1 package frozen puff pastry, completely thawed
- 3 dark beers (I use Guinness)
- 1 cup low sodium chicken broth
- 1 cup light brown sugar, packed
- 2 heaping tablespoons Emeril's Bayou Blast spice
- 2 tablespoons unsalted butter (for caramelizing onions)
- 6 large Vidalia onions (recipe follows)
- ¼ cup granulated sugar (for caramelizing onions)
- 1 cup white wine (for deglazing)
- 2 cups Pepper Jack cheese, shredded or grated
- ¼ cup water (for egg wash)
- 1 egg, beaten (for egg wash)
- A pinch of Kosher salt
- Optional: Dijon mustard and/or duck sauce (for dipping)

# Beer-Simmered Kielbasa with Caramelized Onions and Cheese in Puff Pastry

## YIELD: MAKES 28 KIELBASA

### Kielbasa Directions:

♦ In a 4 quart stock pot or Dutch oven, add the kielbasa, dark beer, chicken broth, light brown sugar, and 2 tablespoons of Emeril's Bayou Blast spice. Stir well. Bring the mixture to a boil and then reduce the heat to low, letting it simmer for 10 minutes. Remove pot from the heat and allow the mixture to cool, about 10 minutes.

♦ Remove the cooled kielbasa from the liquid and, on a cutting board, slice into 1 inch thick pieces. Set the sausage rounds aside.

### Caramelized Onions Directions:

♦ Trim the ends off each onion and then halve them through the middle. Remove the peels and slice into half-moon shapes. Using a cast iron skillet or heavy Dutch oven, over medium-low heat, melt 2 tablespoons of unsalted butter and add the onions. Sprinkle the onions with salt and ¼ cup of granulated sugar. Stir the onions often until they are a dark mahogany and reduced. Do not let them burn. This will take 50-60 minutes. Deglaze the pan periodically with ¼ cup of a white wine as the onions cook. Set onions aside in a bowl to cool.

### Puff Pastry Assembling Directions:

♦ Preheat oven to 375 degrees Fahrenheit.

♦ Roll out each sheet of puff pastry on a well-floured, marble cutting board. Halve the pastry sheets and then halve them again (to make quarters). Cut a piece of pastry approximately 4 inches long and 2 inches wide and place it flat on your cutting board.

♦ Leaving about ½ inch space from the end, place one piece of sliced kielbasa over the rolled-out puff pastry. Add a tablespoon of the caramelized onions and sprinkle the mixture with 2 tablespoons of Pepper Jack cheese.

♦ Seal the puff pastry by rolling it on the cutting board like a jelly roll and then pinching both ends shut. Mix the water and egg together to form an egg wash. With a pastry brush, "paint" the puff with the egg wash. Repeat for each pastry. Position pastries 1 inch apart on a cookie sheet. Bake in the oven for 25-30 minutes, or until golden brown and "puffed up." Watch these closely as they will burn very quickly if left unattended.

♦ Serve on a decorative platter with dipping sauces in bowls.

# Appetizer

The origin of naan bread dates back to ancient Asia around 1300 B.C. and continues to be popular in places like India and Pakistan to this day. The first time I cooked with naan, I was catering for a rather large cocktail party. Our clients said they wanted us to make a different kind of pizza to pass around to their guests. So, my cooks and I came up with this fabulous idea. We cooked our barbecued chicken thighs on an outside grill along with the naan. Then, we topped the naan with mozzarella cheese and some fresh basil and cilantro and finished it under a hot broiler oven for a few minutes. We cut everything up into pretty slices and served. All of the guests were very pleased! These are also great appetizers to bring to your next football tailgate party!

## Ingredients:

- 4 naan flatbreads (regular or whole wheat)
- 6 chicken thighs, boneless and skinless
- 1 cup sweet barbecue sauce (p. 193)
- 2 tablespoons Emeril's Bayou Blast spice
- 2 tablespoons extra virgin olive oil
- 2 cups mozzarella cheese, shredded
- ½ cup red onion (1 medium red onion), minced finely
- ½ cup fresh basil leaves, chopped coarsely or torn by hand
- ½ cup fresh cilantro, chopped coarsely or torn by hand
- Freshly cracked black pepper, to taste

CHEF CARDIE'S

# Grilled Barbecued Chicken, Cheese, and Fresh Herbs on Naan Bread

YIELD: SERVES 8-10

## Directions:

♦ In a mixing bowl, stir together the 2 tablespoons of Emeril's Bayou Blast with 2 tablespoons of olive oil. Add the chicken thighs and toss them in the bowl, coating the chicken on all sides. Let the chicken rest for 5 minutes at room temperature before grilling or sautéing.

♦ Preheat oven to 350 degrees Fahrenheit.

♦ Place the chicken thighs on a grill that has been preheated or in a sauté pan on the stovetop over medium high heat. Cook the chicken for 4 minutes per side. After cooking for 2 minutes, "paint" the chicken with barbecue sauce, flip them over, and repeat the process once more.

♦ Place the chicken thighs in an oven-proof baking dish and cook in the preheated oven for 10 minutes. Once done, remove the thighs from the oven and let them cool for 10 minutes.

♦ Place the naan breads on the same hot grill or in the preheated oven. Cook them for at least 2 minutes per side. Do not burn the bread!

♦ Chop or slice the chicken thighs into bite-sized pieces. Cover each flatbread with grilled chicken pieces. Scatter the shredded mozzarella cheese over the chicken. Scatter the minced red onion and freshly chopped herbs over the top. Season with freshly cracked black pepper.

♦ Set oven to the broiler mode.

♦ Place the "decorated" naan onto a large cookie sheet (2 at a time). Place them under the broiler for no more than 3 minutes. Watch very carefully to prevent burning. Remove from the oven when the cheese has melted and bubbled on top. Let cool for a few minutes.

♦ Using a pizza cutter or sharp knife, slice the naan into 6 small pieces per flatbread. Serve two slices per person as an appetizer.

# Appetizer

Have you ever seen those pricey beef cuts at your local butcher counter or Costco and wondered, "Why is beef tenderloin or chateaubriand so darn expensive?" Well, technically, beef tenderloin is a small muscle, not often used by the animal, so it is the most tender part of the meat. There is only a small amount of it (about 5 pounds), raising its desirability. The fillet mignon you dine on at fancy restaurants is a cut directly from the whole beef tenderloin. Now you know some culinary facts that you can share with friends! I remember, quite vividly, making several trays of the pictured classic and delicious appetizer for a catered, formal birthday party at the Jersey Shore. My staff went to walk around with the sliders but only seconds later, one of my staff returned to the kitchen with an empty tray and said, "Chef Cardie, the piranhas have officially escaped!" Yes, they were that good!

## Horseradish Sauce Ingredients:

- ½ cup horseradish, grated (jarred is fine but fresh is preferable)
- 1 cup sour cream
- ¼ cup mayonnaise
- 1 heaping tablespoon Dijon mustard
- 1 teaspoon white wine vinegar
- Optional: ½ cup fresh dill, chopped coarsely (for garnish)
- A pinch of Kosher salt and lots of freshly cracked black pepper, to taste

## Beer Tenderloin Ingredients:

- 1 (5 pound) beef tenderloin
- ¼ cup extra virgin olive oil
- 2 heaping tablespoons Emeril's Bayou Blast spice
- Lots of freshly cracked black pepper
- 2 freshly baked French breads, cut into ½ inch thick slices (see Chef's Note)

# Grilled Beef Tenderloin Sliders with Homemade Horseradish Cream

YIELD: SERVES 10-12

## Horseradish Directions:

♦ In a small bowl, whisk together the listed ingredients until the mixture is smooth and creamy. Taste it and adjust ingredients or seasonings to your preference. Refrigerate the cream sauce, covered, for at least 4 hours before serving.

## Beef Tenderloin Directions:

♦ With a sharp paring knife, trim the beef tenderloin of any excess fat and "silver skin."

♦ Place the meat on a wooden cutting board or in a large marinating pan. Rub ¼ cup of olive oil and 2 tablespoons of Emeril's Bayou Blast spice over the meat. "Massage" the spice and oil into the meat. Season with lots of black pepper. Let meat rest at room temperature for 30 minutes.

♦ Over a preheated outdoor grill set to medium-high, place the beef tenderloin on sideways to cook, untouched, for 6 minutes. Using tongs, carefully turn the meat over and grill the other side for another 6 minutes in the same manner. Repeat this process once more while ensuring the tenderloin sides are also grilled or browned. The meat is ready when an instant meat thermometer placed in the center of the tenderloin reads 130 degrees Fahrenheit. Remove the meat and immediately wrap it in aluminum foil. Let it rest for 20 minutes before carving.

♦ Slice the rested tenderloin into ½ inch pieces and place them atop the ½ inch slices of French bread (see Chef's Note). Using a teaspoon, top with a dollop of reserved horseradish sauce and garnish with a small amount of freshly chopped dill.

> *Chef's Note:  For a special version of this appetizer, use my recipe for cheesy garlic bread (p. 129), as the base for the beef instead of plain French bread.*

> *Chef's Note:  Please do not overcook beef tenderloin. In order to achieve its full flavor profile, this expensive cut of meat must not be cooked above medium-rare.*

# Appetizer

I can almost promise you that this special drink will make your guests do a genuine double take! Prepare to hear: "Huh?" "You did *what* with the lemons and limes?" "You *grilled* them?" "Why doesn't it look like a traditional lemonade?" That is the beauty and originality of it all! I think that even your kids will be impressed with this one and they can make this drink with you and sell it on the curb for an extra fifty cents!

## Ingredients:

- ½ cup freshly squeezed lemon juice (about 6 large lemons)
- ½ cup freshly squeezed lime juice (about 6 large limes)
- 1 (small) head fresh ginger, peeled and pieces sliced
- 8 cups cold water
- ¼ cup liquid lemon juice concentrate
- 1 cup granulated sugar
- Lemon slices, not grilled (for garnish)
- Lime slices, not grilled (for garnish)
- Optional: any good vodka (for making it a cocktail)

# Grilled
# Citrus and Ginger
# Lemonade

## Directions:

♦ Cut each lemon and lime in half through the center. Place each half flesh-side down on a preheated grill over medium-high heat. Grill the lemons and limes for about 5 minutes, or until nice grill lines have formed. Remove the fruit with tongs and transfer them to a holding pan. Let them cool for 5 minutes.

♦ Using a lemon reamer, juice the lemon and lime halves into a 3 quart pitcher.

♦ Pour 4 cups of cold water into a soup pot along with ¼ cup of liquid lemon concentrate. Add the sliced ginger and granulated sugar. Bring the mixture to a full boil and stir until the sugar has fully dissolved, about 8 minutes. Remove from the heat and let the mixture cool for at least 15 minutes.

♦ Strain the cooled sugar and ginger mixture through a fine mesh sieve into the pitcher with the lemon and lime juice. Discard the solid slices of ginger. Pour 4 cups of cold water into the pitcher. Stir the ingredients well.

*Chef's Note: You can add ice cubes to the pitcher to chill everything rapidly. However, I like to make this recipe a day ahead and chill it in the refrigerator.*

♦ When ready to serve, garnish each drink with slices of lemon, lime, or both!

*Chef's Note: This drink will have a slightly darker color to it than any other lemon or lime drink because the fruit has been grilled. One of my best friends just told me that she added some quality vodka to her individual servings and it was one of the best cocktails she had ever tasted!*

# Appetizer

It is simply amazing what one can learn by observing someone else cook something special. My brother, Loren, does not profess to be a trained gourmet chef, but he is a top-notch cook, especially when you get him anywhere near an outdoor grill! Many years ago, I watched him do this recipe on his nice, big grill when he lived in Clifton, New Jersey. He asked me if I had ever tasted grilled clams casino before and I told him that I had not. I do not know why exactly, but I was a bit skeptical at first. However, after the first bite of this incredible appetizer, I was "hooked" for life! I write that this recipe serves about 8 people, but believe me, I could eat the entire batch of clams by myself! Do not forget to purchase the slightly larger Cherrystone clams from your trusted fish monger. Thanks for creating this dish for me, Bro! I love reminiscing about all of the great times we have shared together and I look forward to creating many more good days with you in the future!

## Ingredients:

- ◆ 30 Cherrystone clams, soaked in cold water for 30 minutes (see Chef's Note)
- ◆ 12 slices thick smoky bacon
- ◆ 1 cup unsalted butter (2 sticks), softened to room temperature
- ◆ 2 large red or green peppers (I use one of each), chopped
- ◆ 1 large Vidalia onion (or 2 medium onions), chopped finely
- ◆ ¼ cup good white wine
- ◆ Juice from 1 lime
- ◆ 2 teaspoons Old Bay seasoning
- ◆ 1 tablespoon or a few shakes of Tabasco sauce or Frank's Hot Sauce
- ◆ 1 cup breadcrumbs (I use Panko) (additional breadcrumbs may be needed)
- ◆ Freshly cracked black pepper, to taste
- ◆ 1 whole lemon, quartered or sliced (for garnish)
- ◆ Fresh curly parsley, chopped (for garnish)

# Grilled
# Clams Casino

YIELD: SERVES ABOUT 8

## Directions:

♦ Preheat outdoor grill to medium-high heat.

> *Chef's Note:* *Once removed from the soaking water, it is imperative to scrub each clam lightly with a wire kitchen brush under cold, running water before you begin grilling. This will ensure that there are no sand particles in your clams. Discard any opened or cracked clams.*

♦ Cook the bacon slices in a large sauté pan over medium heat until browned and crispy, about 10 minutes. Drain on paper towels. Once cooled, crumble bacon with your fingers. Set aside.

♦ In a mixing bowl, make casino butter by combining the softened butter, chopped peppers, chopped onion, white wine, lime juice, Old Bay seasoning, some hot sauce, and the reserved crumbled bacon. Season with plenty of freshly cracked black pepper. Mix everything well. Cover the bowl with plastic wrap and refrigerate for 1 hour.

> *Chef's Note:* *The mixture of butter and ingredients you have just made is called, "compound butter." To fresh freeze the butter for future use, shape it into an "oval mound" and cover with plastic wrap. The butter can be kept frozen for at least 3 months.*

♦ When ready, place clams directly onto the grill and close the lid. After about 5 minutes, check on the clams. They should be opening. As they open, transfer them individually to a large platter. Let cool for about 5 minutes. Any unopened clams after grilling are to be discarded.

♦ Once they can be handled, carefully pull the top shell off of each clam and discard the shell. With a sharp paring knife, slightly loosen the clam meat from the bottom shell. Then, using a tablespoon, mound a portion of the casino butter on top of each clam half. Cover each butter mixture with a sprinkling of Panko breadcrumbs (roughly 2 teaspoons).

♦ Return the clams to the grill. Shut the lid and cook for approximately 6 minutes, or until the clam tops are browned and bubbly. Garnish with some lemon slices and a sprinkling of chopped curly parsley. Serve immediately.

# Appetizer

How many of you know the wonderful feeling of being at a lavish cocktail party and seeing a tray of delicious meatballs with toothpicks coming toward you? I do not know about you, but I really enjoy watching people who are trying to balance their drink with one hand while attempting to reach for more than one meatball at the same time! Who needs to be entertained by (the now defunct), Ringling Brothers and Barnum & Bailey Circus when you can have *that* as your side show? Of course, after my own balancing acts, I have to take my shirt and tie to the local dry cleaners, but that is beside the point. The point is that these delicious hors d'oeuvres are so worth it. I could not resist including my own "kicked-up" version in this cookbook, especially since they can be enjoyed year-round. I hope that you make these for your family and friends and think of me "juggling" right alongside you!

## Meatball Ingredients:

- ½ pound ground beef
- ½ pound ground veal
- ½ pound ground pork
- 1 teaspoon dried thyme
- 1 teaspoon dried rosemary
- 1 teaspoon dried parsley
- ½ cup breadcrumbs, seasoned
- ¼ cup olive oil
- 4 large garlic cloves, minced very finely
- 2 large eggs, beaten well
- 2 tablespoons Worcestershire sauce
- ½ cup Parmesan Reggiano cheese, grated
- Plenty of freshly cracked black pepper, to taste
- 2 heaping tablespoons Emeril's Original Essence spice
- Optional: Flat leaf parsley, finely chopped (for garnish)

## Sauce Ingredients:

- 4 tablespoons unsalted butter (½ stick)
- 4 tablespoons all-purpose flour
- 1 cup rich beef stock (p. 87)
- 1 cup heavy cream
- 2 teaspoons dried rosemary
- 2 teaspoons dried thyme
- 2 teaspoons garlic powder (not garlic salt)
- 2 tablespoons Worcestershire sauce
- A few good shakes any hot sauce (such as Tabasco or Frank's)
- Plenty of freshly cracked black pepper, to taste

# "Kicked-Up"
# Swedish
# Meatballs

## Meatball Directions:

♦ Preheat oven to 425 degrees Fahrenheit.

♦ In a large mixing bowl, mix the three meats well with the all of the listed ingredients. Make sure the spices and cheese are especially well distributed. Using your hands, form round meatballs (1½ inches in diameter), and set them into an oven-proof baking dish that has been greased with non-stick spray.

♦ Place the meatballs into the oven and bake for 25 minutes without turning. Once well browned, remove from the oven and let them cool for 15 minutes.

## Sauce Directions:

♦ In a 3 quart Dutch oven, over medium-high heat, melt 4 tablespoons of unsalted butter with the 4 tablespoons of all-purpose flour to form a small roux. Whisk the roux together constantly for 5 minutes, or until it begins to turn a light brown. Do not burn the roux.

♦ Slowly whisk in the beef stock and stir until the mixture has begun to thicken slightly, about 2 minutes. Stir in the heavy cream, dried rosemary, dried thyme, garlic powder, Worcestershire sauce, and a few good shakes of your favorite hot sauce. Cook for 3 more minutes, stirring the sauce often to prevent burning or clumping. Once done, season everything with plenty of freshly cracked black pepper.

♦ Return the browned meatballs to the Dutch oven and coat them well on all sides with the heated sauce. Using a slotted spoon, place the meatballs carefully onto a pretty serving platter and spoon more of the sauce over the top of them. Place individual toothpicks through each meatball and garnish the top with some finely chopped flat leaf parsley.

*Chef's Note: If you wish to serve these meatballs as a dinner entrée, you can cook some thin spaghetti or egg noodles (following the directions on the box), and place the meatballs and sauce right over the top of the pasta.*

# Appetizer

The credit for this barbecued shrimp recipe goes to the one and only, Chef Emeril Lagasse, who serves this delightful shrimp appetizer at most of his restaurants in Las Vegas and New Orleans. I recently cooked this dish for a major fundraising dinner we catered for the Tennessee Valley Coalition for the Homeless in Knoxville, Tennessee. We tweaked the recipe by serving the shrimp over a small bed of linguini and my head cook, Jim Fuller, reduced an incredible sauce for hours on end and finished it by adding in a few Guinness dark beers. Sorry, Chef Emeril, but it was delicious and you would have been extremely proud of your student for "kicking it up a notch!"

## Ingredients:

- 3 pounds large or jumbo shrimp in their shells (16-20 shrimp per pound)
- 4 tablespoons New Orleans Creole or Cajun Seasoning, divided
- 5 tablespoons olive oil, divided
- 1 cup onions, chopped
- 6 tablespoons garlic, minced
- 3 bay leaves
- 3 lemons, quartered
- 2 cups water
- 2 (12 ounce) dark stout beers (I use Guinness)
- 1 cup Worcestershire sauce (I use Lea and Perrins)
- 1 cup white wine
- 1 cup heavy cream
- 4 tablespoons unsalted butter (½ stick), cold
- Freshly cracked black pepper
- 1 cup combination of green onions and flat leaf parsley, both chopped (for garnish)
- Optional: spaghetti or linguini

CHEF CARDIE'S

# New Orleans Barbecued Shrimp

YIELD: SERVES 10-12

## Directions:

- Peel and devein the shrimp, leaving only their tails attached. Reserve the shrimp shells. Using your hands, coat the shrimp in 2 tablespoons of Creole Seasoning. Sprinkle them with freshly cracked black pepper. Refrigerate for at least 45 minutes, or until sauce base has been made.

- In a large pot or Dutch oven, over high heat, add 3 tablespoons of olive oil. When the oil is hot, add the onions and garlic. Sauté for 5 minutes. Then, add the reserved shrimp shells, 2 tablespoons of Creole Seasoning, 3 bay leaves, quartered lemons, 2 cups of water, 2 dark beers, 1 cup of Worcestershire sauce, 1 cup of white wine, and plenty of black pepper. Stir well and bring the mixture to a boil. Reduce the heat and simmer slowly for 30 minutes uncovered. Remove from the heat and allow the stock to cool for about 20 minutes.

- Strain the mixture through a mesh sieve into another pot. There should be about 3-4 cups of sauce at this time. Place over high heat, bring to a boil, and then simmer until thick, syrupy, and dark brown. This takes roughly 25 minutes and makes about 2 cups of rich sauce base.

- In a large skillet over medium-high heat, add the remaining 2 tablespoons of olive oil. Once hot, add and sauté the seasoned shrimp, occasionally shaking the skillet, for 3-5 minutes, or until the shrimp have turned opaque. Set the pan aside once the shrimp have cooked.

  *Chef's Note: When we were in Tennessee, we cooked the seasoned shrimp on cookie sheets in an oven at 350 degrees Fahrenheit for about 15 minutes with great results!*

- Pour 1 cup of cream into the barbecue sauce base. Stir and simmer for 5 minutes. Using tongs, transfer the shrimp to a warm platter. Just before serving, whisk into the sauce the 4 tablespoons of unsalted butter. You will end up with about 2 cups of barbecue sauce.

- Mound the shrimp in the center of a platter. Spoon the sauce over the shrimp and around the plate. Garnish with green onions and parsley. Serve over a bed of cooked spaghetti or linguini.

# Appetizer

If you think the shrimp cocktail in the picture looks as if they are being served in large martini glasses, you would be correct. I did a major catering job at the Jersey Shore and we were going for a little dramatic effect. We even ordered these gorgeous Gulf shrimp from a New Orleans-based company called, "Louisiana Crawfish Company" (LAcrawfish.com). The fresh seafood from the Gulf Coast cannot be beat so do yourself a favor and check them out! I also recommend that you set some shrimp aside for yourself because this crowd-pleaser never lasts for very long!

## Shrimp Boil Ingredients:

- ♦ 5 pounds large shrimp (16-20 count per pound), peeled, cleaned, and deveined with tails left intact
- ♦ 2 cups cold water
- ♦ 2 (12 ounce) beers (I use Budweiser)
- ♦ 1 cup white wine
- ♦ 6 large garlic cloves, peeled and left whole
- ♦ 1 package crab boil (such as Zatarains)
- ♦ 3 whole sprigs fresh thyme
- ♦ 3 whole sprigs fresh rosemary
- ♦ 2 bay leaves
- ♦ Juice from 2 whole lemons (use lemons as well)
- ♦ 2 tablespoons Tabasco sauce or Frank's Hot Sauce

## Spicy Cocktail Sauce Ingredients:

- ♦ 2 cups good tomato catsup
- ♦ 2 tablespoons fresh lemon juice
- ♦ 2 tablespoons prepared horseradish
- ♦ 2 tablespoons Worcestershire sauce
- ♦ 2 large garlic cloves, peeled and minced
- ♦ 1 tablespoon Tabasco sauce or Frank's Hot Sauce

## Remoulade Sauce Ingredients:

- ♦ 2 cups mayonnaise
- ♦ 2 tablespoons Dijon mustard
- ♦ 2 tablespoons whole grain mustard
- ♦ 2 teaspoons fresh capers
- ♦ 2 tablespoons flat leaf parsley, chopped
- ♦ 3 garlic cloves, minced finely
- ♦ 1 tablespoon Worcestershire sauce
- ♦ 2 teaspoons mild paprika
- ♦ 1 heaping tablespoon Emeril's Bayou Blast spice
- ♦ 1 tablespoon or a few good shakes of Tabasco sauce or Frank's Hot Sauce
- ♦ 2 tablespoons fresh lemon juice
- ♦ 2 green onions, chopped finely (some green and all of the white)

# New Orleans Shrimp Cocktail with Two Dipping Sauces

YIELD: SERVES 10-12

## Shrimp Boil Directions:

♦ In a large stockpot, over high heat, add all listed ingredients **except for** the shrimp and let pot reach a boil. Lower the heat to medium. Put a well-fitting lid on the pot and let the mixture simmer for at least 30 minutes. After that time, add the shrimp and close the lid again. Cook the shrimp for 10 minutes without removing the lid.

♦ Shut off the heat and drain the shrimp with a large colander in the sink. Discard the herb sprigs. Place shrimp into a large bowl and refrigerate for at least 1 hour, or until well chilled.

*Chef's Note: I make my shrimp and sauces the day before my cocktail party. I store the cooked shrimp in zip-lock bags and put my sauces in bowls covered with plastic wrap.*

## Spicy Cocktail Sauce Directions:

♦ Stir everything in a mixing bowl until well blended. Chill well before serving.

## Remoulade Sauce Directions:

♦ Stir everything in a mixing bowl until well blended. Chill well before serving.

# Appetizer

What ever happened to good, old-fashioned popovers? Do you remember your mom baking these for you when you were a kid? "No," you say? Well then, have I got a recipe for you! A popover is the American version of the British recipe, Yorkshire pudding. Of course, with this recipe, we are not including the meat drippings from a luscious, prime rib of beef. Instead, you will be making a delicate, savory, semi-sweet, and mouth-watering treat that you will want to make for your family time and time again. I am also giving you the recipe for a simple strawberry butter to spread over the warm popovers. Good luck trying to eat just one!

## Popover Ingredients:

- 1 cup whole milk
- 1 cup all-purpose flour
- 1 teaspoon salt
- 1 teaspoon baking powder
- 2 large eggs, at room temperature
- 2 tablespoons unsalted butter, melted (plus 1-2 tablespoons for greasing muffin tins or crème brulee cups)
- 1 teaspoon vanilla extract

## Strawberry Butter Ingredients:

- ½ cup unsalted butter (1 stick), softened to room temperature
- ½ cup powdered sugar
- 1 cup fresh strawberries, chopped

# Popovers with Strawberry Butter

---
## YIELD: MAKES 6 LARGE
---
### OR 12 SMALL POPOVERS

## Popover Directions:

♦ Place the 1 cup of milk in a saucepan. Over medium-low heat, warm the milk slightly. Do not over-simmer or boil it. The milk should be warm to the touch. Let cool to room temperature.

♦ In a mixing bowl, whisk together the flour, salt, and 1 teaspoon of baking powder.

♦ Crack 2 large eggs into a mixing bowl and, using a handheld whisk or an electric mixer, beat the eggs for 2 minutes, or until fluffy and light in color. Slowly drizzle in the cup of milk, 2 tablespoons of melted butter, and 1 teaspoon of vanilla extract. Whisk or beat well.

♦ Add the flour mixture to the egg mixture and whisk or beat for another 2 minutes, or until all flour has been absorbed and combined. Let batter rest for 10 minutes at room temperature.

♦ Preheat oven to 450 degrees Fahrenheit.

> *Chef's Note: At this point, some recipes recommend that you warm your muffin tins or crème brulee cups in the oven for 5 minutes before adding the batter. This helps the popovers "pop" and expand more easily.*

♦ Coat a 12 serving muffin tin *or* 6 individual, 6 ounce crème brulee cups (if you want larger popovers), with buttered cooking spray and some additional melted butter. Fill cups halfway to the top with the batter. Place the tins or cups onto a lined cookie sheet and into the oven.

♦ Bake popovers for 15 minutes. Then, immediately reduce the heat to 350 degrees Fahrenheit and bake for an additional 20 minutes, or until the popovers have turned golden brown on the outside. Do not open the oven door during the baking process.

♦ Remove popovers from the oven and let them cool for about 5 minutes before "popping" them out of the cups. Serve on a pretty platter along with strawberry butter on the side.

## Strawberry Butter Directions:

♦ In a mixing bowl, cream the butter with a handheld mixer until it is whipped and smooth. Stir in the powdered sugar and mix using a spatula or handheld mixer on low speed.

♦ Fold in the chopped strawberries. Mix well until the butter is light pink in color and creamy.

> *Chef's Note: Popovers are best served fresh from the oven. If they must be made ahead, warm them in an oven at 350 degrees Fahrenheit until warm and crispy, about 5 minutes.*

> *Chef's Note: Frozen baked popovers will keep in an airtight bag or container for up to 3 months. To reheat, transfer the popovers directly from the freezer to a cookie sheet and bake at 350 degrees Fahrenheit for about 8 minutes.*

# Appetizer

This is a recipe that gets me quite emotional as it was a favorite of my late father-in-law, Camillo (Rock) Gentile and my late brother-in-law, Rocky Gentile. These grilled clams were on their mind whenever we got together. As both were residents of the Jersey Shore and coastal Florida, they both knew how to be connoisseurs of good steamers and succulent Cherrystone clams! I loved cooking for them and I will forever be indebted to these two great men for the love, kindness, and friendship they bestowed on my life. I dedicate this recipe to their memories

## Ingredients:

♦ 50 fresh Cherrystone clams

♦ 6 large garlic cloves, minced

♦ 1 cup unsalted butter (2 sticks), melted

♦ 2 tablespoons Old Bay Seasoning Mix

♦ Juice from 2 whole lemons (zest from 1 of those lemons)

♦ 1 tablespoon or a few good shakes of Tabasco sauce or Frank's Hot Sauce

♦ 3 whole sprigs fresh thyme, leaves removed and chopped finely

♦ 3 whole sprigs rosemary, leaves removed and chopped finely

♦ ¾ (standard, 750 milliliter) bottle champagne (Chef drinks the other ¼ of the bottle)

♦ Kosher salt and freshly cracked black pepper, to taste

♦ ½ cup combination of red and green bell peppers (one of each), chopped finely (for garnish)

♦ Fresh parsley, chopped finely (for garnish)

♦ Optional: French bread loaf

# Rocky's
# Grilled Cherrystone Clams in
# Champagne and Garlic Butter Sauce

## Directions:

♦ Let clams soak in a large pot of ice water for at least 30 minutes. Scrub each clam's outer shell with a small kitchen brush and rinse under cold water. Place scrubbed clams into a clean pot with fresh ice water for an additional 20 minutes.

♦ Place pot of clams over medium-high heat on a preheated grill (indoor or outdoor). Covering with the lid, cook clams until they have just opened, about 8 minutes.

   *Chef's Note: Discard any clams which have not fully opened.*

♦ In a small Dutch oven, add the unsalted butter, Old Bay Seasoning, lemon juice, minced garlic, hot sauce, lemon zest, and fresh herbs. Pour in the champagne and stir well to blend. Bring the mixture to a boil and then reduce the heat and simmer for 15 minutes. The sauce should begin to "reduce" and thicken slightly. Add salt and freshly cracked pepper, to taste.

♦ Spread the grilled clams onto a large, festive platter and pour sauce directly over the top. Garnish the clams with chopped red and green bell peppers and fresh parsley.

♦ Crusty French bread can be included on the side for sopping up the champagne sauce.

# Appetizer

What cookbook would be complete without a deviled egg recipe that can be used for your upcoming cocktail party? This is not your run-of-the-mill, deviled egg recipe either. It has chunks of fresh shrimp in it as well as a touch of spicy curry powder, giving this appetizer a distinct and "kicked-up" flavor! Make plenty of these because they will not last for very long at your gathering!

## Ingredients:

♦ 6 large eggs

♦ ½ pound fresh shrimp (12 small cocktail shrimp *or* 6 large shrimp cut in half), peeled, deveined, and cooked in 2 cups of boiling salted water for about 5 minutes, or until they turn pink or opaque

♦ 1 tablespoon white wine vinegar (for cooking eggs)

♦ 2 tablespoons Kosher salt (for cooking eggs)

♦ 1 tablespoon garlic (about 2 large garlic cloves), minced finely

♦ 1 tablespoon Old Bay seasoning

♦ 4 green onion stalks (mainly the white part but also a bit of the green), chopped

♦ ½ cup mayonnaise (I use Hellman's)

♦ 1 tablespoon Dijon mustard

♦ 1 tablespoon any good curry powder

♦ Juice from ½ lemon

♦ 2 good shakes any hot sauce (such as Tabasco or Frank's)

♦ Freshly cracked black pepper, to taste

♦ Red (not smoked) paprika (for garnish)

♦ Fresh chives, chopped (for garnish)

# Shrimp Curried
# Deviled Eggs

YIELD: MAKES 12 EGGS

## Perfectly Cooked, Hard-Boiled Eggs Directions:

♦ Lay your large eggs flat in a large pot or Dutch oven (with a tight-fitting lid). Fill the pot with cold water, covering the eggs by 1 inch. Add 1 tablespoon of white wine vinegar to the water along with 2 tablespoons of Kosher salt. Over medium-high heat, let the water and eggs reach a full boil. Once it does, remove the pot from the heat, cover it tightly, and let it sit undisturbed for 10 minutes. Immediately drain the eggs with a colander over the sink and plunge the eggs into a larger bowl filled with ice water. Once cool enough to handle, peel the eggs and slice them in half lengthwise.

   *Chef's Note: You can hard boil and even peel the eggs the day before. Just make sure that they are left whole, tightly wrapped, and then stored in the refrigerator.*

## Deviled Eggs Directions:

♦ Remove the egg yolks from each egg and place them in a metal mixing bowl. Mash the yolks using the back of a spoon or fork. Position the egg white halves on a serving platter. Set both egg halves aside.

♦ Add to the egg yolk bowl, 1 tablespoon of minced garlic, the Old Bay seasoning, and chopped green onions. Combine well. Then whisk in the mayonnaise, Dijon mustard, curry powder, juice from ½ a lemon, a few dashes of hot sauce, and plenty of freshly cracked black pepper. Ingredients should be whisked together well.

♦ Add the cooked shrimp pieces to the mixing bowl. With a rubber spatula, fold the cooked shrimp into the mixture. Do not break the shrimp pieces apart.

   *Chef's Note: This is the time to taste your mixture to see what else is may need. More garlic? More pepper or hot sauce? Adjust seasonings accordingly.*

♦ Mound about 2 tablespoons of the shrimp mixture onto each egg half.

♦ Sprinkle each egg with a pinch of red paprika for some color contrast and then top each egg with a few pieces of freshly chopped chives. Refrigerate the platter of eggs for at least 30 minutes before serving.

# Appetizer

I was introduced to this recipe many years ago at a barbecue hosted by my sister, Nancy, and was hooked after just one bite. Her best friend and next-door neighbor arrived with a big, electric crockpot filled with seasoned cream cheese and jumbo lump crabmeat and I knew, right away, that I needed to add this to my repertoire, but with my own twists. I am still asked to bring this appetizer to parties and when I arrive, I am greeted with "Ooh, the crab dip is in the house!" so I like to have fun with it and have my "talking point" dish make its own statement. As you can see, I once used it to welcome 2013 and other times, the messages have been for specific loved ones. People are always asking, "How do you make this so good, Cardie?" Well, I am finally sharing one of my most prized culinary "secrets" with you so that you can make this recipe all by yourself!

## Ingredients:

- 2 (8 ounce) containers jumbo lump crabmeat (I use Phillips)
- 2 packages cream cheese with chives, softened (I use Philadelphia)
- 6 large Vidalia onions, sliced and caramelized (recipe follows)
- 2 tablespoons unsalted butter (for caramelizing onions)
- ¼ cup granulated sugar (for caramelizing onions)
- At least 1 cup white wine (for deglazing)
- 2 large garlic heads, roasted (recipe follows)
- 2 teaspoons olive oil (for roasting garlic)
- ½ tablespoon dried herbs (for roasting garlic)
- 4 tablespoons Emeril's Bayou Blast spice, divided
- Juice and zest from 2 whole lemons, divided
- 3 green onions or scallions, caramelized and minced finely (recipe follows)
- 3 whole sprigs thyme, leaves removed and minced finely
- 3 whole sprigs rosemary, leaves removed and minced finely
- 2 tablespoons or a few good shakes of Tabasco or Frank's Hot Sauce
- Kosher salt and freshly cracked pepper, to taste
- Fresh flat leaf parsley, chopped finely (for garnish)
- French bread or miniature rye bread, sliced (for dipping)

- 4 large red and green peppers
- 2 tablespoons Worcestershire sauce
- ½ cup mayonnaise
- ½ cup sour cream
- ½ cup aged cheddar cheese, shredded
- ½ cup Pepper Jack cheese, shredded
- Mild red paprika (for garnish)

# Signature
# New Orleans Jumbo
# Crabmeat Dip

## YIELD: SERVES 10-12

### Caramelized Onions Directions:

♦ Trim the ends off each onion and then halve them through the middle. Remove the peels and slice into half-moon shapes. Using a cast iron skillet or heavy Dutch oven, over medium-low heat, melt 2 tablespoons of unsalted butter and add the onions. Sprinkle the onions with salt and ¼ cup of granulated sugar. Stir the onions often until they are a dark mahogany and reduced. Do not let them burn. This will take 50-60 minutes. Deglaze the pan periodically with ¼ cup of a white wine as the onions cook. Set onions aside in a bowl to cool.

### Roasted Garlic Directions:

♦ Preheat oven to 425 degrees Fahrenheit.

♦ Using a very sharp knife, cut off the top ¼ section of each garlic head, exposing the cloves. Discard any loose paper from the head but do not remove all of it. Lay the garlic heads on a sheet of aluminum foil and place each garlic head clove-side up. Sprinkle with salt and pepper, 1 teaspoon of olive oil per garlic head, and ½ tablespoon of dried herbs (such as rosemary or thyme). Wrap the garlic heads in aluminum foil and seal the package. Place on a baking sheet. Roast garlic for 45 minutes. Once cooled, the garlic cloves can be easily removed using a paring knife or by simply squeezing the garlic heads with your hands.

### Roasted Peppers Directions:

♦ Place each bell pepper over an open gas flame on the stovetop or place them on a very hot grill. "Blister," or darken, the outer skins of the peppers on all sides, turning them frequently for about 10 minutes. Remove the peppers and place them into a brown paper bag. Roll up the bag and let the peppers sit for about 15 minutes. Remove the peppers from the bag and use your fingers to help peel off the outer skin. Then chop the peppers and combine.

### Crabmeat Dip Directions:

♦ Preheat oven to 350 degrees Fahrenheit.

♦ In a large mixing bowl, add the softened cream cheese, mayonnaise, and sour cream. Using a handheld mixer or metal spoon, stir the mixture until well blended. Blend in 2 tablespoons of Emeril's Bayou Blast, the caramelized onions, Worcestershire sauce, cheddar cheese, Pepper Jack cheese, thyme and rosemary sprigs, juice and zest from 1 of the lemons, hot sauce, and freshly cracked pepper. Taste the seasoned cream cheese and add spices accordingly.

♦ Drain the crabmeat carefully with a colander over the sink. Do not break up the lumps. Add 2 tablespoons of Emeril's Bayou Blast and 1 tablespoon of lemon juice and zest to the crabmeat. Toss gently in the colander. Very gently, fold the crabmeat into the seasoned cream cheese.

♦ In a 9 x 12 inch Pyrex dish, add the ingredients together. Spread them gently so as not to break apart the crabmeat. Place the uncovered dish into the oven and cook for 25 minutes or until the top is brown and bubbly.

♦ Garnish the dip with some reserved green onions and sprinkle with mild red paprika. Serve with sliced French bread or miniature rye bread on the side.

# Appetizer

Here is another recipe that will literally, stop your guests in their tracks at your next cocktail party! If you like blue cheese, Gruyere cheese, and bacon mixed together, this appetizer is for you! Yes, you can substitute cheddar cheese, or even Swiss cheese, if you desire, but there is something about pure Maytag blue cheese and Gruyere cheese that is just so deep and flavorful. Regardless of your choice of cheeses, be sure to make plenty of these stuffed mushrooms to pass around because these little culinary delights never last for very long!

## Ingredients:

♦ 30 large button *or* cremini mushrooms (stems removed, chopped, and reserved separately)

♦ ½ cup Gruyere cheese, grated

♦ ½ cup Maytag blue cheese, crumbled

♦ 1 (8 ounce) package cream cheese, softened (I use Philadelphia)

♦ 12 strips thick smoky bacon

♦ 2 tablespoons unsalted butter

♦ 1 tablespoon Emeril's Bayou Blast spice

♦ 2 Vidalia onions, chopped finely

♦ 1 cup Italian breadcrumbs, seasoned

♦ 4 large garlic cloves, minced very finely

♦ Juice from 1 whole lemon

♦ 1 tablespoon or a few good shakes of Tabasco sauce or Frank's Hot Sauce

♦ A pinch of Kosher salt and freshly cracked black pepper, to taste

♦ 1 whole lemon, quartered (for garnish)

♦ Whole curly parsley sprigs (for garnish)

CHEF CARDIE'S

# Smoky Bacon, Blue Cheese, and Gruyere Cheese Stuffed Mushrooms

YIELD: SERVES 10-12

## Directions:

♦ Preheat oven to 375 degrees Fahrenheit.

♦ On cookie sheets lined with aluminum foil, cook the bacon strips in the oven for about 15 minutes, or until they have browned and become crispy. Do not burn. Remove the bacon and allow it to cool. Chop the bacon coarsely and set it aside in a bowl.

♦ In a large sauté pan, over medium-high heat, add 2 tablespoons of unsalted butter, 1 tablespoon of Emeril's Bayou Blast spice, and the chopped onions and mushroom stems. Cook, stirring frequently, until the onions and stems begin to caramelize. This takes about 15 minutes. Remove the pan from the heat and allow the mixture to cool slightly.

♦ In a large mixing bowl, combine the cream cheese, seasoned breadcrumbs, Maytag blue cheese, grated Gruyere cheese, chopped bacon, onion and mushroom stem mixture, minced garlic, juice from 1 lemon, and a few dashes of hot sauce. Using a rubber spatula, combine or fold the mixture until everything is well integrated. Season with a pinch of Kosher salt and some freshly cracked black pepper.

*Chef's Note: Now is the time to taste the mixture to see what it needs. More hot sauce? More pepper? More garlic? Whatever you would like to add is just fine!*

♦ Spray a large, 9 x 13 Pyrex glass dish with buttered, non-stick cooking spray. Line up the mushrooms evenly so that they lie flat and side-by-side in the baking dish. Stuff each mushroom with one heaping tablespoon of the cheese and bacon mixture.

♦ Bake the mushrooms in the preheated oven for 15 minutes. These will be very hot so let them cool slightly before serving them to your guests. Garnish with whole sprigs of curly parsley and quartered lemon slices scattered around your serving platter (as shown in the picture).

# Appetizer

Do you love steamed mussels as much as I do? If so, then you already know that a good, local fish monger is needed in order to get the freshest and largest mussels available. I am not saying that your supermarket's fish counter is not the best place to get them, but I have not had much luck. Any seafood that sits on crushed ice under hot lights for hours at a time sends out a "caution flag" for me. A store that specializes in solely selling fresh seafood (usually brought in the same day and not frozen), is the best way to proceed. I promise, you will taste the difference. This delightful appetizer will light your taste buds on fire! It is a simple, one pot dish that is very easy to prepare. Oh, do not forget to include some crusty French bread so that you can sop up all of the delicious sauce!

## Ingredients:

- 5 pounds mussels, cleaned (see Chef's Note)
- 2 cups seafood stock (p. 91)
- 2 (13½ ounce) cans coconut milk
- ½ cup freshly squeezed lime juice (juice from about 5 or 6 large limes)
- 2 tablespoons unsalted butter
- 5 large garlic cloves, sliced very thinly
- 3 tablespoons fresh ginger, sliced (about 4 thin slices of peeled ginger)
- 2 tablespoons light brown sugar
- 2 tablespoons any good curry powder
- 2 bay leaves
- 1 tablespoon Old Bay seasoning
- Plenty of freshly cracked black pepper
- ½ cup fresh basil leaves, chopped (for garnish)
- ½ cup fresh cilantro, chopped (for garnish)
- Optional: crusty French bread (for dipping)

# Steamed Mussels in Coconut Lime Broth and Fresh Herbs

## YIELD: SERVES 8-10

### Directions:

*Chef's Note: Your fresh mussels may have a "beard" attached to the front or side of their shell. Simply pull on the "beard" to remove it and then discard. In a large colander, wash your mussels under very cold water and only cook the mussels that are firmly closed. Discard any cracked or slightly opened mussels.*

♦ In a small sauté pan, over medium heat, melt 2 tablespoons of the unsalted butter. Add and slowly cook the sliced garlic cloves and ginger pieces until they begin to caramelize, or turn golden brown, about 5 minutes. Do not burn or scorch the garlic or ginger. Remove from the heat and let this mixture cool for 5 minutes.

♦ The key to this mussel appetizer is the broth, the broth, the broth. In a 3 quart Dutch oven, add the seafood stock, coconut milk, brown sugar, lime juice, curry powder, bay leaves, Old Bay seasoning, reserved garlic and ginger, and plenty of freshly cracked black pepper.

♦ Bring the mixture up to a full boil. Then immediately reduce the heat to medium-low and simmer the sauce for 35 minutes, uncovered, or until the liquid has reduced by half. Add the cleaned mussels to the pot and raise the heat to medium-high. Close the lid of the Dutch oven and steam for 5-6 minutes, or until the mussels have opened completely.

*Chef's Note: Before you add the mussels to the broth, taste the liquid with a teaspoon and adjust seasonings as you see fit.*

♦ Remove pot from the stovetop. Using a slotted spoon, place the mussels onto a pretty silver or white platter. Using a small ladle, spoon the sauce over the top of the mussels. Garnish them with a sprinkling of chopped basil and some chopped cilantro. Serve immediately and enjoy!

# Appetizer

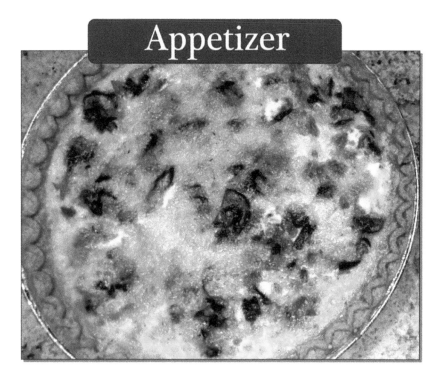

Did you just say to me, "Close your eyes so I can quiche you!?" Did I hear that correctly? Or did you say, "Chef Cardie, please get into your kitchen and bake for me one of your fabulous quiches!?" You can pair slices of this classic French dish with a fresh garden salad and glass or two of good white wine and you will have yourself a meal fit for a "roi." That is the French word for "king!" I am also going to give you the simple instructions for making your own savory, homemade pie crust! Bon appétit mon amis (enjoy your meal, my friends)!

## Quiche Ingredients:

- 1 package wild mushrooms *or* 1 cup combination of shiitake, button, and cremini mushrooms, chopped
- 4 large eggs, beaten well
- ½ cup whole milk
- ¼ cup sour cream
- ½ cup half-and-half *or* heavy cream
- ¼ cup Swiss cheese, grated
- ¼ cup Monterey Jack cheese, grated
- ¼ cup aged cheddar cheese, grated
- ½ cup fresh asparagus tips, chopped roughly
- 2 tablespoons unsalted butter
- 1 tablespoon Emeril's Bayou Blast spice
- ¼ cup green onions, chopped
- 1 tablespoon fresh thyme leaves, minced
- ½ tablespoon garlic powder
- ½ tablespoon onion powder
- Kosher salt and freshly cracked black pepper, to taste

## Pie Crust Ingredients:

- 1½ cups all-purpose flour (plus additional flour for rolling dough)
- 1 teaspoon Kosher salt
- 1 teaspoon freshly cracked black pepper
- ½ cup unsalted butter (1 stick), cold and cut into tablespoons
- 4 tablespoons cold water
- 1 package dry white lentils (for prebaking crust)

# Three Cheese Quiche
# with Asparagus and
# Wild Mushrooms

**YIELD: 1 LARGE QUICHE**

## Pie Crust Directions:

♦ Place the flour, salt, and pepper into the bowl of a food processor and pulse to combine well. Add the cold butter, 2 tablespoons at a time, and pulse until the mixture resembles coarse breadcrumbs. While the machine is running, drizzle in the cold water, processing until the dough comes together and forms a ball. Transfer the dough to a slightly floured surface and roll out into a flat disc shape. Cover it with plastic wrap and refrigerate for at least 1 hour.

♦ Preheat oven to 400 degrees Fahrenheit.

♦ Remove the disc of dough from the refrigerator and let it sit at room temperature for about 20 minutes. Roll out the dough to about ¼ inch thickness on a floured, marble cutting board. Lay the dough into a 10 inch quiche pan and crimp and trim the excess edges of the dough. Cut a piece of parchment paper large enough to cover the bottom portion of the quiche crust. Using the package of white lentil beans as pie weights, cover the parchment paper with the beans to prevent the crust from rising.

♦ Place the crust onto a cookie sheet and into the oven to bake for 15 minutes. Remove from the oven. Remove the lentil beans and parchment paper. Place the quiche crust back into the oven, uncovered, for another 15 minutes, or until it turns golden brown.

> *Chef's Note: I save the dry lentil beans in a zip-lock bag and use them each time I make a pie crust for my quiche. You can make your pie crust the day prior to lessen any stress or worry.*

## Quiche Directions:

♦ Preheat oven to 350 degrees Fahrenheit.

♦ In a large skillet on the stovetop, over medium heat, melt 2 tablespoons of butter. Add the wild mushrooms, fresh asparagus tips, Emeril's Bayou Blast spice, green onions, and some Kosher salt and freshly cracked black pepper, to taste. Sauté for about 8 minutes. Remove the pan from the heat and allow the mixture to cool slightly.

♦ In a large mixing bowl, combine the beaten eggs, milk, sour cream, half-and-half, minced thyme, garlic powder, and onion powder. Whisk everything together until well combined.

♦ Layer the three cheeses on the bottom portion of the quiche crust. Pour the mushroom and asparagus mixture over the top of the cheese and spread lightly with a rubber spatula. Carefully and slowly pour the egg and cream mixture into the quiche pan. Make sure that you do not overflow the pie crust.

♦ Return the quiche to the cookie sheet and bake for 30-35 minutes without opening the oven door. Test for doneness by inserting a toothpick into the center of the quiche. If it comes out clean, you are good to go! Remove the quiche and allow it to set for about 10 minutes.

# Salads

# Salad

I dedicate this simple and delicious recipe to my older son, Charlie. Even as a young boy, he loved ordering tuna fish sandwiches whenever he got the opportunity. Most of the time, I opened a regular can of that store-bought albacore tuna, dumped it into a mixing bowl, added plenty of celery; onions; and mayonnaise; and sandwiched the mixture between two, toasted pieces of white bread. Voila! Your typical tuna fish sandwich! However, as I became a more innovative and creative chef, I began asking myself questions about how to liven up the recipe. What about using fresh Ahi tuna from the local fish market? How about adding some chopped sour apples and wonderful herbs and spices to the mix? Now we are talking! So, the next time you go shopping for your child's tuna fish salad ingredients, skip the canned aisle and try this recipe instead! I guarantee that your kids will be singing your praises!

## Ingredients:

- 12 ounces fresh Ahi tuna steaks (from fish counter at your local market)
- 1 tablespoon olive oil
- 2 tablespoons unsalted butter
- ½ cup celery, diced finely
- ½ large Vidalia onion, chopped finely
- ½ (small) jar red pimentos, drained of liquid and chopped finely
- ½ cup Granny Smith apple (1 large apple), unpeeled and diced finely
- 2 heaping tablespoons Old Bay seasoning
- 2 teaspoons roasted garlic powder (not garlic salt)
- 1 (small) package fresh basil leaves, chopped finely
- A few good shakes any hot sauce (such as Tabasco or Frank's)
- At least ½ cup mayonnaise, to taste
- Plenty of freshly cracked black pepper, to taste
- 1 bunch radicchio lettuce (for garnish or serving base)

CHEF CARDIE'S

# Charlie's
# Ahi Tuna Salad with
# Granny Smith Apples

### YIELD: SERVES ABOUT 6

## Directions:

♦ In a large, non-stick skillet, over medium-high heat, add the olive oil and unsalted butter. Sear the tuna steaks on the first side until lightly browned, about 3 minutes. Turn with a spatula or tongs and sear for another 2 minutes, or until cooked to your preference. Transfer the tuna to a plate and let it rest, undisturbed, for 5 minutes.

> *Chef's Note: I like to cook my tuna steaks to medium-rare. They should be cooked on the outside until nice and browned but left a bit "pink" on the inside. This will preserve the wonderful taste of the Ahi tuna itself.*

♦ In a large mixing bowl, add the celery, onions, pimentos, Granny Smith apples, Old Bay seasoning, roasted garlic powder, chopped basil, and a few good shakes of your favorite hot sauce. Mix the ingredients together well.

♦ Flake the fish with your fingers or cut the cooled tuna steaks into ½ inch chunks. Add to the mixing bowl. Add at least ½ cup of mayonnaise and plenty of freshly cracked black pepper. Using a rubber spatula, fold the mayonnaise into all of the ingredients until everything is mixed to a smooth consistency.

♦ With a serving spoon, place a desired amount of the tuna salad into individual leaf "bowls" of your radicchio lettuce.

> *Chef's Note: A radicchio lettuce bundle is shaped like a small bowl. Each segment of the lettuce pulls apart and forms a cute, little edible bowl for serving.*

# Salad

A few things about Caesar Salad before we begin. I am sorry to disappoint you, but the dish was named after its "inventor," Italian chef, Cesare Cardini around 1923…not Julius Caesar. When it is prepared correctly, it is a delicious, culinary dream. Those wrinkled fast food packets you see are a poor representation. A surefire way to impress a special someone is to follow these instructions when making your salad. The romantic rewards you may reap will have you wanting to make it often!

## Caesar Salad Ingredients:

- 1 tablespoon Kosher salt
- 2 large garlic cloves, peeled and left whole
- Juice from ½ lemon
- 2 tablespoons red wine vinegar
- 1 tablespoon dry mustard (I use Colman's)
- 1 large egg yolk
- 1 tablespoon Worcestershire sauce
- ¼ cup good olive oil
- 1 package Romaine lettuce hearts, cut into 2 inch pieces
- ¼ cup fresh parmesan cheese, grated
- ½ cup French bread croutons (recipe follows)
- Kosher salt and freshly cracked black pepper, to taste
- Optional: 2 small anchovy fillets (buy Italian gourmet if including)

## Herbed & Parmesan Croutons Ingredients:

- 1 large loaf crusty French bread, cut into 1½ inch sized cubes
- ½ cup unsalted butter (1 stick), melted
- ½ cup fresh parmesan cheese, grated
- 4 garlic cloves, minced finely
- 1 tablespoon fresh thyme leaves, minced finely
- 1 tablespoon flat leaf parsley, minced finely

# Classic Caesar Salad
# with Herbed and Parmesan
# Croutons

## Classic Caesar Salad Directions:

*Chef's Note: Do not make this salad using large, metal mixing bowls. Invest in a good, wooden salad bowl.*

♦ Add 1 tablespoon of salt to the center of the wooden bowl. Add the 2 garlic cloves on top and, pressing firmly with the back of a fork or metal spoon, begin to make a paste. Mix well for about 2 minutes, or until the garlic begins to fall apart. Remove any large garlic pieces with your spoon and discard.

♦ If desired, add the anchovy fillets and break them up in the garlic and salt mixture.

♦ Using a small wire whisk or the back of your spoon, add the lemon juice, red wine vinegar, dry mustard, egg yolk, and Worcestershire sauce. Combine items well.

♦ In a very slow stream and stirring constantly, add the olive oil to form an emulsion. This will finalize the liquid components of the Caesar dressing. Whisk in the parmesan cheese.

♦ Add the chopped Romaine lettuce hearts to the bowl and using tongs, toss the lettuce leaves, lightly coating or "kissing" them with the Caesar dressing. Do not "drown" the leaves in the dressing. Season with Kosher salt and freshly cracked black pepper.

♦ Top the salad with freshly baked, grated parmesan cheese croutons. Mix everything once more. Serve in a pretty salad bowl or dish of your choice.

## Herbed and Parmesan Croutons Directions:

♦ Preheat oven to 350 degrees Fahrenheit.

♦ Place the melted butter, parmesan cheese, minced garlic cloves, and fresh herbs into a large, metal salad bowl. Stir well. Season with Kosher salt and fresh pepper. Add the French bread cubes and using tongs or your clean hands, coat the bread on all sides.

♦ Position the bread cubes on a cookie sheet lined with aluminum foil. Bake in the oven for 15-18 minutes. Watch very carefully to avoid burning the croutons.

# Salad

Here is a fun and creative salad for you to make during the "dog days" of summer. I just love grilled corn-on-the-cob and I simply love to grill fresh, green and yellow zucchini. It goes fantastically with a few chopped Jersey tomatoes, grilled Bermuda red onion, some fresh basil leaves, and a bit of olive oil mixed with fresh lime juice and zest. Add it all together and you have got yourself a beautiful little side dish. For a dramatic presentation, I put this salad right on top of my oven-baked flounder fillets and serve. Delicious and beautiful to the eye as well!

## Ingredients:

- 6 ears fresh corn, husked and cleaned
- 4 fresh (large) zucchinis (2 green and 2 yellow), split lengthwise
- 1 medium red Bermuda onion, halved
- ½ cup good olive oil (plus 2 tablespoons to grill corn and zucchini)
- 2 tablespoons Emeril's Bayou Blast spice
- 4 large Jersey tomatoes, cut in half and then diced into 1 inch cubes
- 2 tablespoons granulated sugar
- 1 tablespoon dry mustard (I use Colman's)
- Juice and zest from 2 large limes
- 2 tablespoons balsamic vinegar
- 1 tablespoon white wine vinegar
- ¼ cup fresh basil leaves, chopped finely (for garnish)
- A pinch of Kosher salt and freshly cracked black pepper, to taste

# Grilled Corn, Red Onion, and Zucchini Summer Salad

## Directions:

♦ Place the husked and cleaned corn, sliced zucchini, and red onion halves into a large roasting pan. Sprinkle the corn, zucchini, and onion with 2 tablespoons of olive oil and mix with the 2 tablespoons of Emeril's Bayou Blast spice. Toss the vegetables in the mixture until they are coated on all sides.

♦ Place the corn over a hot grill and rotate by a half turn every 1 minute, or until the corn has caramelized on all sides, about 10 minutes. Place the sliced zucchini and red onion halves on the grill, grilling for 2 to 3 minutes per side. Remove them from the grill when they have caramelized. This should take approximately 8 minutes.

*Chef's Note: Grilling the corn will take a few minutes longer than the zucchini or red onion. Grill the corn first, remove it from the grill, and then tend to the zucchini and red onion.*

♦ On a clean cutting board, cut the grilled zucchini into pretty, half-moon slices and put them into a salad bowl. Chop the grilled red onion halves into bite-sized pieces and add them to the bowl. Add the diced tomatoes. Using a sharp knife, remove the kernels and add to the bowl.

*Chef's Note: The easiest way to remove kernels is to first cut the corn in half. Then stand each ear of corn on a clean kitchen towel. Slice the corn in a downward motion, letting the grilled kernels fall into the cloth so that they can be poured into the bowl.*

♦ In another mixing bowl, add the granulated sugar, dry mustard, lime juice, lime zest, balsamic vinegar, and 1 tablespoon of white wine vinegar. Stir well with a whisk. In a slow stream, add the ½ cup of olive oil to form an emulsion. Whisk vigorously until the dressing comes together. Season with a pinch of Kosher salt and freshly cracked black pepper.

♦ Carefully pour about 3 tablespoons of the dressing over the reserved vegetables in the bowl. Toss the vegetables gently in the liquid with tongs.

*Chef's Note: This salad is especially delicious if you let everything chill for a few hours before serving. I make my salad in the morning and refrigerate it until the party begins but it can even be made two days in advance and kept refrigerated in an airtight container.*

♦ Garnish your plates with ½ cup of chopped basil leaves. Serve the salad well chilled.

# Salad

I "invented" this special salad many years ago while working weekends at a well-known, Bergen County, New Jersey restaurant. I wanted the menu to include a creative salad which could also serve as an entrée. This fresh and colorful presentation passed with flying colors with both the owners *and* customers! There are two key words to note here: "fresh fish!" My mother and culinary teachers could not emphasize enough how important it is to smell the fish that you are buying. As Emeril Lagasse would say, "If your seafood doesn't smell like the fresh ocean, go with the lamb chops." I recommend seafood lovers try this recipe at home. You and everyone else will absolutely love it!

## Ingredients:

♦ 3 pounds large shrimp (16-20 per pound), peeled and deveined

♦ 2 pounds fresh wild Alaskan salmon fillets, cut in half and then into 2 inch squares

♦ 2 pounds large sea scallops

♦ 1 heaping tablespoon Old Bay seasoning

♦ ½ cup olive oil (plus at least 3 tablespoons for seasoning and sautéing the fish)

♦ 2 tablespoons unsalted butter

♦ 4 garlic cloves, crushed and minced finely

♦ Juice from 2 large lemons

♦ Juice from 2 large limes

♦ 1 heaping tablespoon Dijon mustard

♦ 2 tablespoons granulated white sugar

♦ 2 tablespoons white wine vinegar

♦ 1 package fresh Romaine lettuce hearts, chopped coarsely

♦ 1 head iceberg lettuce, chopped coarsely

♦ 1 head radicchio lettuce, chopped coarsely

♦ 2 pints fresh blackberries

♦ 2 large Jersey tomatoes, cut in half and then sliced

♦ 2 Vidalia onions, cut in half and then sliced thinly

♦ Fresh cilantro, chopped finely (for garnish)

♦ Kosher salt and freshly cracked black pepper, to taste

# Grilled Shrimp, Wild Salmon, and Scallop Seafood Salad with Blackberries

## Directions:

♦ In a large mixing bowl, add the shrimp, scallops, and wild salmon. Season the seafood with 1 tablespoon of Old Bay seasoning and 3 tablespoons of olive oil. Move the fish around gently and do not break up the seafood itself.

♦ In a large, cast iron pot, over medium-high heat, melt 2 tablespoons of unsalted butter. Add and cook the scallops, without turning them over, for 3 minutes. Flip scallops with a spatula and continue cooking for 3 additional minutes. Transfer the scallops to a warm plate or bowl. Add the wild salmon fillets to the pan and cook them for 2 minutes on each side. Remove the salmon pieces and add them to the cooked scallops. Add in the large shrimp and cook each side for 3 minutes. They will turn pink or opaque when they are done cooking. Add the shrimp to the scallops and salmon.

*Chef's Note: You may need more butter or olive oil when sautéing the seafood.*

♦ In another mixing bowl, combine the minced garlic, lemon juice, lime juice, Dijon mustard, granulated sugar, and white wine vinegar. Stir vigorously with a wire whisk to incorporate everything. Slowly drizzle in ½ cup of olive oil, whisking constantly, to form an emulsion. Season the dressing with Kosher salt and freshly cracked black pepper.

♦ To assemble the salad for serving, lay down a blanket of all three lettuces on the bottom of each serving plate. Top the lettuce leaves with a small handful of fresh blackberries, a few slices of chopped tomato, and a few thin slices of Vidalia onion. Add a heaping portion of the mixed seafood. Spoon or ladle over a few tablespoons of the reserved salad dressing. Garnish each plate with freshly chopped cilantro. Serve immediately.

*Chef's Note: You can preassemble the plates with the blackberries, lettuces, tomatoes, and onions. However, I would keep the seafood and salad dressing chilled in the refrigerator until your guests are ready to be served.*

# Salad

There is a simple reason why potato salad is often served at get togethers: it is delicious! The key rule for this recipe is to not overcook your potatoes! Mushy potatoes are no good! Nada! Nyet! Nein! Simply follow the "yellow brick road" by way of these instructions to create a wonderful side dish which can accompany almost any meal!

## Ingredients:

- ♦ 4 pounds baby Yukon gold potatoes (about 1½ bags), unpeeled
- ♦ 4 large eggs (recipe follows)
- ♦ ¼ cup Kosher salt (for boiling eggs and potatoes), divided
- ♦ 1 tablespoon white wine vinegar (for boiling eggs)
- ♦ 1 bunch sliced scallions (white), and half of the green parts, chopped
- ♦ 2 tablespoons green onion, chopped
- ♦ ½ cup dill pickles (about 5 large pickles), chopped finely
- ♦ 8 slices smoky bacon, cooked, cooled, and chopped
- ♦ 1 tablespoon Emeril's Original Essence spice
- ♦ 1 (small) jar red pimentos, chopped
- ♦ 2 cups prepared mayonnaise
- ♦ Juice from 1 lemon
- ♦ ¼ cup Dijon mustard
- ♦ ½ small red onion, chopped
- ♦ Salt and freshly cracked black pepper, to taste
- ♦ Paprika (for garnish)
- ♦ Optional: 2 tablespoons capers, drained
- ♦ Optional: fresh flat leaf parsley, chopped finely (for garnish)
- ♦ Optional: additional green onions, chopped (for garnish)

# Homemade Irish
# Potato Salad

**YIELD: SERVES ABOUT 8**

## Perfectly Cooked, Hard-Boiled Eggs Directions:

♦ Lay your large eggs flat in a large pot or Dutch oven (with a tight-fitting lid). Fill the pot with cold water, covering the eggs by 1 inch. Add 1 tablespoon of white wine vinegar to the water along with 2 tablespoons of Kosher salt. Over medium-high heat, let the water and eggs reach a full boil. Once it does, remove the pot from the heat, cover it tightly, and let the pot sit undisturbed for 10 minutes. Immediately drain the eggs with a colander over the sink and place the eggs into a larger bowl filled with ice water.

## Potato Salad Directions:

♦ In a larger pot filled with cold, salted water, over high heat, let the brine reach a full boil. Add the unpeeled potatoes and cook for 20 minutes, or until fork tender. Remove the potatoes from the water and drain them with a colander. Let them cool slightly. Place potatoes in a 1 gallon zip-lock bag and allow them to cool and harden for 2 hours in the refrigerator.

♦ In a large mixing bowl, add the green onions, pickles, capers, bacon, Emeril's Original Essence, pimentos, mayonnaise, juice from 1 lemon, mustard, and chopped red onion. Whisk the ingredients together thoroughly.

♦ Carefully remove the outer shells from the chilled eggs and roughly chop or slice them. Add the eggs to the bowl. Using a very sharp knife, quarter the larger potatoes and halve the smaller sized ones. Mix well with the other ingredients. Add salt and black pepper, to taste.

♦ Garnish the top of your salad with finely chopped flat leaf parsley or chopped green onion (or both). Sprinkle on a bit of red paprika for extra color. Serve this salad chilled.

*Chef's Note: I make my potato salad and coleslaw (p. 61), the day before my party. That way, the flavors have a chance to fuse together.*

# Salad

I have had the good fortune of growing up and spending more than half of my life's summers on the Jersey Shore. I lived first in Normandy Beach, then Mantoloking Dunes, and now Point Pleasant Beach with my wife. There is nothing like the fresh seafood and creamy coleslaw synonymous with that area. My earliest childhood recollections of this coleslaw are from the famous (and adored), Wharfside and Lobster Shanty restaurants. These great establishments are still going strong and more importantly, they still serve this delicious side salad. Here is my take on it!

## Ingredients:

- ½ head green cabbage, cut and shredded (see Chef's Note)
- ½ head purple cabbage, cut and shredded (see Chef's Note)
- 2 cups mayonnaise (I use Hellman's)
- ¼ cup white granulated sugar
- ¼ cup brown sugar, packed
- Juice from 1 lemon
- 2 tablespoons rice wine vinegar
- 2 tablespoons prepared horseradish, grated
- 1 teaspoon onion powder
- 1 teaspoon celery salt
- 1 teaspoon dry mustard (I use Colman's)
- ½ cup carrots, grated
- Paprika (for garnish)
- Kosher salt and freshly cracked black pepper, to taste

# Jersey Shore
# Coleslaw

## Directions:

♦ Except for the shredded cabbage, place all of the ingredients into a large mixing bowl and whisk until everything has been well combined. The sugar must completely dissolve in the mixture. Taste to see what the dressing might need and adjust according to your taste buds.

*Chef's Note: If you want to make life easier, most supermarkets carry packages of multicolored shredded coleslaw. These can be used to avoid using a sharp box grater. Two packages will feed about 8 people.*

♦ Add the shredded cabbage to the mixing bowl and using tongs, toss everything to combine well. Chill the finished coleslaw in the refrigerator for 1 hour before serving.

♦ Decorate your plate with lettuce leaves for a more dramatic and colorful presentation.

*Chef's Note: I sometimes use a nice and round metal food mold to present this dish. This mold can be found in just about any gourmet market or store.*

# Salad

I have been enjoying delicious egg salads and salads for as many years as I have been alive (and that is a pretty long time)! My mother often made me this special recipe for my school lunch while I was growing up in Upper Montclair, New Jersey. Packed with my egg salad sandwich on soft, Wonder bread were some ruffled potato chips and a Yoo-Hoo chocolate milk to wash it all down. Do you remember those days or am I dating myself again? Anyway, even at a young age, I appreciated and looked forward to my mom's food. Somehow and someway, Mom did her own special thing; nothing was the "norm" or "same old thing" for this amazing lady. She would see a Monet but paint a Picasso! Of all things, she would add a tablespoon of curry powder and a teaspoon of ground cumin to give this salad a different kind of zing. I promise you, the spices are not overpowering or off-tasting in any way. Please try this recipe with your own kids and see what they think! I honestly believe you will receive some great grades on your next report card!

## Ingredients:

♦ 8 hardboiled eggs, peeled and chopped coarsely (recipe follows)

♦ 1 tablespoon white wine vinegar

♦ 2 tablespoons Kosher salt

♦ ½ cup real mayonnaise

♦ 5 green onions, sliced thinly

♦ ½ cup celery, sliced finely

♦ At least 1 tablespoon any good curry powder, to taste

♦ 1 heaping tablespoon Emeril's Original Essence spice

♦ 2 teaspoons celery salt

♦ 2 teaspoons garlic powder (not garlic salt)

♦ A few good shakes any hot sauce (such as Tabasco or Frank's)

♦ 1 teaspoon cumin, ground

♦ 1 tablespoon Dijon mustard

♦ Juice from ½ lemon

♦ Plenty of freshly cracked black pepper, to taste

♦ Optional: 1 tablespoon Spanish paprika (not the smoked kind) (for garnish)

♦ Optional: radicchio lettuce leaves (for garnish or serving base)

# CHEF CARDIE'S
# Mom's
# Curried
# Egg Salad

YIELD: SERVES ABOUT 6

## Perfectly Cooked, Hard-Boiled Eggs Directions:

♦ Lay your large eggs flat in a large pot or Dutch oven (with a tight-fitting lid). Fill the pot with cold water, covering the eggs by 1 inch. Add 1 tablespoon of white wine vinegar to the water along with 2 tablespoons of Kosher salt. Over medium-high heat, let the water and eggs reach a full boil. Once it does, remove the pot from the heat, cover it tightly, and let it sit undisturbed for 10 minutes. Immediately drain the eggs with a colander over the sink and place the eggs into a larger bowl filled with ice water. Once cool enough to handle, peel the eggs and chop them coarsely.

## Egg Salad Directions:

♦ In a large mixing bowl, whisk together the mayonnaise, green onions, celery, curry powder, Emeril's Essence spice, celery salt, garlic powder, hot sauce, ground cumin, Dijon mustard, and lemon juice. Fold in the chopped eggs and season the salad with plenty of freshly cracked black pepper.

♦ Garnish the salad with 1 tablespoon of Spanish paprika (not the smoked kind). Cover the salad with plastic wrap and chill in the refrigerator for at least 1 hour before serving.

*Chef's Note: This egg salad can be served on a regular bed of mixed salad greens or you can make an incredible sandwich on whole wheat, Italian, or French bread. You can also use radicchio lettuce leaves shaped like little serving "bowls" and present your salad in a more "dramatic" fashion!*

# Salad

Do you love peaches as much as I do? You can enjoy this recipe year-round with either fresh summer peaches or canned peaches during the wintertime. Pairing beautifully with fresh and meaty avocados, this delightful side salad will impress your family and guests and bring sunshine to your day. The tasty dish, topped with a lemon and lime vinaigrette, is great on its own, but it can also go right on top of your fresh fish fillets or oven-baked, barbecued chicken breasts to create a dramatic and delicious culinary presentation!

## Ingredients:

♦ 3 large avocados, peeled, sliced in half lengthwise, and center pit removed (see Chef's Note)

♦ 6 large peaches, unpeeled, halved, and center pit removed (fresh or canned)

♦ ½ cup olive oil, divided

♦ 1 tablespoon Emeril's Original Essence spice

♦ ½ cup brown sugar, packed

♦ 2 medium Vidalia onions, peeled and then quartered

♦ 2 medium red bell peppers, seeds removed and halved lengthwise

♦ Juice from 1 large lemon

♦ Juice from 2 large limes

♦ 1 tablespoon white wine vinegar

♦ 1 tablespoon granulated sugar

♦ 2 tablespoons balsamic vinegar

♦ 1 tablespoon dry mustard (I use Colman's)

♦ 2 tablespoons fresh cilantro leaves, chopped (for garnish)

♦ A pinch of Kosher salt and freshly cracked black pepper, to taste

# Peach, Red Pepper, and Avocado Salad with Citrus Vinaigrette

## Directions:

♦ Preheat oven to the broiler setting.

♦ Place the peach halves, quartered onions, and red pepper halves into a large roasting pan and coat them with ¼ cup of olive oil, 1 tablespoon of Emeril's Essence spice, and ½ cup of brown sugar. Toss everything to coat well. Place the roasting pan under the broiler and cook for 15 minutes, or until the peaches and vegetables have browned and caramelized. Do not let the mixture burn. Remove from the oven and let everything cool for about 10 minutes.

> *Chef's Note: If you would prefer to grill your peaches, be my guest. Each side can be grilled over medium heat for about 3 minutes. Do not let them burn, but rather, caramelize. Remove and cool once done.*

♦ Once cooled, chop the onions and bell peppers into 1 inch chunks. Slice the cooked peach halves in half again and add everything to a large, silver mixing bowl.

♦ Using a tablespoon, and going around the outer edges in a slow, circular motion, gently remove the inside of each avocado half. Dice the "meat" of the avocados into 1 inch cubes and add to the bowl of peaches and vegetables. Set aside.

> *Chef's Note: An avocado is at its freshest when it can be squeezed easily or has a bit of "give" to it. Do not purchase avocados that are as hard as rocks. It means that they are not ripe and are therefore, unusable.*

♦ To create your salad dressing, in another mixing bowl, whisk together the juices from 1 large lemon and 2 large limes. Blend in the 1 tablespoon of white wine vinegar, 1 tablespoon of granulated sugar, balsamic vinegar, dry mustard, a pinch of Kosher salt, and freshly cracked black pepper, to taste. Mix together well. In a slow stream, drizzle in the remaining ¼ cup of olive oil, whisking continuously to create an emulsion.

♦ Spoon the dressing over the peaches and vegetables. Gently fold everything together using a rubber spatula. Do not break up the avocado or peaches with a heavy metal spoon. Garnish the top of the salad with 2 tablespoons of chopped cilantro leaves. Serve this salad chilled.

> *Chef's Note: This is another dish that can be easily made the night before or morning of your big event. Just make sure that the ingredients are sealed in either an airtight container or large salad bowl covered tightly with plastic wrap and are stored in the refrigerator.*

# Salad

A coulis is simply a puree of fruit or vegetables to make a dressing or garnish. I apologize for the fancy culinary term, but your guests will be quite impressed by your talents and knowledge! It is fun to make all different kinds of salads, but I had a blast making this one at a summer demonstration I did called, "Lettuce Celebrate," at Kings Cooking Studios. At the time, I used fresh mangos (which were in season), but you can easily make this salad with peaches as well. This recipe really stands out because so many people enjoy lobster with fruit. If you do too, then this all-seasons dish is for you!

## Poached Salad Ingredients:

- ♦ 4 large avocados, very ripe
- ♦ 2 (10 ounce) frozen lobster tails, thawed in refrigerator
- ♦ 2 cups dry white wine
- ♦ ½ cup cold water
- ♦ ½ cup Vidalia onions (2 medium or 1 large), sliced
- ♦ Juice from 2 lemons, divided (for lobster and avocados)
- ♦ 2 bay leaves
- ♦ 2 heaping tablespoons Old Bay seasoning
- ♦ Juice and zest from 1 large orange
- ♦ 2 packages leafy green lettuce (I use a combination of butter and iceberg lettuce)
- ♦ 2 cups peaches, sliced into 1 inch chunks
- ♦ ½ cup green pepper (about 1 large pepper), chopped finely
- ♦ ½ cup red pepper (about 1 large pepper), chopped finely
- ♦ ½ cup red Bermuda onion, minced finely
- ♦ Salt and freshly cracked black pepper, to taste
- ♦ Optional: cilantro, chopped (for garnish)
- ♦ Optional: garlic bread (p. 129)

## Peach Honey Coulis Ingredients:

- ♦ 1 (15 ounce) can peaches *or* 2 (large) fresh peaches, peeled, pitted, and cut into 1 inch chunks
- ♦ 2 tablespoons freshly squeezed lemon juice (about ½ lemon)
- ♦ 2 tablespoons freshly squeezed lime juice (about ½ lime)
- ♦ ¼ cup freshly squeezed orange juice
- ♦ 4 large garlic cloves
- ♦ 4 tablespoons honey
- ♦ 2 teaspoons cinnamon
- ♦ ½ teaspoon nutmeg, grated
- ♦ 2 good shakes of Tabasco sauce or Frank's Hot Sauce
- ♦ 2 tablespoons granulated sugar
- ♦ Salt and freshly cracked black pepper, to taste

# Poached Lobster and Avocado Salad with Peach and Honey Coulis

YIELD: SERVES 8-10

## Peach Honey Coulis Directions:

♦ Place all ingredients into a blender or food processor and puree, scraping down the sides a few times. Strain the pureed ingredients through a fine wire mesh sieve into a bowl or small pot. Press down with a small, rubber spatula to release the liquids from any remaining solids before discarding. Refrigerate the dressing for at least 1 hour before serving.

## Poached Lobster Directions:

♦ In a 3 quart Dutch oven, add the 2 cups of white wine, ½ cup of water, sliced Vidalia onions, juice from 1 of the lemons, 2 bay leaves, Old Bay seasoning, orange juice, and orange zest. Place on the stovetop over medium heat and let the mixture reach a low simmer.

♦ Set the lobster tails onto a cutting board and, with a very sharp knife, slice the thawed tails down lengthwise, creating two halves. Place the halved lobster tails into the pot, shell-side down, and simmer them gently for about 15 minutes. Remove the lobster from the liquid and set aside to cool. Once cool, slice the lobster meat into diagonal slices about ½ inch thick.

*Chef's Note: Remember, a simmer is when the water does not reach the boiling point. Do not overcook your lobster tails.*

## Poached Lobster and Avocado Salad Directions:

♦ Peel and cut the avocados lengthwise and remove the pit with a sharp knife. Cut the avocados into decorative slices. Squeeze the juice from the remaining lemon over the avocados so they do not brown or "oxidize." Arrange the avocado slices over the lettuce greens you have placed in individual bowls or on a large serving platter.

♦ In a bowl, mix the lobster meat, peach chunks, chopped green and red bell peppers, and minced red onion together. Using a tablespoon, drizzle the peach coulis dressing over the top of the salad without "drowning" it. Season with a pinch of Kosher salt and lots of freshly cracked black pepper.

♦ Garnish with a sprinkling of chopped parsley and cilantro. Serve with slices of warm garlic bread (p. 129), on the side and pair with a good glass of fruity Chardonnay!

# Salad

There are many delicious seafood salads out there but this one tops my list! Although it is a popular dish in New Orleans, classic Shrimp Louie is credited as first being made in the early 1900's by Louis Davenport, a hotel owner and restaurateur from the West Coast. I never had Mr. Davenport's version, but my mother used her "kicked-up" Russian dressing with spicy chili sauce, fresh Jersey tomatoes, ripe avocados, and hard-boiled eggs to make the best Shrimp Louie I have ever eaten. It inspired this recipe! You must make this salad for your family or a luncheon with your best friends!

## Shrimp Louie Ingredients:

- 3 pounds large Gulf shrimp (16-20 per pound), cooked, peeled, and deveined
- 1 stick butter, melted (for cooking shrimp only)
- 1 heaping tablespoon Old Bay Seasoning (for cooking shrimp only)
- 3 ripe avocados, halved, pit removed, and cut into slices
- 8 large eggs, hardboiled (recipe follows), cooled and sliced or cut into quarters
- 1 tablespoon white vinegar (for cooking eggs only)
- 2 tablespoons Kosher salt (for cooking eggs only)
- 2 heads crisp iceberg lettuce
- 3 large cucumbers, peeled and cut into ½ inch slices
- 6 large beefsteak Jersey tomatoes, sliced in half and then cut into quarters
- 1 cup black olives, pitted

## Shrimp Louie Dressing Ingredients:

- 1½ cups mayonnaise
- ½ cup catsup
- ¼ cup hot and spicy chili sauce
- 3 tablespoons pickle relish
- 2 tablespoons Worcestershire sauce
- Juice from 1 lemon
- Kosher salt and freshly cracked black pepper, to taste
- 1 additional lemon, sliced thinly (for garnish)
- Optional: 1 bunch fresh chives (for garnish)

# Shrimp Louie
# Salad

OR 8 SMALL PLATES

## Shrimp Louie Directions:

♦ Evenly divide the iceberg lettuce, cucumbers, avocados, eggs, tomatoes, cooked shrimp, and black olives between 6 large salad plates.

## Perfectly Cooked, Hard-Boiled Eggs Directions:

♦ Lay your large eggs flat in a large pot or Dutch oven (with a tight-fitting lid). Fill the pot with cold water, covering the eggs by 1 inch. Add 1 tablespoon of white wine vinegar to the water along with 2 tablespoons of Kosher salt. Over medium-high heat, let the water and eggs reach a full boil. Once it does, remove the pot from the heat, cover it tightly, and let it sit undisturbed for 10 minutes. Immediately drain the eggs with a colander over the sink and place the eggs into a larger bowl filled with ice water. Once cool enough to handle, peel the eggs and slice them.

## Shrimp Directions:

♦ Please refer to this book's shrimp cocktail recipe for cooking instructions (p. 33). If necessary, you can purchase freshly cooked and peeled shrimp from your local fish monger. They will let you sample a shrimp in order to ensure its freshness.

> *Chef's Note: For a more dramatic presentation, I place my fresh shrimp (peeled and uncooked), onto a hot grill for about 3 minutes per side. While they cook, they are brushed with 1 stick of melted butter that is seasoned with a heaping tablespoon of Old Bay seasoning. Once off the grill, I cover and refrigerate the shrimp for a few hours, or even overnight.*

## Shrimp Louie Dressing Directions:

♦ Place the listed ingredients into a large mixing bowl. Whisk vigorously until well combined. Chill the Louie dressing in the refrigerator for at least one hour before serving. I make my dressing the night prior.

♦ Spoon the chilled dressing over the top of the assembled salad. Garnish with some chopped chives and lemon slices.

# Salad

This is one of the dishes that I made for the sold-out cooking class, "Lettuce Celebrate" at Kings Cooking Studios in Short Hills, New Jersey. The audience took home the recipe for this light, yet satisfying salad that day and now I am sharing it with all of you. It is a tangy and sweet salad with a bit of crunch that is just perfect and very refreshing to eat during the hot summer months.

## Ingredients:

- 2 small shallots, peeled and sliced
- ¼ cup sherry vinegar
- ¼ cup rice wine vinegar
- ¼ cup lemon juice
- 3 tablespoons honey (I use Sue Bee)
- 2 teaspoons Kosher salt
- ½ cup extra virgin olive oil
- 2 cucumbers, peeled, seedless, and cut into small nickels
- 2 cups fresh jicama, peeled of brown skin and shredded or grated
- 3 cups watermelon, cut into small cubes
- 3 cups honeydew melon, cut into small cubes
- Freshly cracked black pepper, to taste
- 2 tablespoons fresh mint, chopped, divided (1 tablespoon reserved for garnish)

# Sweet and Tangy Melon and Jicama Slaw

YIELD: SERVES 8-10

## Directions:

♦ Soak the shallots in the ¼ cup of sherry vinegar for 15 minutes. This will remove some of the sharp onion flavor from the shallot.

♦ Combine the shallots and sherry vinegar with the rice wine vinegar, lemon juice, honey, and salt and pepper. Slowly whisk in ½ cup of olive oil to create an emulsion. Then, add 1 tablespoon of chopped fresh mint to the mixture. Set the dressing aside.

♦ In a separate bowl, combine the cucumbers, jicama, watermelon, and honeydew melon. Pour the dressing over the fruit and vegetables and lightly toss. Do not over mix or break up the melon pieces.

♦ Seal the mixture in an airtight container and refrigerate overnight. Garnish with the remaining 1 tablespoon of chopped mint. Serve chilled.

# Salad

The Waldorf-Astoria, located in New York City, is arguably one of the finest hotels in the world. This historic and elite hotel has housed presidents and world leaders alike since it opened in March 1893. The hotel has been closed since 2017 due to extensive renovations but they plan to reopen sometime in 2020 as both a hotel and an apartment complex. I am not sure why people cannot leave history alone but I guess life goes on! Speaking of history, in 1896, this wonderful and refreshing salad was invented by a simple restaurant worker named "Oscar Tschirky." He became known as, "Oscar of the Waldorf," and his salad became a worldwide phenomenon. So, when you have a taste this fruity and delicious salad, you will actually be taking a bite out of world-class history!

## Salad Ingredients:

- 1 cup dried cranberries
- 1 cup hot water
- 1½ cups mayonnaise (I use Hellman's)
- 3 tablespoons sour cream
- 2 teaspoons granulated sugar
- 2 tablespoons fresh lemon juice (juice from 1 large lemon)
- 4 Granny Smith apples, peeled, cored, and cut into ½ inch cubes
- 1 cup celery, sliced thinly
- 1½ cups red grapes (seedless), cut in half
- ½ cup candied walnuts *or* pecans, chopped (recipe follows) (be mindful of allergies)
- Large lettuce leaves (for plating)
- 2 pinches of Kosher salt and plenty of freshly cracked black pepper, to taste

## Candied Walnuts Ingredients:

- ½ cup walnuts *or* pecans (be mindful of allergies)
- 3 tablespoons unsalted butter
- ¼ cup granulated sugar

# Waldorf Salad
# with Candied Walnuts

YIELD: SERVES 8

## Salad Directions:

◆ In a medium-large sized mixing bowl, soak the cranberries in hot water until they soften and plump, about 10 minutes. Drain the cranberries with a colander, pat them dry, and set aside.

◆ In another mixing bowl, whisk together the mayonnaise, sour cream, granulated sugar, and fresh lemon juice. Add the apple cubes, sliced celery, halved grapes, and reserved cranberries. Season with a pinch or two of Kosher salt and lots of freshly cracked black pepper. Mix the ingredients with your gloved hands to incorporate everything well.

◆ On individual salad plates, arrange whole pieces of lettuce leaves. Spoon the salad over the lettuce and form a "vertical tower" for a beautiful presentation. Sprinkle or garnish the salad with candied walnuts (recipe follows).

## Candied Walnuts Directions:

◆ In a medium sized sauté pan or small Dutch oven, over medium-low heat, melt the unsalted butter and granulated sugar. Stir the sugar and butter until a brown caramel has formed, about 5 minutes. Be very careful not to burn this mixture. Immediately add the chopped walnuts or pecans to the mixture and stir for 1 minute to coat.

◆ Carefully transfer the walnuts (or pecans), to a baking sheet covered with parchment paper. Using a rubber spatula, separate the walnuts to prevent them from sticking together. Once completely cooled, chop the walnuts finely for a pretty garnish.

> *Chef's Note: Candied walnuts or pecans can be stored in an airtight container for several weeks.*

# Soups

# Soup

I simply love cooking with roasted garlic and I love the look and taste of oven-roasted cauliflower. Put these two things together and you get a delightful, tasty soup that can be served either hot or cold. I have prepared this soup for formal dinner parties and as a starter for a simple family meal, both to high acclaim. You will need to use a hearty chicken stock for this recipe so please, refer to the one on page 89. You will be so pleased that you did!

## Ingredients:

- 2 whole heads fresh cauliflower, cut apart to attain the florets only
- 3 large garlic heads, roasted (recipe follows)
- 4 tablespoons olive oil, divided (plus 3 teaspoons for roasting garlic)
- ½ tablespoon dried herbs (for roasting garlic)
- 2 tablespoons Emeril's Bayou Blast spice
- 2 large Vidalia onions, peeled and chopped
- 5 large celery stalks, cleaned and chopped
- 3 large carrots, peeled and chopped into ¼ inch cubes
- 1 cup any good white wine
- 12 cups rich chicken stock (3 quarts) (p. 89)
- 2 bay leaves
- 4 sprigs fresh thyme, leaves removed and minced finely
- 1 cup half-and-half
- ½ cup all-purpose flour (for roux)
- ½ cup unsalted butter (1 stick) (for roux)
- Kosher salt and freshly cracked black pepper, to taste
- Flat leaf parsley *or* chopped chives, minced (for garnish)

# Cream of Cauliflower Soup with Roasted Garlic

## Roasted Garlic Directions:

♦ Preheat oven to 425 degrees Fahrenheit.

♦ Using a very sharp knife, cut off the top ¼ section of each garlic head, exposing the cloves. Discard any loose paper from the head but do not remove all of it. Lay the garlic heads on a sheet of aluminum foil and place each garlic head clove-side up. Sprinkle with salt and pepper, 1 teaspoon of olive oil per garlic head, and ½ tablespoon of dried herbs (such as rosemary or thyme). Wrap the garlic heads in aluminum foil and seal the package. Place on a baking sheet. Roast garlic for 45 minutes. Once cooled, the garlic cloves can be easily removed using a paring knife or by simply squeezing the garlic heads with your hands.

## Soup Directions:

♦ Preheat oven to 400 degrees Fahrenheit.

♦ Place cauliflower florets in a large mixing bowl and toss them in 2 tablespoons of olive oil and 2 tablespoons of Emeril's Bayou Blast spice. Place the florets in a roasting pan and bake them for 25 minutes. Once golden brown, remove them and set aside.

♦ In a large sauté pan or Dutch oven, over medium heat, add the other 2 tablespoons of olive oil and the chopped onions, celery, and carrots. Cook for 10-12 minutes. Season the vegetables with Kosher salt and freshly cracked black pepper, to taste. Set the pan aside.

♦ In a 4 quart Dutch oven or soup pot, over medium heat, add and stir the wine and chicken stock together. Add in the reserved roasted garlic, 2 bay leaves, thyme, reserved onion mixture, and all but one roasted cauliflower (reserve for garnish). Bring the mixture to a full boil and then reduce the heat to medium-low. Simmer for 15 minutes. Let the soup cool slightly before the next step.

♦ In a food processor fitted with a steel blade or a blender, ladle in 3 cups of the soup at a time. Puree each batch of soup until everything is well blended. Add each batch of the pureed soup into a clean soup pot simmering over medium-low heat. Once you have pureed the entire mixture, add in the half-and-half. Combine well.

> *Chef's Note: To thicken soup, cook ½ cup of flour and 1 stick of unsalted butter in a sauté pan over medium heat to form a "blonde" roux. Stir the roux for about 10 minutes, let it cool slightly, and add a tablespoon at a time to the pureed soup to attain the desired consistency.*

♦ Garnish the soup with the reserved, roasted cauliflower floret along with some freshly chopped flat leaf parsley or chives. Serve hot or cold.

# Soup

I took six years of French in high school and college but one of the only things I know how to say is, "Oui, Oui, monsieur!" However, I *do* know that the French's onion soup makes for a classic dining experience that will impress your family and guests. With the melted Fontina cheese and garlic croutons, this is nearly a complete meal in itself!

## Ingredients:

- 10 (large) sweet Vidalia onions, caramelized (recipe follows)
- 10 tablespoons unsalted butter (1 stick and 2 tablespoons), divided
- ¼ cup granulated sugar (for caramelizing onions)
- 2 cups white wine, divided
- 1 loaf crusty French bread, 22 inches long (for croutons)
- 2 teaspoons Kosher salt (plus salt for caramelizing onions)
- 2 tablespoons olive oil
- 4 garlic cloves (about 2 tablespoons), minced
- 2 tablespoons fresh parsley, minced
- 6 cups low sodium beef broth (1½ quarts)
- 2 cups low sodium chicken broth
- 2 tablespoons French Cognac (1 full jigger)
- 5 whole thyme sprigs
- 2 bay leaves
- 2 cups Fontina cheese, shredded or grated

# French Onion Soup with Garlic Croutons and Fontina Cheese

## YIELD: SERVES 10-12

## Caramelized Onions Directions:

♦ Trim the ends off each onion and then halve them through the middle. Remove the peels and slice into half-moon shapes. Using a cast iron skillet or heavy Dutch oven, over medium-low heat, melt 2 tablespoons of unsalted butter and add the onions. Sprinkle the onions with salt and ¼ cup of granulated sugar. Stir the onions often until they are a dark mahogany and reduced. Do not let them burn. This will take 50-60 minutes. Deglaze the pan periodically with ¼ cup of a white wine as the onions cook. Set onions aside in a bowl to cool.

## Garlic Croutons Directions:

♦ Preheat oven to 350 degrees Fahrenheit.

♦ Slice the French bread into rounds about ¼ inch thick. In a bowl, add 2 teaspoons of salt, 2 tablespoons of freshly minced garlic, 2 tablespoons of minced parsley, and 1 stick of softened butter. Combine these ingredients to form a compound butter. Spread the mixture liberally on one side of the French bread slices and line them up, side by side, on a baking sheet. Bake the slices for about 3-4 minutes, or until they become toasty brown. Set aside.

## Soup Directions:

♦ In a Dutch oven, over medium heat, add 2 tablespoons of olive oil. Add the beef broth, white wine, chicken broth, French Cognac, fresh thyme sprigs, and bay leaves. Then simmer over medium-low heat for 30 minutes. Remove the thyme sprigs and bay leaves once done. Ladle the mixture into 10-12 broiler-proof soup crockpots or 8 ounce ramekins. Over the top of each soup, add the garlic bread croutons. Then top with 4 tablespoons of grated Fontina cheese.

♦ Place your oven rack in the top third of the oven and heat the broiler. Position the crockpots or ramekins on a foil-covered baking sheet under the broiler for about 3 minutes, or until the cheese browns and melts completely. Watch these carefully and do not burn!

*Chef's Note: The soup (without the melted cheese and bread), can be kept warm for up to an hour before company arrives.*

# Soup

I love Bermuda and encourage you to visit there if ever given the chance. The friendliness and hospitality abounding from its people is unmistakable and unforgettable. Their food is pretty darn good too! This island paradise holds a special place in my heart because my parents often traveled there for their getaways. One of my most treasured memories is enjoying a private, gourmet lunch with my late mother at The Four Ways, one of Bermuda's finest restaurants. Mom was "my date" for the afternoon and I remember us having wonderful conversations at that  table. It was there and then that I first savored this fish chowder, one of the best soups I have ever had! The song lyrics may be, "Bermuda is another world," but this soup is "out of this world!" Mom kicked hers up to notches unknown that day with lots of hot sherry pepper sauce but I had not yet acquired my similar taste for spicy food. However, I recently had the pleasure and honor of making the spicy version for the prestigious, Diamond Club luncheon at Sandals, Barbados. The 30+ people present sang my praises and could not eat it fast enough! I know my mother would be proud and touched that this recipe and our "love story" is included. I also know you and your family will enjoy this special dish! It is easy to make, you do not have to fly across the Atlantic to purchase the ingredients, and it will bring Island splendor to your home!

## Ingredients:

- 3 pounds mixed white fish fillets (such as cod, sea bass, or red snapper), skin and bones removed and cut into 1 inch cubes or "chucks"
- 2 pounds medium shrimp (20-25 count per pound), peeled and deveined
- 4 tablespoons unsalted butter (½ stick)
- 2 tablespoons olive oil
- 1 leek (white and pale green parts only), rinsed under cold water and chopped finely
- 6 cups rich seafood stock (p. 91)
- 1 (24 ounce) can chopped tomatoes, seeded, with juice
- 4 tablespoons corn-starch mixed with 4 tablespoons of water (for thickening)
- 2 heaping tablespoons Outerbridge's sherry pepper sauce (found online)
- 1 cup any good white wine

- 2 medium Vidalia onions, chopped finely
- 2 large green bell peppers, chopped finely
- 4 large celery ribs, chopped finely
- 4 large carrots, chopped finely
- 5 large garlic cloves, minced
- 1 (small) can tomato paste
- 3 bay leaves
- 1 teaspoon allspice, ground
- 1 teaspoon clove, ground
- 2 teaspoons dried thyme
- 2 teaspoons dried rosemary
- 3 tablespoons Worcestershire sauce
- 1 cup dark Bermudian rum (I use Gosling's)
- Freshly cracked black pepper, to taste
- Flat leaf parsley, chopped finely (for garnish)

# Island
# Fish Chowder

## Directions:

♦ In a 6 quart Dutch oven, over medium-high heat, add 4 tablespoons of unsalted butter and 2 tablespoons of olive oil. Add and cook the onions, bell peppers, leeks, celery, carrots, and garlic until softened or "translucent," about 10 minutes.

♦ Stir in the seafood stock, chopped and seeded tomatoes, and 1 cup of good white wine. Bring to a boil. Then reduce the heat to medium-low and simmer the mixture, uncovered, for 30 minutes.

♦ Add in the fish chunks, tomato paste, bay leaves, allspice, clove, thyme, rosemary, and plenty of freshly cracked black pepper, to taste. Simmer another 25 minutes.

> *Chef's Note: By design, the fish will fall apart during the simmering process. Do not worry. It is not overcooked.*

♦ Mix the cornstarch and water together to form a "slurry." Stir it into the soup to thicken. Simmer, stirring occasionally for another 2-3 minutes.

♦ Stir in the 2 pounds of uncooked shrimp, Worcestershire sauce, and dark rum. Gently simmer for another 25 minutes, uncovered. Remove the soup from the heat and let it sit, covered with a tight-fitting lid, for an additional 30 minutes (without peeking).

♦ Remove the lid and add 2 heaping tablespoons of sherry pepper hot sauce to the soup. Stir to blend well.

♦ Ladle the chowder into pretty soup bowls and top with a sprinkling of finely chopped flat leaf parsley. Serve immediately.

> *Chef's Note: Like any good homemade soup, this chowder is best when prepared the day or morning before it is needed. This allows the wonderful flavors to blend together! The cooked seafood will not spoil overnight as long as the soup is refrigerated. Simply reheat over medium-low heat and serve piping hot!*

# Soup

In June 2019, I had the honor and privilege of serving as Executive Chef for a benefit dinner sponsored by the Tennessee Valley Coalition for the Homeless. The night was unforgettable and the event raised thousands of dollars for homeless war veterans. Our first course was the delightful bacon and potato soup pictured here. Our Southern friends loved this hearty and filling soup and it got our dinner off to a fabulous start. Each diner received this recipe that night and I even heard one tell her husband, "Honey, I'm making this for our next Tennessee University football tailgate party!"

## Ingredients:

- ◆ 12 slices smoky bacon
- ◆ 11 tablespoons unsalted butter, divided (for sautéing vegetables and making a roux)
- ◆ 3 (large) sweet Vidalia onions, peeled and chopped
- ◆ 6 large celery stalks, chopped
- ◆ 3 large green peppers, seeded and chopped
- ◆ 8 garlic cloves, minced
- ◆ 3 tablespoons Emeril's Creole Essence
- ◆ ½ cup all-purpose flour (for roux)
- ◆ 12 cups rich chicken stock (3 quarts) (p. 89) *or* 3 (32 ounce) boxes low sodium chicken stock
- ◆ 3 (12 ounce) dark lager beers (I use Irish Guinness)
- ◆ 12 large red russet potatoes, washed and cubed
- ◆ 4 cups fresh, aged cheddar cheese, grated
- ◆ 3 cups half-and-half
- ◆ Kosher salt and freshly cracked black pepper, to taste
- ◆ Fresh flat leaf parsley, chopped (for garnish)
- ◆ Fresh green onions, chopped (for garnish)

# New Orleans
# Beer, Cheese, and
# Potato Soup

YIELD: ABOUT 4 QUARTS

## Directions:

♦ Preheat oven to 400 degrees Fahrenheit.

♦ On a cookie sheet lined with parchment paper, position the bacon slices side-by-side without them overlapping one another. Bake for 15-18 minutes, or until crisp. Do not burn. Remove bacon from oven and drain on paper towels. Let cool. Chop into small pieces and set aside.

♦ In a large sauté pan, over medium heat, add 3 tablespoons of unsalted butter and lightly sauté, or "sweat," the chopped Vidalia onions, celery, and green peppers for 5 minutes. Add the minced garlic and 3 tablespoons of Emeril's Creole Essence spice. Stir everything well for another 3 minutes.

♦ In another saucepan or sauté pan, over medium heat, melt the 1 stick of unsalted butter with ½ cup of flour to form a roux. Stir the butter and flour for 10 minutes, or until a nice "blonde" roux has formed. Set the mixture aside to cool.

♦ In a 6 quart pot or Dutch oven, over high heat, add the 12 cups of chicken stock, 3 Guinness beers, and cubed red potatoes. Bring liquids to a full boil and immediately reduce the heat to medium-low. Simmer the potatoes for 20 minutes, or until they are fork tender. Do not let the potatoes turn to mush.

♦ Add to the pot, the cooked vegetables, chopped bacon, and grated cheddar cheese. Stir well to combine. Add Kosher salt and freshly cracked black pepper, to taste. Stir in 3 cups of half-and-half. Adjust seasonings accordingly.

> *Chef's Note: The soup should be fairly thick. However, if you desire to thicken it further, stir in one tablespoon at a time of the cooked and cooled roux until the desired consistency is reached.*

♦ Ladle the soup into decorative bowls. Garnish each serving with a tablespoon each of chopped parsley and green onions.

# Soup

I made the pictured recipe for a quaint restaurant in my hometown, Zaferon Grill, and it was a huge success with customers. We all know New England has their own clam chowder. Why is this not an option for New Orleans? Instead of bacon, I use sliced and browned andouille sausage and add it to a pot of "goodies." When paired with crusty French bread, it makes for a full meal. You can also make this soup and freeze it in quarts for later use. I took some with me to a football tailgate party, heated it in a pot over a charcoal fire, and served. How long did it last? I am sure you guessed correctly!

## Ingredients:

- 8 pounds fresh little neck clams *or* 4 pounds gourmet canned clams (I use Bar Harbor or Italian imported), chopped
- 6 cups clam juice or seafood stock (1½ quarts) (p. 91)
- 3 pounds New Orleans andouille *or* chorizo sausage
- 2 cups white wine (for clams)
- 2 cups cold water (for clams)
- 10 garlic cloves, peeled and minced, divided
- 4 tablespoons Old Bay Seasoning, divided
- Juice from 2 lemons (for clams)
- 1 head fresh, flat leaf parsley, ½ chopped (for recipe) *and* ½ minced finely (for garnish)
- 3 cups leeks (about 4 large leeks, white and some green parts), chopped
- 4 cups sweet Vidalia onions (about 6 onions), chopped
- 4 cups celery (1 whole bunch), chopped
- 1 stick unsalted butter (for roux)
- 2 packages fresh thyme, leaves minced finely
- 2 packages fresh rosemary, leaves minced finely
- 1 cup all-purpose flour (plus ½ cup for roux)
- 4 cups low sodium chicken stock (1 quart)
- 4 pounds golden russet potatoes, quartered
- 2 (16 ounce) packages frozen corn, thawed
- Kosher salt and freshly cracked black pepper, to taste

- 2 tablespoons olive oil
- 4 bay leaves
- 2 cups half-and-half
- 4 cups heavy cream

# New Orleans
# Clam Chowder

YIELD: ABOUT 4 QUARTS

## Fresh Clams Directions:

♦ Fill the bottom of a good sized stock pot with 2 cups of white wine, 2 cups of cold water, 5 minced garlic cloves, 2 tablespoons of Old Bay Seasoning, the juice from 2 lemons, and a few tablespoons of chopped flat leaf parsley. Raise the heat to high and boil the mixture. Reduce the heat to medium-high and add the fresh clams. Close the pot with a tight lid. Allow the clams to steam open, without peeking, for 10 minutes. Transfer the clams to a large bowl or platter with a slotted spoon and set aside.

   *Chef's Note: Discard any clams which have not fully opened. Once the clams are cooled, remove them from their shells and chop them coarsely. Set aside.*

## Soup Directions:

♦ Slice the andouille sausage into thin, ½ inch, nickel-sized pieces. In a preheated sauté pan, over medium heat, add 2 tablespoons of olive oil and cook the sausage until browned on all sides, approximately 8 minutes. Remove the sausage with a slotted spoon and drain on paper towels. Do not drain the fat from your pan.

♦ Add the leeks, onions, and celery to the pan. Sauté for about 7 minutes, or until the vegetables become translucent. Do not brown this mixture. While sautéing, sprinkle the vegetables with salt, pepper, and 1 tablespoon of Old Bay seasoning.

♦ Stir in the remaining 5 garlic cloves, bay leaves, thyme, and rosemary. Dust the vegetable mixture with 1 cup of all-purpose flour. Cook for at least 5 minutes, forming a bit of a roux. Stir in the chicken stock, seafood stock, quartered potatoes, and corn kernels. Bring the mixture to a rapid boil. Immediately reduce the heat to low and simmer until potatoes are fork tender, about 25 minutes.

♦ Add the half-and-half, heavy cream, and reserved chopped clams. Re-season with Kosher salt, freshly cracked black pepper, and a bit of Old Bay seasoning as needed. Stir well.

   *Chef's Note: To thicken chowder, cook ½ cup of flour and 1 stick of unsalted butter in a sauté pan over medium heat to form a "blonde" roux. Stir the roux for about 10 minutes, let it cool slightly, and add a tablespoon at a time to the soup to attain the desired consistency.*

♦ Before serving, stir in 4 tablespoons of minced parsley. Ladle into shallow bowls or soup cups.

# Soup

This is a very good thing to make on a lazy Sunday. All you have to do is let this stock cook over medium-low heat for about 6 hours. Once you are finished, you can freeze the stock and use it to make delicious soups and gravies. This beef stock can also be frozen in ice cube trays so that you can add a few cubes at a time to your soups and gravies.

## Ingredients:

- 6 pounds beef bones *or* a combination of beef and veal bones (ask butcher for both)
- 6 large carrots, washed and cut into chunks
- 6 large celery stalks, washed and cut into chunks
- 6 large onions, peeled and cut into chunks
- 2 (4 ounce) cans tomato paste
- 4 tablespoons olive oil (for sautéing vegetables)
- 1 bouquet garni (parsley, bay leaf, rosemary, and thyme tied together with kitchen twine into a cheese cloth)
- 6 quarts cold water (or enough to completely cover the meat bones)
- ¼ cup  white wine or water (for deglazing)

# Rich
# Beef Stock

YIELD: ABOUT 3-4 QUARTS

## Directions:

♦ Preheat oven to 425 degrees Fahrenheit.

♦ Place the veal and beef bones into a large roasting pan and smear them all over with the tomato paste. Brown the bones in the oven for 1 hour.

♦ While the bones cook, in a Dutch oven, over medium-high heat, add 4 tablespoons of olive oil. Add the listed vegetables. Stir and caramelize the vegetables for 20 minutes

♦ Place the cooked bones and vegetables into a 4 gallon stock pot on the stovetop over low heat. Deglaze the roasting pan and scrape off all of the brown bits on the bottom of the roasting pan using some wine or water. Add these juices to the stockpot!

♦ Add enough water to cover the stockpot's contents (about 6 quarts). Add the bouquet garni and raise the heat to high until the mixture reaches a rapid boil. Immediately reduce the heat and skim off the fat that has risen to the top. Do not cover the stockpot with a lid at any time. Simmer for approximately 6 hours. Add water to keep the bones covered as needed.

   *Chef's Note: It is imperative to skim the fat off of the stock's surface every 30 minutes.*

♦ After 6 hours, let the mixture cool. De-fat the stock one final time. Store the stock in 1 quart containers in the freezer. If you are using it sooner, the stock will keep in tightly sealed quart containers in the refrigerator for about 3 or 4 days.

# Soup

I am quite aware that there are a lot of chicken stocks on the market today (low sodium ones and others), but I "bother" with the work because there is nothing that quite compares to a homemade stock. Like the beef stock listed in this cookbook (page 87), this concoction can be frozen and stored away for up to two months and be used for all sorts of soups and gravies. Your kids will go bonkers for the chicken noodle soup that you can invent using this semi-dark and luscious chicken stock!

## Ingredients:

♦   5 pounds chicken backs and necks (ask butcher for both)

♦   4 tablespoons olive oil (plus olive oil for coating chicken)

♦   5 large carrots, washed and cut into chunks

♦   5 large celery stalks, washed and cut into chunks

♦   5 large onions, peeled and cut into chunks

♦   ½ cup wine or water (for deglazing)

♦   5 quarts cold water or enough to completely cover the meat bones

♦   1 bouquet garni (parsley, bay leaf, rosemary, and thyme tied together with kitchen twine into a cheese cloth)

# Rich

# Chicken Stock

YIELD: ABOUT 4 QUARTS

## Directions:

♦ Preheat oven to 400 degrees Fahrenheit.

♦ Place the chicken backs and neck bones into a large roasting pan. Coat them with a bit of olive oil. Brown the bones in the oven for 1 hour.

♦ While the chicken bones are cooking, set a Dutch oven on the stovetop over medium-high heat. Add 4 tablespoons of olive oil and the listed vegetables. Stir and caramelize the vegetables for 20 minutes.

♦ Place the cooked bones and vegetables into a 4 gallon stock pot on the stovetop over low heat. Deglaze the roasting pan and scrape off any brown bits on the bottom of the roasting pan using some white wine or water. Add this to the stockpot!

♦ Add enough water to cover the stockpot's contents (about 5 quarts). Add the bouquet garni and raise the heat to high until the mixture reaches a rapid boil. Immediately reduce the heat and skim off the fat that has risen to the top. Do not cover the stockpot with a lid at any time. Simmer for approximately 4 hours. Add water to keep the bones covered as needed.

> *Chef's Note: It is imperative to skim the fat off of the stock's surface every 30 minutes.*

♦ After 4 hours, let the mixture cool. De-fat stock one final time. Store the stock in 1 quart containers in the freezer for up to 3 months. If you are using it sooner, the stock will keep in tightly sealed quart containers in the refrigerator for about 3 days.

# Soup

I have mentioned in this cookbook, several times, that it is extremely important to have a good relationship with your local fish monger. The person standing behind the counter will have no problem selling you fresh fish bones, fresh shrimp shells, fresh lobster shells, or fresh crab shells for a fairly cheap price. You do not want to purchase any shellfish remnants that are over a day or two old. If you do, your entire house will stink and the stock itself will taste rancid and fishy. So, make sure that your shells smell just like the wild blue ocean! With this stock, you can make some incredibly tasty gourmet soups like shrimp or lobster bisque (p. 95), or New England clam chowder!

## Ingredients:

- ◆ 4 pounds fish bones *or* seafood shells (a collection of fish bones from cod, halibut, salmon, and others *or* a combination of crab, lobster, and shrimp shells *or* a combination to your liking!)
- ◆ 3 tablespoons olive oil
- ◆ 2 Vidalia onions, peeled and quartered
- ◆ 4 carrots, unpeeled and chopped into 2 inch chunks
- ◆ 5 large celery stalks, chopped into 2 inch chunks
- ◆ Cloves from 2 large garlic heads, unpeeled, chopped roughly
- ◆ 1 (small) can tomato paste
- ◆ 16 cups cold water (4 quarts)
- ◆ 2 cups white wine
- ◆ 1 tablespoon dried rosemary
- ◆ 1 tablespoon dried thyme
- ◆ 1 tablespoon dried basil

# Rich

# Seafood Stock

---

**YIELD: ABOUT 3 QUARTS**

---

## Directions:

♦ In a wide, 6 quart stockpot or Dutch oven, over medium-high heat, add the olive oil. Sauté the onions, carrots, celery, garlic cloves, tomato paste, and seafood shells (or fish bones), for about 12 minutes, stirring vigorously and continuously. The vegetables and fish bones should just begin to "caramelize," or turn slightly brown in color.

*Chef's Note: My fish monger sells me (cheaply), a 4 pound halibut fillet bone without the head. It takes a bit of time to carve the fish bones into 3 inch chunks for the seafood stock but the effort is well worth it in the end.*

♦ Add the 16 cups of cold water, 2 cups of white wine, and 3 dried herb ingredients to the pot. Bring the mixture to a full boil and then immediately reduce to a low simmer. Let the mixture simmer uncovered for 3-3½ hours.

*Chef's Note: Occasionally, you will want to de-fat your seafood stock with a large kitchen spoon during the cooking process. Simply "skim off" and discard the fat from the fish bones or shells that rises to the top of the stock as it appears.*

♦ After this time, remove the pot from the heat and let the stock cool for at least 45 minutes. Strain the broth through a fine mesh sieve into another pot or Dutch oven. Discard the leftover bones (or shells), and vegetables. This should leave about 3 quarts of rich seafood stock.

♦ Use the stock immediately or place it into individual quart containers with tight fitting lids. The stock can be kept refrigerated for up to 3 days or frozen for up to 6 months.

*Chef's Note: As mentioned earlier, this seafood stock can be used for your next New England clam chowder or shrimp or lobster bisques (p. 95). You can also cook down a cup or two of this stock over medium-high heat for 30 minutes and add ¼ cup of heavy cream, plenty of freshly cracked black pepper, and 1 heaping tablespoon of Old Bay seasoning to create an unforgettable sauce for your stuffed flounder!*

# Soup

This is one of the special occasions where I will be revealing some of my most treasured culinary secrets. Many autumns ago, my lovely wife, Lynne, asked me to concoct a "pumpkin-anything" recipe. The first few attempts at a gourmet pumpkin soup found their way to the bottom of our trash compactor and were probably scarier than most of the Halloween decorations in the neighborhood. However, things began to come together as I started experimenting with roasted garlic, fresh herbs, cinnamon, nutmeg, maple syrup, and even curry powder. I made this soup as part of our 2019 Thanksgiving dinner and my son and wife were doing some silly dances while signaling their total approval and appreciation! This terrific Fall soup pairs well with buttered biscuits too (page 137)!

## Ingredients:

- 1 (32 ounce) can pumpkin puree
- 1 (16 ounce) can pumpkin puree
- 1 (14 ounce) can coconut milk
- 12 cups chicken stock (3 quarts) (p. 89)
- 3 tablespoons unsalted butter (for sautéing) (plus 2 sticks for roux)
- 3 tablespoons olive oil, divided (plus 4 teaspoons for roasting garlic)
- 4 large Vidalia onions, chopped
- 8 large celery stalks, washed and sliced into chunks
- 1 package *or* 2 tablespoons fresh thyme leaves
- 1 package *or* 2 tablespoons fresh rosemary sprigs
- 4 large garlic heads, roasted (recipe follows)
- ½ cup real maple syrup (not the stuff you put on pancakes)
- 3 tablespoons Saigon cinnamon
- 1 teaspoon fresh nutmeg, grated
- 2 heaping tablespoons any good curry powder (I use Madras)
- 4 good shakes any hot sauce (such as Tabasco or Frank's)
- 1 cup all-purpose flour (for roux)
- ½ tablespoon dried herbs (for roasting garlic)
- Kosher salt and freshly cracked black pepper, to taste
- Chopped chives (for garnish)

- ½ cup sour cream (for garnish)
- ½ cup roasted pumpkin seeds (can find at health food stores) (recipe follows) (for garnish)
- Optional: buttered biscuits (p. 137)

93

# Signature
# Pumpkin Soup

YIELD: ABOUT 3 QUARTS

## Roasted Garlic Directions:

♦ Preheat oven to 425 degrees Fahrenheit.

♦ Using a very sharp knife, cut off the top ¼ section of each garlic head, exposing the cloves. Discard any loose paper from the head but do not remove all of it. Lay the garlic heads on a sheet of aluminum foil and place each garlic head clove-side up. Sprinkle with salt and pepper, 1 teaspoon of olive oil per garlic head, and ½ tablespoon of dried herbs (such as rosemary or thyme). Wrap the garlic heads in aluminum foil and seal the package. Place on a baking sheet. Roast garlic for 45 minutes. Once cooled, the garlic cloves can be easily removed using a paring knife or by simply squeezing the garlic heads with your hands.

## Roasted Pumpkin Seeds Directions:

♦ Preheat oven to 350 degrees Fahrenheit.

♦ Using your hands, coat the pumpkin seeds with 2 tablespoons of olive oil. Spread the seeds on a sprayed cookie sheet lined with aluminum foil. Bake for about 10-12 minutes, or until seeds begin to brown. Do not burn the seeds. Remove them from the oven and let cool.

## Pumpkin Soup Directions:

♦ In a large sauté pan, over medium-high heat, melt the unsalted butter and add 1 tablespoon of olive oil. Add and cook the onions, celery, rosemary, and thyme leaves for about 12 minutes. Remove vegetables from the pan and put them and the roasted garlic cloves into a blender. Add 2 cups of the chicken stock. Puree the mixture until everything has reached a liquid or soupy consistency. Set aside.

♦ In a 6 quart Dutch oven or large soup pot, over low-medium heat, add the remaining 10 cups of chicken stock and 48 ounces of pumpkin puree. Stir well for 5 minutes. Then stir in the pureed onion, celery, herbs, and roasted garlic mixture.

♦ Add the coconut milk, maple syrup, cinnamon, nutmeg, curry powder, and a few dashes of hot sauce, to taste. Continue to stir the mixture. Do not burn the pot bottom or the soup itself.

♦ Taste the soup and adjust seasonings accordingly. Adding some Kosher salt and freshly cracked black pepper will finish the soup up nicely.

> *Chef's Note: To thicken soup, over medium heat, cook 1 cup of flour and 2 sticks of unsalted butter in a sauté pan for 20 minutes, stirring continuously, to form a "brunette" roux. Let it cool slightly and add a tablespoon at a time to the soup to attain the desired consistency.*

♦ Serve the soup in deep bowls. Garnish with a handful of roasted pumpkin seeds, chopped chives, and a dollop of sour cream.

# Soup

I dedicate this recipe to my oldest son, Mr. Charles G. Mortimer IV (lovingly known to everyone as, "Charlie"). He may have inherited his formal family name at birth but he also inherited a burning desire to be a prominent player in the restaurant industry. Growing up, Charlie watched me cook for him countless times, both professionally and at home. When he went to college, he earned a degree in hotel and restaurant management. Since that time, he has worked numerous jobs in the food and beverage industry and has developed into a proven leader in today's business world. As a young boy, Charlie had a real affinity for lobster, so I made this simple, yet authentic, lobster bisque for him. Now he orders this soup almost every time we go out to eat. However, the last time we were dining at a restaurant that offered the bisque, he did not order it or even mention it. I said, "Char, the lobster bisque is calling your name!" He replied, "No thanks, Dad. It's nowhere close to what you make for me." Ah, loyalty and love works for me every time! Please make some lasting and priceless culinary memories with your own kids!

## Ingredients:

- 1½ cups lobster meat (canned or fresh from fish monger), chopped, divided
- 5 cups seafood (shellfish) stock (1¼ quarts) (see Chef's Note)
- ½ cup button mushrooms, chopped
- 3 tablespoons unsalted butter (plus 2 sticks for roux)
- ½ cup Vidalia onion, chopped
- ½ cup celery, chopped
- 2 large carrots, peeled and chopped
- 1 tablespoon Old Bay seasoning
- 2½ cups half-and-half
- ½ cup sweet sherry
- A few good shakes any hot sauce (such as Tabasco or Frank's)
- 1 cup all-purpose flour (for making roux)
- Freshly cracked black pepper, to taste
- 1 bunch fresh chives, chopped (for garnish)
- Optional: crusty French bread

# Simple and Rich
# Lobster Bisque

◆———————————————◆

◆———————————————◆

## Directions:

*Chef's Note: To make this soup even more special, please use the seafood stock recipe on p. 91. Store-bought stock can be used but it is not the same as making and enjoying your own.*

◆ In a large saucepan or 3 quart Dutch oven, over medium-low heat, melt the 3 tablespoons of unsalted butter. Add the chopped mushrooms, onions, celery, and carrots. Cook and stir until the vegetables are tender, about 12 minutes.

◆ Stir in the seafood stock as well as 1 heaping tablespoon of Old Bay seasoning. Bring mixture to a full boil and then reduce the heat to low, simmering the soup for 15 minutes. Remove from the heat and let it cool for approximately 10 minutes.

◆ Pour the mixture into the container of a blender or food processor that is fitted with a steel blade (you might have to do this in stages). Add in 1 cup of the chopped lobster meat. Put the lid on the food processor or blender and process until mixture is smooth and silky.

◆ Return soup to the pot or Dutch oven and, over low heat, stir in the half-and-half and sweet sherry. Season with some freshly cracked black pepper and a few dashes of hot sauce. Add the remaining ½ cup of chopped lobster meat. Stir frequently until thickened, about 30 minutes.

*Chef's Note: To thicken soup, over medium heat, cook 1 cup of flour and 2 sticks of unsalted butter in a sauté pan for 20 minutes, stirring constantly, to form a "brunette" roux. Let it cool slightly and add a tablespoon at a time to the soup to attain the desired consistency.*

◆ Ladle the soup into pretty serving bowls and garnish the top with chopped chives. Serve the soup with a nice tossed salad and some crusty French bread on the side for a complete meal.

# Soup

Preparing this recipe does require quite a bit of time and some good, old-fashioned patience but it is so worth it in the end. This pea soup can be made ahead of time and then frozen for up to 2 months. Please do not buy canned soup that tastes like the tin can in which you purchased it. Make your very own homemade concoction and watch your kids come running into the kitchen to ask, "What smells so wonderful?" It is a fabulous recipe to prepare during the cold and blustery winter!

## Ingredients:

- 5 cups fresh, dried split peas
- 3 quarts cold water
- 2 tablespoons olive oil (for sautéing vegetables)
- 3 onions, chopped
- 5 large celery stalks, chopped
- 5 large carrots, peeled and chopped
- ½ cup all-purpose flour
- 2 tablespoons Emeril's Bayou Blast spice
- 12 cups chicken stock (3 quarts) (p. 89)
- 2 large and meaty ham hocks (from local butcher)
- 1 bouquet garni (parsley, bay leaf, rosemary, and thyme tied together with kitchen twine into a cheese cloth)
- Kosher salt and freshly cracked black pepper, to taste
- Optional: No more than ½ cup of flour and 1 stick of unsalted butter (for roux) (see Chef's Note)
- Optional: A sprinkling of parmesan cheese per bowl (for garnish)

# Split Pea Soup
# with Vegetables and
# Ham Hock

## Directions:

♦ In a large stockpot, cover 5 cups of dried split peas with 3 quarts of very cold water. Soak the peas for at least 6 hours and then drain over the sink with a colander. Rinse them and repeat the process for a total soaking time of 12 hours. I do this process overnight.

♦ In a 4 or 5 quart Dutch oven, over medium heat, add 2 tablespoons of olive oil and sauté the onions, celery, and carrots for 15 minutes. Dust the vegetables with ½ cup of all-purpose flour mixed with 2 tablespoons of Emeril's Bayou Blast spice. Continue to stir until all of the flour and spice has been cooked out, about 5 minutes. Set aside to cool slightly.

♦ In a 3 or 4 quart soup pot, over medium heat, slowly add and stir in the 4 quarts of chicken stock, ham hocks, reserved and drained split peas, reserved vegetable mixture, and bouquet garni. Stir well to combine. Season with some Kosher salt and freshly cracked black pepper. Simmer the soup for 90 minutes, stirring occasionally, or until the peas and vegetables are soft and the ham hock has begun to fall apart. Do not burn the bottom of the soup pot during the simmering process!

♦ After 90 minutes, discard the bouquet garni. Carefully remove the 2 ham hocks and place them onto a wooden cutting board. With a sharp knife, remove the meat from the ham bones, chop it into bite-sized pieces, reserve some for garnish, and return the meat to the soup pot.

> *Chef's Note: If you wish to thicken your soup base, simply put equal parts of flour and butter into a sauté pan over medium heat to form a "blonde roux." Whisk the mixture for 5 minutes, stirring constantly. Add 1 tablespoon of the roux at a time to the soup to reach your desired consistency.*

♦ Ladle the soup into nice serving bowls and garnish the top of each with the reserved chopped ham and a sprinkling of parmesan cheese.

# Soup

This recipe is for all of the vegetable lovers out there! I made this soup at a cooking class I taught at Morris Knolls High School in Rockaway, New Jersey. The room was packed with curious, interested, and very hungry high school students and by the time I finished the demo, I saw many of them licking their chops! Every young person received a cup of this soup and a freshly baked, buttered roll on the side. It was pure heaven to be in the room and I will never forget how appreciative the students were that I was able to attend their great school and give them a copy of this recipe!

## Ingredients:

- 8 large white onions, caramelized (recipe follows)
- 4 tablespoons unsalted butter (½ stick), divided
- ¼ cup granulated sugar (for caramelizing onions)
- 1 cup white wine (for deglazing)
- Cloves from 4 large garlic heads, roasted (recipe follows)
- 2 tablespoons olive oil (plus 4 teaspoons for roasting garlic)
- ½ tablespoon dried herbs (for roasting garlic)
- 4 cups mixed mushrooms (e.g. cremini, button, wild, and portobello), sliced
- 1 heaping tablespoon Emeril's Bayou Blast spice
- 3 cups corn kernels (from 6 fresh ears of corn or thawed, frozen corn)
- 3 green zucchinis, cut in half and then into ½ inch slices
- 3 large cucumbers, peeled, seeded, and sliced thinly
- 6 large celery stalks, chopped finely
- 1 tablespoon fresh thyme, chopped finely
- 1 tablespoon fresh rosemary, chopped finely
- 6 cups tomato juice or V-8
- 6 cups low sodium vegetable stock (1½ quarts)
- Kosher salt and freshly cracked black pepper, to taste
- 1 bunch fresh chives, chopped (for garnish)

CHEF CARDIE'S

# Vegetable Soup with
# Roasted Garlic, Caramelized Onions,
# and French Herbs

## YIELD: ABOUT 3 QUARTS

### Caramelized Onions Directions:

♦ Trim the ends off each onion and then halve them through the middle. Remove the peels and slice into half-moon shapes. Using a cast iron skillet or heavy Dutch oven, melt 2 tablespoons of unsalted butter over medium-low heat and add the onions. Sprinkle the onions with salt and ¼ cup of granulated sugar. Stir the onions often until they are a dark mahogany and reduced. Do not let them burn. This will take 50-60 minutes. Deglaze the pan periodically with ¼ cup of a white wine as the onions cook. Set onions aside in a bowl to cool.

### Roasted Garlic Directions:

♦ Preheat oven to 425 degrees Fahrenheit.

♦ Using a very sharp knife, cut off the top ¼ section of each garlic head, exposing the cloves. Discard any loose paper from the head but do not remove all of it. Lay the garlic heads on a sheet of aluminum foil and place each garlic head clove-side up. Sprinkle with salt and pepper, 1 teaspoon of olive oil per garlic head, and ½ tablespoon of dried herbs (such as rosemary or thyme). Wrap the garlic heads in aluminum foil and seal the package. Place on a baking sheet. Roast garlic in oven for 45 minutes. Once cooled, the garlic cloves can be easily removed using a paring knife or by simply squeezing the garlic heads with your hands. Chop cloves coarsely and set aside.

### Vegetable Soup Directions:

♦ In a large frying pan, over medium-high heat, add 2 tablespoons of unsalted butter. Gently sauté the mixed mushrooms for about 10 minutes. Add 1 tablespoon of Emeril's Bayou Blast and season the mushrooms with Kosher salt and freshly cracked black pepper, to taste. Stir well. Place the cooked mushrooms into a separate bowl and set aside.

♦ In the same pan, add 2 tablespoons of olive oil. Sauté the corn kernels, zucchini, cucumbers, and celery until they turn a light-colored brown, about 12 minutes. Stir in the caramelized onions and garlic. Add the chopped thyme and rosemary. Slowly pour in the tomato juice (or V-8), and low sodium vegetable stock.

♦ Bring the mixture up to a boil, uncovered. Reduce the heat to medium-low and simmer gently for 35 minutes, stirring often. Do not burn.

♦ Serve soup in pretty crockpots or bowls and garnish with chopped chives on top. This soup can be served hot or cold.

# Sides

# Side

Do you love zucchini? Oh boy! Have I got a delightful side dish for you! In truth, I do not deserve the bragging rights for this recipe. They belong to Andrea Sartori, one of my best friends and also my personal trainer. She is an amazing, talented woman in and out of her private gym in Little Falls, New Jersey. She has always taken a great interest in my health and welfare and like her husband, Mike, has been an avid supporter and wonderful taste-tester for this cookbook. Recently, Andrea asked if she could contribute a healthy and enjoyable dish to my collection of recipes. I told her, "If you don't write one for me, then I won't publish the damn cookbook!" I hope that she will thank me by allowing me to do three less leg squats in her gym in the future (fat chance that will happen)! Even if I do not receive this act of mercy, including this recipe is worth it. Andrea told me it is simple to make and that once you start eating these zucchini noodles (hot or cold), you will not be able to put the bowl down. Even your kids will love this side because they will be able to eat their veggies like string candy!

## Ingredients:

- ♦ 4 large or 6 medium green zucchinis (yellow zucchini can also be used)
- ♦ 3 tablespoons unsalted butter
- ♦ 1 tablespoon garlic (about 3 large cloves), minced finely
- ♦ 1 tablespoon "Better Than Bouillon" (chicken base variety) (found at any major grocery store)
- ♦ ½ cup fresh parmesan cheese, grated (see Chef's Note)

# Andrea's

# Special

# Zucchini Noodles

## YIELD: SERVES ABOUT 6

### Directions:

♦ Using a "spiralizer" tool or good vegetable peeler, "peel" the whole zucchinis lengthwise to form thin strips that resemble "noodles."

> *Chef's Note:  While crafting your noodles, be careful not to peel the seeded areas of the zucchini.*

♦ In a large sauté pan, over medium heat, add the unsalted butter and minced garlic. Stir the butter and garlic mixture for 2 minutes. Do not scorch or burn the garlic.

♦ Add the zucchini noodles to the pan along with 1 tablespoon of "Better Than Bouillon." Stir together well for 3-4 minutes but not so hard as to break apart the noodles.  Fold in ½ cup of parmesan cheese and stir to combine for 1 additional minute. Serve immediately.

> *Chef's Note:  Andrea has a valid point about parmesan cheese. Pre-grated parmesan cheese tends to "ball up" or get "clumpy" or "waxy." Buy a small block of real parmesan cheese and use your vegetable peeler to attain nice strands to mix right into the zucchini noodles.*

When I was a young boy, my late mother would remind me that eating spinach would make me as strong as my cartoon idol, Popeye! So I did what I was told and ate all of my vegetables (or at least, most of them)! This is a side dish that goes well with nearly any meal you can dream of and it is also quite healthy! Oh my goodness, did I just say healthy? No one told me how good spinach would be with fresh lemon juice, sautéed garlic, and grated parmesan cheese mixed in with it! OMG! Shut the front door and enjoy!

## Ingredients:

- ♦ 3 large packages baby spinach leaves, stems removed
- ♦ 2 tablespoons olive oil
- ♦ 6 large garlic cloves, sliced very thinly
- ♦ ½ cup dry white wine
- ♦ Juice and zest from 1 large lemon
- ♦ 2 tablespoons unsalted butter
- ♦ ¼ cup fresh parmesan cheese, grated, to taste
- ♦ Kosher salt and freshly cracked black pepper, to taste
- ♦ 1 additional lemon, sliced (for garnish)

# Baby Spinach with
# Lemon Zest, Sliced Garlic, and
# Grated Parmesan Cheese

## YIELD: SERVES 8-10

### Directions:

♦ In a 4 quart Dutch oven, over medium heat, add 2 tablespoons of olive oil and sauté the sliced garlic for about 3 minutes. You want the garlic to turn golden brown without it burning. Remove the garlic with a slotted spoon and set it aside in a small bowl.

♦ Add to the pot, the baby spinach leaves, white wine, juice from 1 lemon, a pinch of Kosher salt, and some freshly cracked black pepper. Cover the pot with a tight lid or aluminum foil for exactly 5 minutes. Do not peek under the lid during this process.

♦ Uncover the pot and add the 2 tablespoons of unsalted butter, sautéed garlic slices, and lemon zest. Stir for an additional 1 minute, or until the spinach has completely wilted. Transfer to a bowl or warm plate and add the ¼ cup of freshly grated parmesan cheese over the top.

♦ Garnish with a few fresh lemon slices and serve.

# Side

Do these maple syrup, smoky bacon, and brown sugar Brussels sprouts look appetizing to you? My maple-glazed Brussels sprouts are not the mushy and off-tasting sprouts you may had once or twice in your life. I made this side dish for my Christmas dinner one year. I was not sure if there would be any "takers," but I decided to give it a shot. When I went to get myself a serving, they were already gone! I think it was my older son, Charlie, who said, "Great new dish, Dad. Where the heck did that come from?" Try this easy recipe for your next holiday dinner. You will be very pleased with the results and you will get some wonderful reviews at the dinner table!

## Ingredients:

- 3 pounds smaller Brussels sprouts *or* 2 pounds larger Brussels sprouts, root end trimmed and then halved lengthwise
- 6 slices thick, smoky bacon, slices halved
- 1 heaping tablespoon Emeril's Bayou Blast spice *or* any "kicked up" all-purpose spice
- ¼ cup canola oil
- 4 tablespoons unsalted butter (½ stick)
- 4 heaping tablespoons light brown sugar, packed
- 2 tablespoons apple cider vinegar
- 2 good shakes any hot sauce (such as Tabasco or Frank's)
- ¼ cup pure maple syrup (not the commercial one used on pancakes)
- Freshly cracked black pepper, to taste

# Bacon and Maple-Glazed Brussels Sprouts

### YIELD: SERVES 8-10

## Directions:

♦ In a large sauté pan, over medium heat, cook the bacon slices until crispy. Remove the bacon, drain them on paper towels, and set aside to cool. Once cooled, chop the bacon coarsely and set aside in a small bowl.

♦ Toss the sprouts in 1 heaping tablespoon of Emeril's Bayou Blast or any all-purpose spice.

*Chef's Note: Do not include any tougher outer leaves of the Brussels sprouts which may have fallen apart on the cutting board.*

♦ Pour out all but 1 tablespoon of bacon fat from the sauté pan. Over medium-high heat, add the canola oil to the remaining bacon fat and heat until it is shimmering and very hot. Add the Brussels sprouts to the pan and let them sizzle and brown for 2 minutes. Shake the pan often so the sprouts do not stick to the bottom of the hot pan. Using tongs or a spatula, turn the sprouts over and let them brown and caramelize on the second side for 1 more minute.

♦ Add the 4 tablespoons of unsalted butter and 4 tablespoons of brown sugar. Stir until the brown sugar has melted and the Brussels sprouts begin to glisten in the caramel sauce, about 1 more minute. Pour in 2 tablespoons of apple cider vinegar, a few shakes of hot sauce, and the maple syrup. Continue to cook, stirring the sprouts for an additional 1 minute, shaking the pan continually.

*Chef's Note: Please be careful not to overcook the Brussels sprouts. If you do, they begin to emit an acrid, off-tasting smell. Discard the vegetables if they become overcooked.*

♦ Using a metal slotted spoon, transfer the Brussels sprouts to a baking dish. Raise the stovetop heat to high and let the sauce reach a full boil. Cook for an additional 1 minute.

♦ Pour the heated and bubbling sauce over the Brussels sprouts. Season with plenty of freshly cracked black pepper. Garnish the sprouts with the crumbled smoky bacon and serve immediately.

*Chef's Note: The Brussels sprouts can easily be made a day or two prior to being needed. When ready to serve, remove them from the refrigerator, let them warm to room temperature, and reheat them in a preheated oven at 325 degrees Fahrenheit for about 15 minutes.*

# Side

This is another easy and delicious recipe that you can enjoy all year-round. Halved, baked onions with a splash of balsamic vinegar and grated parmesan cheese go fabulously with rib eye steaks (page 187). You know those "bloomin' onion" things you order at certain steakhouses? No offense to them, but this recipe is better by far, trust me! Serve these onions on a pretty platter and then take notice of the approving smiles from everyone in the room!

## Baked Onions Ingredients:

- 6 large Vidalia onions, cut in half through the root-end and then peeled
- 1½ cups fresh Parmesan Reggiano cheese, grated
- 3 tablespoons good balsamic vinegar
- ¼ cup drinkable white wine
- ¼ cup light brown sugar, packed
- 1 tablespoon roasted garlic powder (not garlic salt)
- A few good shakes any hot sauce (such as Tabasco or Frank's)
- ¼ cup good olive oil
- A pinch of Kosher salt and freshly cracked black pepper, to taste
- 1 bunch fresh chives, chopped (for garnish)

## Russian Dressing Ingredients:

- At least ½ cup any good catsup
- 1 cup mayonnaise (I use Hellman's)
- 3 fresh dill pickles, chopped finely
- 1 tablespoon Worcestershire sauce
- 1 teaspoon onion powder
- 1 teaspoon garlic powder
- A few good shakes any hot sauce (such as Tabasco or Frank's)
- Freshly cracked black pepper, to taste

# Baked Vidalia Onions
# with Parmesan

YIELD: SERVES 6-8

## Baked Onions Directions:

- Preheat oven to 425 degrees Fahrenheit.

- In a large mixing bowl, whisk together the parmesan cheese, balsamic vinegar, white wine, brown sugar, garlic powder, hot sauce, and a pinch or two of Kosher salt with plenty of freshly cracked black pepper. Slowly drizzle in the olive oil to create an emulsion. Using tongs or your clean hands, gently add the onion halves and coat them in the liquid on all sides.

- Line a large baking sheet with aluminum foil and coat with non-stick buttered cooking spray. Place each onion half cut-side down on the sheet and bake for 50 minutes, or until the onions have caramelized on all sides.

- Remove the onions carefully with tongs and place them, cut-side up, on a silver platter or large serving plate. Garnish with freshly chopped chives on top and serve.

*Chef's Note: Feel free to serve this side to your guests with a dipping sauce (recipe follows). These baked onions will fall apart by themselves. You simply dip the pieces into homemade Russian dressing and enjoy! I promise that they will not last for very long!*

## Russian Dressing Directions:

- In a large metal bowl, whisk together the catsup, mayonnaise, chopped pickles, Worcestershire sauce, onion powder, garlic powder, and a few dashes of hot sauce. Add plenty of freshly cracked black pepper, to taste. Blend thoroughly, taste, and adjust dressing to your preference. Cover the bowl with plastic wrap and refrigerate for at least 1 hour before serving.

# Side

You may know by now that I spent a great deal of time cooking and having amazing adventures in the deep South, where many dishes are slow-cooked. I learned so much meeting and working alongside great chefs in New Orleans, Alabama, and Georgia and this included how to remain patient while creating these types of recipes. This tasty side dish will *not* consume your time like slow-cooking a beef brisket for at least 15 hours. However, it is still a Southern classic full of charm and when paired with the aroma and flavor of real apple cider and smoky bacon, you will have attained superstar status from your family and friends.

## Ingredients:

- ♦ 8 slices smoky bacon, sliced into ½ inch squares
- ♦ 2 large bunches fresh kale leaves, tough stems torn off and discarded
- ♦ 2 cups Vidalia onion (about 3 medium onions or 2 large onions), chopped coarsely
- ♦ 3 large garlic cloves, minced finely
- ♦ ¼ cup white wine (for deglazing)
- ♦ 2 tablespoons granulated sugar
- ♦ 1 heaping tablespoon Emeril's Bayou Blast spice *or* any good all-purpose spice
- ♦ ½ cup pure apple cider *or* concentrated apple juice
- ♦ 2 tablespoons apple cider vinegar
- ♦ ½ cup chicken stock (p. 89)
- ♦ Freshly cracked black pepper, to taste

CHEF CARDIE'S

# Braised Kale
# with Bacon and
# Apple Cider

YIELD: SERVES 8

## Directions:

♦ In a 6 quart Dutch oven, over medium heat, add the bacon pieces, stirring them until well browned, about 8 minutes. Remove the bacon with a slotted spoon and drain on paper towels. Do not drain the bacon fat from the Dutch oven.

♦ Add the chopped onions and sauté them until tender or translucent, about 12 minutes. When the onions are about halfway done cooking, add the minced garlic, white wine (to deglaze any remnants sticking to the pot bottom), and 2 tablespoons of granulated sugar.

♦ While the onions are cooking, sprinkle the chopped kale in a mixing bowl with 1 heaping tablespoon of Emeril's Bayou Blast spice. Add the kale to the Dutch oven, pressing down with your hands so that the kale fits. Add the apple cider (or apple juice), apple cider vinegar, and chicken stock to the pot. Bring ingredients to a boil and then immediately reduce the heat to low. Simmer the kale, covered, for 35 minutes without peeking. Turn the heat off and let the kale rest in the pot, covered, for an additional 15 minutes.

♦ Uncover the pot and stir the cooked kale in the remaining liquid to combine. Add plenty of freshly cracked pepper. Place the kale in a nice serving bowl or onto a pretty serving platter. Sprinkle the top of the kale with the cooked smoky bacon and serve immediately.

*Chef's Note: The braised kale can be made a day or two ahead and reheated in an oven at 325 degrees Fahrenheit for about 20 minutes. Do not add the bacon topping until you are ready to serve the final dish.*

# Side

My late mother-in-law, Edna Gentile, was a fabulous cook and wonderful lady who cared deeply about her immediate and extended family, which included her closest friends. I would spend hours watching her show off her culinary "magic" in her Jersey Shore home and learning from her as she cooked for anyone who walked through the door. From her fantastic, Italian tomato sauce to her fresh blue crab and lobster boils, everything this woman cooked put a huge smile on everyone's faces. This delicious cauliflower recipe is simple to make but as Edna and many other chefs have told me, it is the simplest and freshest ingredients that produce the best tasting meals. This is a side dish you simply must try. Thank you, Mom Gentile! I will never forget you!

## Ingredients:

- ♦ 2 heads fresh cauliflower, tough stems discarded, florets separated
- ♦ Juice from 1 whole lemon
- ♦ 8 garlic cloves, mashed down and minced finely
- ♦ 4 good shakes any hot sauce (such as Tabasco or Frank's)
- ♦ ½ cup any good olive oil
- ♦ 1 cup Italian breadcrumbs, seasoned
- ♦ 1 cup fresh Parmesan Reggiano cheese, grated
- ♦ A pinch of Kosher salt and lots of freshly cracked black pepper, to taste
- ♦ Fresh flat leaf parsley, minced (for garnish)
- ♦ 1 whole lemon, sliced (for garnish)

# Edna's
# Roasted Cauliflower with
# Parmesan, Lemon, and Garlic

## YIELD: SERVES 6-8

### Directions:

♦ Preheat oven to 375 degrees Fahrenheit.

♦ In a large mixing bowl, whisk together the lemon juice, minced garlic, and a few dashes of hot sauce. In a very slow stream, add the olive oil to form an emulsion. Whisk well and add a pinch of Kosher salt and freshly cracked pepper, to taste.

♦ Add the cauliflower florets to the bowl and toss them in the liquid, coating the cauliflower on all sides. Sprinkle in the cups of breadcrumbs and parmesan cheese. Mix together well.

♦ Using a cookie sheet (lined with aluminum foil), or large Pyrex dish that has been coated with non-stick cooking spray, place the cauliflower florets in the preheated oven. Bake until they turn golden brown, about 35-40 minutes. Do not burn the cauliflower. Watch them closely after 30 minutes of cooking time.

   *Chef's Note: Make sure that each floret lies flat on the bottom of the baking dish or cookie sheet. Do not overlap them or stack on top of one another.*

♦ Remove the cauliflower florets from the oven and allow them to cool for about 10 minutes. Garnish with a sprinkling of freshly minced parsley and lemon slices. Serve immediately.

   *Chef's Note: My wife, Lynne, reminded me that Edna heated a large sauté pan over medium-high heat and cooked and browned her cauliflower on the stovetop that way. Both the stovetop and conventional oven methods do this recipe justice.*

# Side

Please do not turn to the next page just yet. There is no reason to be scared of making Hollandaise sauce! These easy instructions will tell you exactly how to make an elegant and delicious side dish that will impress both your family and friends. Hollandaise sauce is quite simple to whip up and once you get the hang of it, you will be using this sauce on many other recipes. Did someone just order eggs Benedict?

## Ingredients:

♦ 2 pounds fresh asparagus (about 2 large bunches), root or "woody" ends trimmed and then slightly peeled (optional)

♦ ½ cup unsalted butter (1 stick)

♦ 3 large egg yolks

♦ 1 teaspoon Kosher salt (for Hollandaise)

♦ ¼ cup freshly squeezed lemon juice (juice from 1 large lemon)

♦ 1 teaspoon warm water (for keeping sauce intact, if needed)

♦ ¼ cup olive oil

♦ ½ cup fresh parmesan cheese, grated (plus 2 tablespoons for garnish)

♦ 1 teaspoon roasted garlic powder

♦ 1 heaping tablespoon Emeril's Original Essence spice

♦ Kosher salt and freshly cracked black pepper, to taste

♦ Fresh flat leaf parsley, chopped (for garnish)

♦ 1 lemon, sliced thinly (for garnish)

# Grilled (or Baked) Asparagus with Parmesan Cheese and Hollandaise Sauce

## YIELD: SERVES ABOUT 8

### Hollandaise Directions:

♦ Melt the unsalted butter in a saucepan or in the microwave. Place the 3 egg yolks, 1 teaspoon of Kosher salt, and ¼ cup of lemon juice into a blender and pulse. With the blender motor running, slowly add the melted butter. Blend until smooth, stopping to scrape down the sides as needed. Transfer the sauce to a bowl.

*Chef's Note: Hollandaise sauce is notorious for separating if not immediately used. If it does separate, simply add 1 teaspoon of warm water and whisk it into the sauce to prevent it from coming apart.*

### Asparagus Directions:

♦ In a large mixing bowl, toss the trimmed asparagus in ¼ cup of olive oil along with the ½ cup of parmesan cheese, roasted garlic powder, Emeril's Original Essence spice, and freshly cracked black pepper. Toss to coat the asparagus well on all sides.

#### Grilled Asparagus:

♦ Heat up an outdoor grill to medium-high heat. Alternatively, you can cook your asparagus in a grill pan or iron skillet on the stovetop over medium-high heat. Place the asparagus on the grill and leave them, without turning, for 2 minutes. Then, turn the asparagus and allow it to grill for 2 more minutes on the other side. Immediately remove the al dente asparagus and place them in a casserole dish for serving.

#### Baked Asparagus:

♦ Preheat oven to 425 degrees Fahrenheit. Put the asparagus in a 9 x 13 inch Pyrex dish and place it in the oven to cook for 12 minutes. There is no need to turn over the asparagus. Immediately remove the al dente asparagus and place them in a casserole dish for serving.

*Chef's Note: Asparagus should be cooked until it is slightly al dente (Italian for, "to the tooth"). It should be cooked but still slightly crispy. Do not overcook the asparagus.*

### Serving Directions:

♦ Spoon the warm Hollandaise sauce over the middle portion of the asparagus and season with a pinch of Kosher salt and plenty of freshly cracked black pepper, to taste. Garnish with the 2 tablespoons of parmesan cheese and a bit of flat leaf parsley in the middle for color. A few thin lemon slices can also be positioned around the edges of your serving platter as a pretty garnish. Serve immediately.

*Chef's Note: You may cover and keep your grilled (or baked) asparagus in the oven on "warm only." However, they must not remain there for more than 10 minutes or you will end up eating mushy and soggy asparagus.*

Put this simple and "out-of-this-world delicious" recipe on your to-do list, especially during the summer grilling season! This South of the Border recipe with a touch of Tequila, Cotija cheese, and some spice, really "kicks up" this corn to the upper stratosphere. The corn goes fantastically with just about anything, but I especially love serving it with a good steak or with a special seafood dinner!

## Ingredients:

- 12 ears of corn, shucked or husk on (silk off)
- About 4 tablespoons canola oil (for coating corn)
- 1 cup unsalted butter (2 sticks)
- 5 large garlic cloves, minced
- 1 cup fresh Mexican Cotija cheese, grated
- ¼ cup good Tequila
- 2 tablespoons Emeril's Bayou Blast spice
- 2 teaspoons any hot sauce (such as Tabasco or Frank's)
- ¼ cup freshly squeezed lime juice (about 2 large limes)
- 4 tablespoons fresh parsley, minced finely
- Salt and freshly cracked black pepper, to taste

CHEF CARDIE'S

# Grilled Mexican-Herbed Corn on the Cob with Tequila and Cotija Cheese

## YIELD: SERVES 8-10

### Directions:

♦ Using a kitchen pastry brush, coat the peeled and husked corn with canola oil on all sides. On a hot grill, place your corn at a 45 degree angle on the grates and let them cook for 2 minutes, without turning. Rotate the cobs a half turn every 1 minute thereafter, or until all sides have darkened and caramelized. Do not burn the corn! Remove corn from the grill after 15 minutes of cooking and bring them inside. Cover with aluminum foil to keep warm.

♦ In a small pot, over medium heat, melt the unsalted butter. Then stir in the minced garlic, Mexican cheese, ¼ cup of Tequila, Emeril's Bayou Blast spice, hot sauce, lime juice, and minced parsley. Add salt and freshly cracked black pepper, to taste. Using the pastry brush, "paint" the butter sauce all over the corn.

   *Chef's Note: I pour the herbed butter sauce into a large roasting pan and roll the corn in the mixture using tongs.*

♦ Serve the corn immediately or keep warm in an oven at 250 degrees Fahrenheit for no more than 20 minutes.

# Side

I should actually be calling this tasty recipe, "Lynne's Special Mushrooms," since it is, by far and away, my wife's favorite side dish! The alluring combination of fresh mushrooms, garlic, Italian breadcrumbs, some herbs, and red wine is simply mouth-watering. It is also perfect for all meals and seasons. Even people who say they hate mushrooms have come back for seconds with this one!

## Ingredients:

- 8 cups (about 4 pounds) any variety of mushrooms (e.g. shitake, wild, button, or porcini) (see Chef's Note)
- 2 large Vidalia onions, chopped
- 2 tablespoons Emeril's Bayou Blast spice
- 6 large garlic cloves, minced finely
- ¼ cup Worcestershire sauce
- ½ cup good Merlot or your favorite red wine
- 4 good shakes any hot sauce (such as Tabasco or Frank's)
- ½ cup fresh parmesan cheese, grated
- ½ cup Italian breadcrumbs, seasoned
- 2 tablespoons fresh thyme, chopped *or* 1 tablespoon dry spice, crumbled
- 2 tablespoons fresh rosemary, chopped *or* 1 tablespoon dry spice, crumbled
- ½ cup fresh flat leaf or curly parsley, chopped
- A pinch of Kosher salt and lots of freshly cracked black pepper, to taste

# Lynne's Mixed Mushrooms in Red Wine with Breadcrumbs, Garlic, and Parsley

### YIELD: SERVES 8-10

## Directions:

*Chef's Note: You do not need to clean each individual mushroom from the package. Instead, use a paper towel to lightly wipe off any glaring impurities. Do not soak or clean your mushrooms with any kind of liquid or cold water.*

♦ In a large skillet, over medium-high heat, add the onions and 2 tablespoons of Emeril's Bayou Blast spice. Cook for about 10 minutes. Add the mushrooms, garlic, and Worcestershire sauce, and sauté for about 10 minutes, stirring often. The mushrooms should darken and glisten.

♦ Add the red wine and cook until most of the liquid has cooked out of the pan. This will take another 10 minutes. Add 4 good shakes of hot sauce. Sprinkle in the grated parmesan cheese, seasoned breadcrumbs, thyme, rosemary, and chopped parsley. Stir well and season liberally with Kosher salt and freshly cracked black pepper.

*Chef's Note: If need be, the mushroom mixture can be put into a 9 x 13 inch Pyrex casserole dish, placed in the oven, and kept on "warm" for 30 minutes.*

I was originally going to call this my "Drunken Carrot" recipe because it contains some good Irish beer and wonderful Irish whiskey. You do not have to wait until Saint Patrick's Day to make this concoction. Do not worry. The alcohol cooks out entirely, so the kids will not be dancing around the house in kilts, singing "Oh Danny Boy!"

## Ingredients:

♦  3 pounds fresh baby carrots, rinsed, drained, and left whole

♦  3 (12 ounce) bottles good, dark Irish beer (I use Guinness Stout)

♦  ¼ cup Irish whiskey (I use Jameson)

♦  3 tablespoons unsalted butter

♦  ¼ cup real maple syrup (not the commercial one used on pancakes)

♦  ¼ cup pure honey

♦  Juice from 1 large lemon

♦  1½ tablespoons Emeril's Original Essence spice

♦  A pinch or two of Kosher salt and freshly cracked black pepper, to taste

♦  Fresh flat leaf parsley, minced (for garnish)

# CHEF CARDIE'S
# Maple Syrup, Honey, and Irish Whiskey Carrots

YIELD: SERVES ABOUT 8

## Directions:

♦ In a medium pot or Dutch oven, over medium-high heat, add the carrots and cover them with the dark beer. If the carrots are not covered, add beer or a cup of water as needed. Add a pinch of salt and let the carrots come to a boil. Reduce the heat immediately, cover the pot with a lid, and simmer the carrots on low heat for about 20 minutes, or until they are slightly tender. Drain them with a colander and set aside to cool, about 10 minutes.

♦ In a large frying pan, over medium-high heat, melt the unsalted butter. Once the bubbles subside, add the carrots, maple syrup, honey, and juice from 1 lemon. Stir constantly until the carrots begin to caramelize, about 8 minutes.

♦ Remove the pan from the heat and, in a circular motion, slowly add ¼ cup of Irish whiskey. Return the pan to the fire, where it may ignite a small flame. This is simply the alcohol burning off. Stir until the flames have subsided.

♦ Place carrots into a serving bowl and toss them with 1½ tablespoons of Emeril's Original Essence spice. Add freshly cracked black pepper, garnish with flat leaf parsley, and serve.

*Chef's Note: This recipe can also be made ahead of time and re-heated in an oven at 300 degrees Fahrenheit for about 15 minutes.*

# Side

I probably love sweet potatoes more than regular potatoes so please, do me a favor and use "real" maple syrup (not that other stuff you buy to squirt on pancakes). The extra dollar or two that you spend will make all the difference in the world with this fabulous recipe and true holiday hit!

## Ingredients:

♦ 4 large sweet potatoes, peeled, cut lengthwise, and then into 2 inch chunks

♦ ¼ cup canola oil

♦ ½ cup pure maple syrup

♦ 2 teaspoons cinnamon

♦ 1 teaspoon fresh nutmeg, grated

♦ Juice and zest from 1 whole lemon

♦ Kosher salt and freshly cracked black pepper, to taste

♦ Fresh, flat leaf parsley, chopped (for garnish)

♦ Optional: 3 tablespoons butter (for mashed potatoes option)

♦ Optional: ½ cup heavy cream (for mashed potatoes option)

CHEF CARDIE'S

# Maple Syrup-Roasted
# Sweet Potatoes

YIELD: SERVES 8-10

## Directions:

♦ Preheat oven to 400 degrees Fahrenheit.

♦ Line a large baking sheet with aluminum foil. In a large mixing bowl or pot, toss the sweet potato chunks in canola oil. Add a dash of Kosher salt and some pepper. Resume tossing by hand. Place chunks on the baking sheet. Roast for 30 minutes without opening the oven door.

♦ Remove the sheet from the oven and let the potato chunks cool slightly, about 5 minutes. Return the potatoes to the mixing bowl and, using tongs or your clean hands, toss the potatoes in the maple syrup, cinnamon, lemon juice, and nutmeg, coating them on all sides. Roast for another 15 minutes, or until potatoes begin to brown.

   *Chef's Note: For a little dramatic effect (as pictured here), place the potatoes under the broiler for about 3 or 4 minutes, or until they have caramelized.*

   *Chef's Note: For additional flair, mash the cooked potatoes in a Dutch oven. Over medium heat, melt 3 tablespoons of butter with ⅛ cup of heavy cream. Mash them well, or until the desired texture is reached.*

♦ Garnish with chopped parsley and serve immediately.

# Side

The recipe for this cornbread and andouille stuffing came into being when one of my culinary schoolteachers challenged me to add a dash of New Orleans "flair" when creating a special take on a classic stuffing. This side dish, originally prepared with fresh, shucked oysters, went over so well that I later prepared it in front of a sold-out audience at Chef's Lab, a prestigious, culinary instructional kitchen in Montclair, New Jersey. At first, the crowd was a little hesitant about the combination of oysters and stuffing but once they tried it, they could not shove the stuffing into their mouths fast enough! Despite this great response, I understand that oysters are an acquired taste which may not be for everyone and have decided to omit them from this recipe. Everyone should be able to enjoy a delicious stuffing like this one when it graces the table!

## Ingredients:

- 12 (very large) cornbread muffins *or* 2 boxes corn bread mix (baked according to box directions)
- 1½ pounds chorizo *or* andouille sausage (about 5 links), sliced into ¼ inch pieces
- 6 tablespoons unsalted butter, divided
- 2 cups onions, chopped
- 4 tablespoons fresh garlic (about 8 large garlic cloves), chopped finely
- 2 cups celery, chopped
- 1 cup combination of red and green peppers, chopped finely
- 2 tablespoons fresh sage, chopped
- 2 tablespoons fresh thyme, chopped
- 2 tablespoons fresh rosemary, chopped
- 2 tablespoons Emeril's Bayou Blast spice
- 3 large eggs, beaten
- ¼ cup sweet vermouth
- A few good shakes any hot sauce (such as Tabasco or Frank's)
- 2 cups rich chicken stock (p. 89)
- Freshly cracked black pepper, to taste
- Fresh flat leaf parsley, chopped finely (for garnish)

CHEF CARDIE'S
# New Orleans
# Cornbread and Andouille
# Stuffing

YIELD: SERVES 8-10

## Directions:

♦ Preheat oven to 350 degrees Fahrenheit. Lightly grease (cooking spray is fine), a 9 x 13 inch baking dish, such as a large, Pyrex glass dish.

♦ Using your hands, crumble the cornbread or cornbread muffins into bite-sized pieces.

♦ In a large sauté pan or 3 quart Dutch oven, over medium-high heat, add 3 of the tablespoons of unsalted butter. Add the chorizo or andouille slices to the pan and cook them for 8 minutes, or until they have browned on all sides. Once cooked, remove the sausages with a slotted spoon and set them aside on paper towels on top of a plate to drain.

♦ Using the same pan or Dutch oven, melt 3 more tablespoons of unsalted butter. Add the onions, garlic, celery, bell peppers, sage, thyme, rosemary, and 2 tablespoons of Emeril's Bayou Blast spice. Cook for about 8 minutes, or until vegetables soften or become translucent. Do not overcook or brown the vegetables too much. This technique is called, "sweating."

♦ Remove your pan or pot from the heat and allow the vegetables to cool for about 5 minutes. Once cooled, add this mixture to the bread mixture set aside earlier.

♦ In a separate large bowl, combine the 3 beaten eggs, sweet vermouth, hot sauce, 2 cups of rich chicken stock, and the reserved sausage pieces. Season with freshly cracked black pepper, to taste. Stir together well or simply use the best tools in the kitchen, your hands. Combine this with the reserved bread mixture and coat the bread as evenly possible with the liquid. Get your kids involved in the fun!

♦ Place the mixture into the prepared baking dish and cook uncovered for approximately 45 minutes. The stuffing should be golden brown on top and moist on the inside. Let it cool slightly and garnish with some fresh, flat leaf parsley on top. Cut the stuffing into squares or simply scoop out and enjoy!

126

# Side

New Orleans has always been my favorite city in the United States to eat in, work in, and visit. With its blend of cultures, there are no limits to the amazing food that comes out of this beautiful and historic place! Dirty rice has likely been a staple since the Spanish and French founded the "The Big Easy" in the 17th century. For those of you keeping score, Thomas Jefferson purchased Louisiana from the French in 1803. Anyway, this delicious and flavorful side dish is as authentic and classic as it gets, and it goes especially well with chicken or steak. I also love it with a nice piece of sautéed red fish right on top! I promise that you and your family will never eat rice the same way again after tasting this easy-to-prepare and delicious Southern masterpiece!

## Ingredients:

- ½ pound chicken livers (from local butcher)
- 1½ pounds pork sausage (about 5 large links)
- 4 tablespoons unsalted butter
- 1 cup green pepper (about 3 small peppers or 2 large bell peppers), chopped
- ½ cup celery (about 4 large stalks), chopped
- 2 medium Vidalia onions (or 1 large Vidalia onion), chopped finely
- 3 tablespoons fresh garlic (about 5 large cloves), minced
- 1 tablespoon thyme leaves (fresh or dried), chopped finely
- 1 tablespoon parsley (fresh or dried)
- 1 tablespoon basil leaves (fresh or dried) chopped finely
- 4 cups rich chicken stock (p. 89)
- 2 bay leaves
- 1 heaping tablespoon Emeril's Bayou Blast spice
- 2 cups long grain white rice
- 2 or 3 good shakes any hot sauce (such as Tabasco or Frank's)
- 1 bunch green onions, chopped finely (for garnish)
- Freshly cracked black pepper, to taste

CHEF CARDIE'S

# New Orleans
# Dirty Rice

YIELD: SERVES 8-10
————————————————

## Directions:

♦ In a food blender, finely chop or pulse the chicken livers. Remove the outer casings of the sausage and the meat from within. Finely chop the sausage meat with a sharp knife and combine it with the livers.

> *Chef's Note: I know that you are thumbing your nose at the thought of chicken livers being in this dish, but I assure you, they are not off-tasting or gamey in any way. Please do not omit the livers from this recipe.*

♦ In a 4 quart Dutch oven, over medium-high heat, add 4 tablespoons of butter and brown the sausage and chicken livers, approximately 10 minutes. Add the green peppers, celery, Vidalia onions, minced garlic, thyme, parsley, and basil. Sauté the mixture for another 5 minutes. This culinary process is known as "sweating" the vegetables.

♦ Stir into the pot the 4 cups of chicken stock. Add in the 2 bay leaves, Emeril's Bayou Blast spice, and 2 cups of long grain rice. Add a few good shakes of your favorite hot sauce along with lots of freshly cracked black pepper, to taste.

♦ Raise the stovetop heat to high and bring the mixture to a full boil. Immediately, reduce the heat to medium-low and stir the rice. Close the lid of your Dutch oven and allow the mixture to simmer for 25 minutes, or until the rice is completely tender.

> *Chef's Note: After every 10 minutes of simmering, carefully open the lid and stir the rice to prevent sticking or clumping at the bottom of the pot.*

♦ The rice can be put into a large, festive bowl to serve family-style. Garnish the top of the rice with chopped green onions. Serve immediately.

# Side

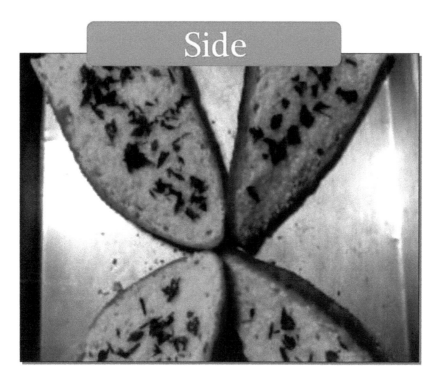

Who does not love garlic bread? From its smell, to its taste, to its texture when it comes out of the oven, warm garlic bread always manages to hit the spot. The real garlic bread lovers (like myself), will absolutely love this creation! It can be served with nearly every recipe in this book and there is always a huge fight to the finish for the last piece!

## Ingredients:

- ♦   2 (large) crusty French breads (each approximately 22 inches long)
- ♦   1 cup unsalted butter (2 sticks), cubed and softened to room temperature
- ♦   2 heaping tablespoons Emeril's Bayou Blast spice
- ♦   1 cup fresh Parmesan cheese, grated
- ♦   5 large garlic cloves, minced finely
- ♦   ¾ cup fresh parsley, minced
- ♦   A pinch of fresh thyme (dry herbs are also suitable)
- ♦   A pinch of fresh rosemary (dry herbs are also suitable)
- ♦   A pinch of Kosher salt

# New Orleans
# Herbed, Parmesan
# Garlic Bread

YIELD: SERVES 8-10

## Directions:

♦ Preheat oven to 350 degrees Fahrenheit.

♦ Slice each French bread in half lengthwise. Then split each half to create four quarters of bread per loaf.

♦ In a large, metal bowl, cream the butter with a spatula and stir in the Emeril's Bayou Blast spice, parmesan cheese, and garlic. Add a pinch of Kosher salt. Using a pastry brush, "paint" the spiced butter on the white side of the slices. Before baking, sprinkle the bread with the minced parsley and a pinch each of fresh thyme and rosemary.

♦ Place the bread on a baking sheet covered with parchment paper or aluminum foil and bake, buttered-side up, in the middle of the oven for 6-8 minutes, or until the bread is golden brown and bubbly.

*Chef's Note: The bread can be wrapped in aluminum foil for baking purposes but I tend to skip this step so I can check how toasty the bread is getting and prevent it from burning (which it can quickly do).*

# Side

Many people think that ratatouille is a Middle Eastern side dish, especially since it goes so well with roasted leg of lamb or lamb shanks. However, ratatouille actually originated from 18th century France and continues to be a very popular recipe there to this day. This is a delicious eggplant and zucchini-based dish immersed in a rich, herbed tomato base. I truly believe that eggplant is an underused vegetable in both our households and local restaurants.; it is wonderful! Try this superb side dish at your next dinner party. I honestly do not think you will have any leftovers!

## Ingredients:

- 5 small Japanese eggplants *or* 3 large eggplants, unpeeled, cut in half and sliced into ½ inch pieces
- 4 tablespoons olive oil, divided
- 2 heaping tablespoons Emeril's Bayou Blast spice, divided
- 1 large red onion, peeled, cut in half, and sliced thinly
- 1 large Vidalia onion, peeled, cut in half, and sliced thinly
- 2 green zucchinis, sliced into ½ inch cubes
- 2 yellow zucchinis, sliced into ½ inch cubes
- 2 red bell peppers, seeds removed and chopped finely
- 2 green peppers, seeds removed and chopped finely
- 2 tablespoons fresh thyme leaves, chopped finely
- 5 large garlic cloves, smashed and minced finely
- 1 (28 ounce) can diced tomatoes (I use Muir Glen)
- 2 cups parmesan cheese, grated
- 3 cups steamed white rice (cooked according to box instructions)
- Fresh flat leaf parsley, chopped (for garnish)
- Freshly cracked black pepper, to taste

# Ratatouille

YIELD: SERVES 8-10

## Directions:

♦ Preheat oven to 350 degrees Fahrenheit. Butter or spray a 9 x 13 inch Pyrex casserole dish.

♦ In a large sauté pan or Dutch oven, over medium heat, add 2 tablespoons of olive oil, the eggplant cubes, and 1 tablespoon of Emeril's Bayou Blast spice, cooking until the eggplant has browned on all sides, about 12 minutes. Remove the eggplant with a slotted spoon, transfer it to a bowl, and set aside.

♦ In the same sauté pan or Dutch oven, over medium heat, add another 2 tablespoons of olive oil. Add the red onion, Vidalia onion, zucchini cubes, chopped red and green peppers, minced thyme leaves, minced garlic, and 1 more tablespoon of Emeril's Bayou Blast spice. Season with plenty of freshly cracked black pepper. Sauté the vegetables for about 15 minutes and transfer to another bowl. Set aside.

♦ Layer the bottom of the prepared casserole dish with the slices of browned eggplant. Coat the top of the eggplant with the onion and zucchini mixture. Top the onions with a coating of diced tomatoes. Top that with a heavy sprinkling of grated parmesan cheese. Repeat this layering process at least twice more, or until you reach halfway up the sides of the dish.

♦ Place the casserole dish into the preheated oven and bake for 45 minutes. Cook your rice during this time. Remove the casserole dish from the oven and let the mixture cool slightly. Spoon the contents generously over a platter filled with steamed white rice and garnish the dish with chopped flat leaf parsley.

# Side

This dish is a real favorite of mine, especially when I am having company over and I want to impress my guests with something extra special! The "pudding" can be prepared a day or two earlier and simply reheated in an oven at 300 degrees Fahrenheit for about 20 minutes. This side dish goes nicely with just about any meat or fish recipe imaginable. For some extra dramatic flair, these ingredients can also be baked and served in individual, 8 ounce buttered ramekins.

## Ingredients:

- 4 pounds fresh corn-on-the cob (about 8 ears) *or* 2 large frozen corn kernel packages, thawed and drained of all excess water (see Chef's Note)
- ½ cup whole milk
- 7 large eggs, whites and yolks separated
- 1 tablespoon freshly cracked black pepper
- 1 tablespoon Emeril's Original Essence spice
- 1 tablespoon dry roasted garlic powder (not garlic salt)
- ½ cup granulated sugar
- 1 (small) can poblano chilis, drained and minced (leftover chilis can be used for garnish)
- 6 tablespoons unsalted butter, cold
- 1 cup all-purpose flour
- 1 teaspoon Kosher salt
- 2 teaspoons baking powder
- 1 cup fresh parmesan cheese, grated
- 1½ cups Monterey Jack cheese, shredded

# Roasted Corn, Cheese, and Poblano Pudding

## YIELD: SERVES 8-10

**Directions:**

*Chef's Note: Fresh corn-on-the-cob should be rubbed with olive oil and then roasted in a hot iron skillet or over a hot grill for about 20 minutes, turning frequently. Thawed kernels of corn should be put on a cookie sheet or baking dish and roasted in an oven at 400 degrees Fahrenheit until they turn slightly brown on top, about 35 minutes. Do not burn or scorch the corn kernels.*

♦ After the corn kernels have roasted and cooled slightly, season them with 1 tablespoon of freshly cracked black pepper, 1 tablespoon of Emeril's Original Essence spice, and 1 tablespoon of roasted garlic powder. Toss the kernels well to combine the spices.

♦ Preheat oven to 350 degrees Fahrenheit. Lightly grease a 9 x 13 inch baking dish.

♦ In a food processor fitted with a steel blade, puree the corn with just enough milk to make it a smooth puree (about ½ cup). Add the 7 egg yolks, sugar, and minced poblano chilis, processing until the mixture is lighter in color and the sugar has dissolved completely. Add the 6 tablespoons of cold butter and process again until smooth and creamy. Scrape down the sides, transfer to a large bowl, and set aside.

♦ In a separate bowl, combine the flour, salt, and baking powder. Stir together well. Using a rubber spatula, fold this mixture into the corn, milk, and poblano mixture. Blend well.

♦ In a metal mixing bowl, add the reserved egg whites and, using an electric handheld blender, beat the egg whites until soft peaks have formed, about 12 minutes. Fold the egg whites into the flour and corn mixture. Add the cheeses and fold them in gently to combine well.

♦ Place mixture into the greased or buttered baking dish. Smooth gently with a rubber spatula.

♦ Place the casserole dish in the oven and bake for 1 hour, or until golden brown on top. Serve slightly warm or at room temperature. Garnish the middle of the casserole with a few leftover poblano chilis and a sprinkling of finely chopped flat leaf parsley.

## Side

This is an easy and delicious side dish that you can enjoy year-round, including during the holidays. Roasted garlic and red bliss potatoes go together like soup and a sandwich, pasta and cheese, peanut butter and jelly, and Sonny and Cher. Well, you get the idea. Some duos just cannot be beat!

### Ingredients:

♦ 2-3 pounds large red bliss potatoes (about 6 potatoes), unpeeled, halved, and chopped into 2 inch chunks

♦ 3 large garlic heads, roasted (recipe follows)

♦ 3 teaspoons good olive oil (for roasting garlic)

♦ ½ tablespoon dried herbs (for roasting garlic)

♦ ¼ cup Kosher salt (for cooking potatoes)

♦ At least ½ cup unsalted butter (1 stick), to taste

♦ 1 tablespoon Emeril's Original Essence spice

♦ ½ cup heavy cream *or* half-and-half (I use a split combination of both)

♦ Kosher salt and freshly cracked black pepper, to taste

♦ 1 small bunch fresh chives, chopped (for garnish)

# Roasted Garlic
# Smashed Potatoes

## YIELD: SERVES ABOUT 8

### Roasted Garlic Directions:

♦ Preheat oven to 425 degrees Fahrenheit.

♦ Using a very sharp knife, cut off the top ¼ section of each garlic head, exposing the cloves. Discard any loose paper from the head but do not remove all of it. Lay the garlic heads on a sheet of aluminum foil and place each garlic head clove-side up. Sprinkle with salt and pepper, 1 teaspoon of olive oil per garlic head, and ½ tablespoon of dried herbs (such as rosemary or thyme). Wrap the garlic heads in aluminum foil and seal the package. Place on a baking sheet. Roast garlic in oven for 45 minutes. Once cooled, the garlic cloves can be easily removed using a paring knife or by simply squeezing the garlic heads with your hands.

### Roasted Garlic Smashed Potatoes Directions:

♦ In a large Dutch oven, add the chopped red potatoes and enough water to cover them. Pour ½ cup of salt into the water. Bring water to a full boil and then reduce the heat and simmer for 15 minutes, or until the potatoes are "fork tender." Remove from the heat. Carefully drain the potatoes with a colander over the sink. Do not rinse the potatoes with cold water.

♦ Return the drained potatoes to the pot and reset to high heat. Stir potatoes for 2 minutes to "dehydrate" them. Reduce heat to medium-low. Add the roasted garlic, butter, and Emeril's Original Essence spice. Using a hand-held potato masher, gently work the garlic and butter into the potatoes. Without "drowning" the potatoes, add the heavy cream until the desired texture is reached (about ½ of a cup). Keep the potatoes a bit lumpy or slightly "smashed."

♦ Season with a pinch of Kosher salt and freshly cracked black pepper, to taste. Serve garnished with freshly chopped chives.

# Side

I was going through the recipes that I had completed for my cookbook when I realized that I did not include one of my favorite things to eat, Southern buttermilk biscuits. If you have ever been to states like Alabama, Georgia, Tennessee, or Mississippi, you would know that biscuits are an important part of every meal. They are eaten during breakfast, lunch, and dinner. Besides having their biscuits with warm butter, our Southern friends like them spread with strawberry jelly or peach preserves. Others use their biscuits to dip into the nearest sauce they can find! Anything goes! These are quite simple to make and you probably have most of the ingredients in your fridge and pantry already (except for perhaps, the fresh buttermilk). Make several batches of these biscuits because they are so delicious! You should also hide some from the kids so that you can save a few for yourself!

## Ingredients:

- 4 cups all-purpose flour, unbleached (plus flour for workstation)
- 4 teaspoons baking powder
- 1 teaspoon baking soda
- 1 teaspoon salt
- 1 cup unsalted butter (2 sticks), cold *or* frozen, cubed *or* grated (see Chef's Note) (plus tablespoons for painting biscuits)
- 2 cups buttermilk (plus tablespoons for painting biscuits)

# Southern Buttermilk Biscuits

---

## YIELD: MAKES 15 BISCUITS

---

### Directions:

- Preheat oven to 450 degrees Fahrenheit.

- Using non-stick butter spray, grease or spray a 9 x 13 inch Pyrex baking pan.

- In a mixing bowl, combine and gently stir the all-purpose flour, baking powder, baking soda, and salt. Add the cubed or grated butter. Using your hands, squeeze or press the butter into the dry mixture until it looks course and clumpy, similar to oatmeal. Try not to leave any big clumps of butter in the bowl.

    *Chef's Note: I saw another chef use this technique in person and it works really well. Freeze the 2 sticks of unsalted butter until you are ready to make the mix. Then, using a handheld grater, grate the sticks of butter into the mixing bowl.*

- Pour in the 2 cups of buttermilk. Using a wooden spoon or rubber spatula, stir and fold in the dough until everything integrates and there is no dry flour remaining. The dough will begin to come off the sides of your mixing bowl.

- Using a plastic or marble cutting board, generously flour the work surface. Transfer the dough to the floured cutting board. Using a wooden rolling pin, shape the dough into a 9 by 13 inch rectangle about 2 inches thick.

- Use a 2 inch biscuit cutter to cut out the biscuits. Position the biscuits close together in the greased baking pan. With a pastry brush, "paint" the tops with a few additional tablespoons of either buttermilk or melted unsalted butter.

- Bake the biscuits for 12-14 minutes. Start checking the biscuits after 12 minutes for doneness. You want them to be plump and golden brown. Serve them right out of the oven!

I made this delicious, green bean casserole recipe while working at a well-known restaurant in Savannah, Georgia and it was a real hit with the customers year-round. My mom had a similar kind of recipe and I think this version comes pretty darn close to imitating hers. The recipe is so good that even your kids will not complain about eating their vegetables! This is truly another fabulous side dish to include on your holiday menu!

## Ingredients:

♦ 2 bags frozen green beans, thawed

♦ 3 cups Vidalia onions (about 4 large onions), sliced and caramelized (recipe follows)

♦ 6 tablespoons unsalted butter (¾ stick), divided (plus butter for greasing baking dish)

♦ ¼ cup granulated sugar (for caramelizing onions)

♦ 1 cup white wine (for deglazing)

♦ 1 cup fresh button mushrooms, sliced in half

♦ 3 cups chicken stock (p. 89)

♦ 1 (10¾ ounce) can cream of mushroom soup

♦ 1 tablespoon Emeril's Original Essence spice

♦ 2 cups cheddar cheese, grated

♦ ½ cup Italian breadcrumbs

♦ Freshly cracked black pepper, to taste

♦ Optional: French's canned fried onion rings (see Chef's Note)

# CHEF CARDIE'S
# Southern Green Bean
# and Caramelized Onion
# Casserole

### YIELD: SERVES 8-10

## Caramelized Onions Directions:

♦ Trim the ends off each onion and then halve them through the middle. Remove the peels and slice into half-moon shapes. Using a cast iron skillet or heavy Dutch oven, melt 2 tablespoons of unsalted butter over medium-low heat and add the onions. Sprinkle the onions with salt and ¼ cup of granulated sugar. Stir the onions often until they are a dark mahogany and reduced. Do not let them burn. This will take 50-60 minutes. Deglaze the pan periodically with ¼ cup of a white wine as the onions cook. Set onions aside in a bowl to cool.

## Green Bean Casserole Directions:

♦ Preheat oven to 350 degrees Fahrenheit.

♦ In a large skillet, over medium-high heat, melt the other ¼ cup of unsalted butter. Sauté the chopped button mushrooms for 8-10 minutes. Remove the pan from the heat. Let the mushrooms cool for a few minutes.

♦ Cook the green beans in the chicken broth for 15 minutes and drain them with a colander over the sink. In a large mixing bowl, combine the green beans, sautéed mushrooms, mushroom soup, caramelized onions, and 1 heaping tablespoon of Emeril's Essence spice. Stir the mixture together well.

♦ Pour the mixture into a well-buttered, 9 x 13 inch Pyrex baking dish. Bake for 25 minutes. Remove the casserole from the oven and top with the grated cheddar cheese and Italian breadcrumbs. If desired, scatter a handful of French's canned onion rings over the top.

   *Chef's Note: This dish can be easily be made the day before your event. If you do make it in advance, delay putting on the cheese, dried onion rings, and breadcrumbs until just before you want to serve the dish.*

♦ Return casserole to the oven and bake for an additional 15 minutes, or until the casserole is hot and the cheese and breadcrumbs have turned golden brown. Serve immediately.

## Side

Do you enjoy broccoli (cooked or uncooked), as much as I do? When I was a kid, I called it, "the stinky vegetable," because when cooked, broccoli tends to emit an interesting kind of odor all to its own! Still, I love eating this healthy and delicious vegetable with just a bit of squeezed lemon and some clarified butter drizzled over the top. A few years ago, I put this casserole on my catering list menu for lunch and dinner parties. It was not initially a dish that flew off the charts. However, due to a lot of good word-of-mouth, this became an often-requested recipe from our loyal clients. Please enjoy this easy and delicious concoction with your family. The casserole makes for an unforgettable side dish for your Thanksgiving and Christmas holiday meals!

## Ingredients:

- 5 cups fresh broccoli (about 3 heads), stems removed (can be used for chicken stock)
- 2 medium Vidalia onions *or* 1 extra-large Vidalia onion, chopped finely
- 3 large garlic cloves, minced
- 2 tablespoons Emeril's Original Essence spice
- ½ cup unsalted butter (1 stick)
- ½ cup all-purpose flour
- 2½ cups whole milk
- ½ cup drinkable white wine
- 1 cup Swiss cheese, shredded
- 1 cup Monterey Jack cheese, grated *or* any other easily grated cheese (e.g. aged cheddar or Pepper Jack)
- 3 large eggs, beaten
- Plenty of freshly cracked black pepper, to taste
- Fresh flat leaf parsley, chopped (for garnish)

# Three Cheese Broccoli Bake

## YIELD: SERVES 8-10

### Directions:

- Preheat oven to 350 degrees Fahrenheit.

- Using a steamer tray or large metal mixing bowl (carefully balanced over a pot of boiling water, filled about halfway up to the top on the stovetop), steam the broccoli florets for about 10-12 minutes, or until tender (but not falling apart). You can retain the steam by either using a large lid or draping a large piece of heavy-duty aluminum foil over the container. Transfer the broccoli from the steamer to another bowl. Season the broccoli with black pepper, minced garlic, and 2 tablespoons of Emeril's Original Essence. Toss the ingredients well to combine.

- In a 3 quart Dutch oven or heavy pot, melt the 1 stick of butter. Whisk in the ½ cup of flour and cook until bubbly and smooth, about 3 minutes. Slowly, add 2½ cups of milk, white wine, and chopped onions, whisking constantly. Bring the mixture to a light boil and immediately reduce the heat to low. Essentially, you have made yourself a classic Bechamel sauce!

  *Chef's Note: When lightly boiling milk or cream, do not leave pot unattended. Heated milk and cream will expand at a rate three times faster than boiling water. This can be dangerous so ensure that children are not around the stovetop.*

- Stir into the mixture the 2 cups of grated cheeses and 3 beaten eggs. Whisk well to combine. Your cream mixture should be nice and thick, but not overly pasty.

- Using a rubber spatula, spread the reserved and steamed broccoli into a 9 x 13 inch Pyrex baking dish. Pour the cheese and milk mixture over the top of the broccoli and gently smooth the top. Do not break up the broccoli florets.

- Cook in the preheated oven for 40-45 minutes, or until the top has turned golden brown and bubbly. Remove, let cool for 5 minutes, garnish with chopped parsley, and serve immediately.

# Side

If you do not like baked potatoes stuffed with sour cream, cheddar, and Pepper Jack cheeses and topped with crispy bacon, you should probably check your blood pressure to see if you are still alive. In other health news, this dish is not for the faint of heart, nor is it for anyone dieting. A healthy recipe? No, I am afraid not! This is a delicious side dish that will make your taste buds do a few somersaults. I know that you might also be thinking about the last time you watched football and had those to-die for potato skins. Well, this recipe is pretty similar to that one, but you get to enjoy the best of both worlds because this recipe gives you a crispy potato skin on the outside and some melt-in-your-mouth mashed potatoes on the inside! Did I just hear you run towards the potato bin?

## Stuffed Potato Ingredients:

♦ 4 large Idaho baking potatoes, washed and dried completely

♦ 2 tablespoons Kosher salt (for rubbing on the outside of the potatoes)

♦ 10 slices thick smoky bacon

♦ 1 tablespoon Emeril's Cajun Essence

♦ 2 teaspoons onion powder (not onion salt)

♦ 2 teaspoons roasted garlic powder (not garlic salt)

♦ ½ cup sour cream

♦ ¼ cup whole milk

♦ 4 tablespoons unsalted butter (½ stick)

♦ ½ cup aged cheddar cheese, grated, divided

♦ ½ cup Pepper Jack cheese, grated, divided

♦ 8 green onions, sliced thinly (use all of the white and light green parts)

♦ Lots of freshly cracked black pepper, to taste

## Yogurt Sauce Ingredients:

♦ 1 cup plain Greek yogurt

♦ Juice from ½ lemon

♦ 1 tablespoon Worcestershire sauce

♦ 1 tablespoon Emeril's Cajun Essence

♦ Plenty of freshly cracked black pepper, to taste

♦ 1 bunch fresh chives, chopped finely (for garnish)

CHEF CARDIE'S

# Twice Stuffed
# Baked Potatoes with
# Spiced Yogurt Sauce

### YIELD: MAKES 8 HALVES

## Stuffed Potato Directions:

◆ Preheat oven to 400 degrees Fahrenheit.

◆ With a fork or a very sharp knife, poke a few holes in and around each potato. Rub the outside of the potatoes with 2 tablespoons of Kosher salt. Place the 4 baking potatoes directly onto the top rack of the oven. Bake for 1 hour and then remove the potatoes with tongs. Let them cool for 15 minutes before handling.

◆ While the potatoes are baking, cook the 10 slices of bacon in the preheated oven until they become nice and crisp, about 18 minutes. Remove and drain the bacon on paper towels and when cool enough, dice, slice, or crumble the bacon. Set it aside in a separate bowl.

◆ After 15 minutes of cooling the potatoes, with a sharp knife, slice each potato in half lengthwise. With a small spoon, carefully scoop out the "flesh" or insides of each potato and transfer to a mixing bowl. Be careful not to break or puncture the potato skins during this process. Set the hollowed skins aside.

◆ In the mixing bowl with potato flesh, add 1 tablespoon of Emeril's Cajun Essence, the onion powder, garlic powder, sour cream, whole milk, unsalted butter, ¼ cup of the aged cheddar cheese, and ¼ cup of the Pepper Jack cheese. Fold in the sliced green onions and finish by adding lots of freshly cracked black pepper, to taste. Using a potato masher or the back of a metal spoon, stir or mash everything together until you attain the desired consistency of mashed potatoes.

◆ Increase the oven temperature to 450 degrees Fahrenheit.

◆ Place each potato half "skin" on an unlined baking sheet and spoon the creamy mixture into each potato half until it is nearly filled to the top. Top each potato with a generous sprinkling of the remaining ¼ cups of aged cheddar and Pepper Jack cheeses. Do not forget to additionally sprinkle on the reserved crumbled or chopped bacon.

◆ Place the baking sheet with stuffed potatoes into the oven for about 12 minutes, or until the cheese on top has completely melted and begins to brown around the top and edges.

◆ Carefully, remove the potatoes from the oven. Let them cool for 10 minutes and then serve on a pretty appetizer plate to your eager and appreciative company!

*Chef's Note: If you are hosting a cocktail party with appetizers, these stuffed potatoes can easily be cut into quarters and passed around on a pretty platter.*

## Yogurt Sauce Directions:

◆ Combine all of the ingredients into a medium sized bowl and whisk to incorporate well. Chill the sauce for at least 1 hour before serving.

## Side

Rice pilaf is another dish with some great, historical roots. Since certain versions date back to ancient Persia, you could say that it has stood the test of time! Besides it being delicious and inexpensive (a fantastic combination), this versatile side dish can be paired with just about any entrée. I learned just how much this was true when I began preparing the colorful recipe at all sorts of restaurants across the country and with my catering company, Cardie Cooks. There are also so many vegetables in it that you could almost serve it as a complete meal! Just make sure to serve some good Italian or French bread alongside it and to wash everything down with some fruity red or white wine!

## Ingredients:

- ◆ 2 heaping tablespoons Emeril's Original Essence spice (for cooking vegetables)
- ◆ 2 tablespoons good olive oil
- ◆ 3 medium carrots (about ½ cup), grated
- ◆ 3 large celery stalks, sliced into ½ inch rounds
- ◆ 1 red bell pepper, chopped finely
- ◆ 2 medium Vidalia onions (or 1 large Vidalia onion), peeled and chopped finely
- ◆ 4 large garlic cloves, minced finely
- ◆ 3 tablespoons unsalted butter
- ◆ 2 tablespoons Worcestershire sauce
- ◆ 2 teaspoons thyme (fresh or dried)
- ◆ 2 teaspoons rosemary (fresh or dried)
- ◆ 2 teaspoons roasted garlic powder (not garlic salt)
- ◆ 3 cups long grain rice
- ◆ 1 (15 ounce) can sweet peas, drained of any liquid
- ◆ 1 (15 ounce) can sweet corn, drained of any liquid
- ◆ 6 cups rich chicken stock (p. 89)
- ◆ Plenty of freshly cracked black pepper, to taste

# Vegetable
# Rice Pilaf

## YIELD: SERVES 10-12

## Directions:

- In a mixing bowl, coat all of the vegetables with the 2 heaping tablespoons of Emeril's Original Essence spice along with 2 tablespoons of good olive oil. Mix with a large spoon to combine everything well.

- In a 4 quart Dutch oven or large soup pot, over medium heat, melt 3 tablespoons of unsalted butter. Cook and stir in the grated carrots, celery, red bell pepper, onions, and garlic until the vegetables begin to soften, about 10 minutes. While the vegetables are sautéing, stir in the Worcestershire sauce, thyme, rosemary, and roasted garlic powder.

- Sprinkle in the 3 cups of long grain rice and stir the rice in the vegetable mixture for an additional 2 minutes. Add the canned peas and corn to the mixture and stir to combine everything well.

- Slowly pour in 6 cups of chicken stock and add plenty of freshly cracked black pepper at the same time. Raise the heat to high and bring the mixture to a full boil. Immediately reduce the heat to low and cover the pot with a tight-fitting lid.

  *Chef's Note: Once the mixture reaches a full boil, scrape the pot with a wooden spoon to dislodge any rice that may have stuck to the sides and bottom.*

- Simmer the rice for 25 minutes without peeking under the lid. Remove the Dutch oven from the heat and allow the mixture to rest, undisturbed (and still covered), for an additional 15 minutes.

- Remove the lid and fluff the rice pilaf with a fork. Spoon onto a nice serving platter or into a 9 x 13 inch Pyrex dish. The dish is plenty colorful so there is no need to add garnish.

# Mains I

# Mains II

# Main

If you gathered all of my closest friends into a room and asked them what their favorite grilled dish is that I make, they would probably say this one. I always make a lot of extra chicken because there is hardly any left for me by the time I finish all of my cooking! These moist and luscious chicken thighs can also be cooked in an oven at 375 degrees Fahrenheit for about 50 minutes. However you choose to prepare them, I think that you will be thoroughly delighted and very proud of yourself!

## Ingredients:

- 16 chicken thighs, bone in and skin on
- 3 pints raspberries (can substitute frozen, unsweetened raspberries if necessary)
- 1 cup any good raspberry jam
- 2 cups tawny port wine
- ½ cup honey
- ¼ cup balsamic vinegar
- Cloves from 3 large heads of garlic, roasted (recipe follows)
- ½ cup New Orleans poultry spice *or* any good chicken spice mix, divided (plus spice for marinade and seasoning the chicken itself)
- A few good shakes any hot sauce (such as Tabasco or Frank's)
- 3 cups buttermilk
- Juice from 1 lemon
- 3 teaspoons olive oil (plus olive oil for drizzling over chicken pieces)
- ½ tablespoon dried herbs (for roasting garlic)
- Kosher salt and freshly cracked black pepper, to taste
- Flat leaf parsley, chopped finely (for garnish)

# 24 Hour Marinated, Buttermilk Grilled Chicken Thighs with Roasted Garlic, Honey, and Raspberry Puree

## YIELD: SERVES 8-10

### Roasted Garlic Directions:

♦ Preheat oven to 425 degrees Fahrenheit.

♦ Using a very sharp knife, cut off the top ¼ section of each garlic head, exposing the cloves. Discard any loose paper from the head but do not remove all of it. Lay the garlic heads on a sheet of aluminum foil and place each garlic head clove-side up. Sprinkle with salt and pepper, 1 teaspoon of olive oil per garlic head, and ½ tablespoon of dried herbs (such as rosemary or thyme). Wrap the garlic heads in aluminum foil and seal the package. Place on a baking sheet. Roast garlic for 45 minutes. Once cooled, the garlic cloves can be easily removed using a paring knife or by simply squeezing the garlic heads with your hands.

### Marinade Directions:

♦ Puree the raspberries in a food processor. Using a fine mesh sieve, over a large bowl, strain, or "seed" the raspberries by pushing them down gently with a spatula. Add the 1 cup of raspberry jam, 2 cups of port wine, ½ cup of honey, ¼ cup of balsamic vinegar, roasted garlic, some poultry spice, and a few shakes of hot sauce. Let the mixture come to a boil and then simmer for 10 minutes to thicken it slightly. Set aside to cool. Check marinade for taste and adjust accordingly. Marinate the chicken thighs as instructed below.

*Chef's Note: Reserve 1½ cups of raspberry puree before marinating the chicken. 1 cup will be for grilling and the other ½ cup will be served alongside the chicken at the table.*

### Directions:

♦ Place in a 1 gallon food storage bag, 8 pieces of chicken, ½ cup of the raspberry marinade, ¼ cup of New Orleans blend poultry spice, and 1½ cups of buttermilk. Seal, press out the air, and marinate the chicken in the refrigerator for at least 24 hours. Repeat this process for the remaining chicken.

♦ Preheat your outside grill and set your indoor oven to 350 degrees Fahrenheit.

♦ Remove the chicken and pat dry using paper towels. Do not rinse them off in the sink. Salt and pepper your pieces well and add some additional spice blend, "massaging" the chicken gently. Drizzle the olive oil over the chicken. Over the medium to hot grill, cook the chicken, skin-side down. Do not turn the pieces for 4 minutes. Flip the chicken over and do not turn for another 4 minutes. Repeat this process at least three more times. The total grilling time should be about 24 minutes.

♦ With 5 minutes remaining in the grilling process, pour 1 cup of the reserved raspberry puree and the juice from 1 lemon into a bowl. Using a clean grill brush or barbecue "mop," evenly smear the raspberry puree onto both sides of the chicken. Remove the chicken from the grill and place the pieces in the oven for 15 minutes while you prepare the rest of your meal.

♦ Garnish the chicken with freshly chopped flat leaf parsley and serve the chicken thighs with ½ cup of raspberry sauce on the side.

# Main

I have entertained and fed many senior citizens, hospital patients, and high school students while performing in well over 100 "Culinary Therapy" shows across the tri-state area. This healthy, delicious, and diabetic-friendly recipe has been showcased several times with the assistance of my son, Charlie. While this is an easy and fun dish to make with your kids, it is even better to eat! Our audiences went crazy for this Asian-inspired recipe and I know that you and your family will as well!

## Marinade Ingredients:

- ♦ 12 chicken thighs, boneless and skinless, cut into 2 inch chunks
- ♦ ½ cup teriyaki sauce
- ♦ 2 tablespoons Emeril's Bayou Blast spice
- ♦ 2 tablespoons garlic powder
- ♦ 1 cup pineapple juice, unsweetened
- ♦ ½ cup light brown sugar, packed
- ♦ 1 jar apricot jelly
- ♦ 2 tablespoons Dijon mustard
- ♦ 4 sprigs fresh thyme leaves, chopped finely
- ♦ 4 sprigs fresh rosemary leaves, chopped finely

## Kabob Ingredients:

- ♦ Wooden or bamboo skewers (immersed in cold water for at least 30 minutes)
- ♦ 2 cups pineapple chunks (fresh or canned)
- ♦ 2 cups mixed green and yellow zucchini, cut into thick, 1 inch chunks
- ♦ 2 cups fresh grape tomatoes
- ♦ Kosher salt and freshly cracked black pepper, to taste
- ♦ Fresh flat leaf parsley, chopped (for garnish)

CHEF CARDIE'S

# 24 Hour Marinated, Grilled Chicken, Pineapple, Zucchini, and Tomato Skewers

YIELD: SERVES 8-10

## Marinade Directions:

♦ Combine the listed marinade ingredients (**except for** the chicken thighs), in a bowl. Stir well. Place the chicken pieces into a 1 gallon zip-lock bag. Reserve at least 1 cup of marinade for basting the next day. Pour in the remaining marinade, seal the bags, shake them well, and refrigerate overnight.

## Kabob Directions:

♦ Alternate skewering the marinated chicken thighs with tomatoes, pineapple chunks, and zucchini chunks. Place the kabobs on a heated and well-oiled grill. Cook for at least 5 minutes before flipping them to the other side. Repeat this process at least three more times, or until the chicken pieces are no longer pink and the juices run clear. A food thermometer should read 165 degrees Fahrenheit.

♦ During the last 5 minutes of cooking, brush the kabobs with the reserved marinade. On a warm platter, season the kabobs with a pinch or two of Kosher salt and plenty of freshly cracked black pepper. Garnish the kabobs with some chopped flat leaf parsley.

# Main

What do they say about pork? It is the "other" white meat? That is somewhat true for most of us but after you make and enjoy this recipe, it will probably be added to your "once a month" meals to prepare for both your family and friends!

## Pork Marinade Ingredients:

- 1 large (at least 5 pound) pork tenderloin
- ½ cup low sodium soy sauce
- 1 cup low sodium chicken broth
- 1 cup white sugar
- 3 tablespoons fresh ginger, grated
- 3 tablespoons fresh garlic, minced
- 2 tablespoons fresh thyme, chopped finely
- 2 tablespoons fresh rosemary, chopped finely
- Juice from 4 large lemons
- 3 tablespoons Dijon mustard
- A pinch or two of Kosher salt and freshly cracked black pepper, to taste

## Mushrooms & Shallots Ingredients:

- 3 pounds fresh cremini mushrooms, stems removed (and saved for soup stock)
- 5 large shallots, peeled and sliced thinly
- 2 tablespoons unsalted butter
- 2 tablespoons olive oil
- ¼ cup Worcestershire sauce
- 1 tablespoon fresh thyme, minced finely
- 4 tablespoons fresh flat leaf parsley, stems discarded, chopped finely
- ½ cup any drinkable red wine (I use a Merlot)
- A pinch of Kosher salt and freshly cracked black pepper, to taste
- Fresh flat leaf parsley, chopped (for garnish)

# 24 Hour Marinated, Pork Tenderloin Smothered with Cremini Mushrooms and Caramelized Shallots

## Pork Marinade Directions:

♦ Combine all of the marinade ingredients (**except for** the tenderloin), into a large bowl and mix well. Trim the pork tenderloin of most of its fat and the "silver skin" on its outside. Place the meat inside a large marinating bag, pour in the marinade, seal the bag tightly, and marinate in the refrigerator for at least 24 hours.

♦ The next day, over an open, hot grill, cook the pork tenderloin for 8 minutes on the first side and 8 minutes on the second side. Shut off the grill, lower the lid, and let the meat cook for another 6 minutes on each side. The internal temperature on a meat thermometer should read 140 degrees Fahrenheit. Let the meat rest for 10 minutes. Slice thinly and serve on a platter covered with the mushroom and shallot mixture (recipe follows).

## Mushroom and Shallots Directions:

♦ In a heavy pan or Dutch oven, over medium heat, melt 2 tablespoons of butter and 2 tablespoons of olive oil. Sauté the sliced shallots for about 15 minutes, stirring constantly. Do not burn the shallots. Once caramelized and golden brown, using a slotted spoon, transfer the shallots to a small bowl and set them aside.

♦ Return the pan to the stovetop. Over medium heat, add the mushrooms and ¼ cup of Worcestershire sauce. Cook the mushrooms for 20 minutes, or until most (if not all), of the liquid has been absorbed and the mushrooms begin to glisten. Add the prepared shallots and finely chopped thyme and parsley to the pan. Add a pinch of Kosher salt and freshly cracked black pepper, to taste. Stir well to combine the ingredients.

♦ Remove the shallots and mushroom mixture from the pan and set aside for a moment. Over medium-high heat, deglaze the pan with ½ cup of red wine and cook the wine down for 5-6 minutes. Pour the reduced wine, mushrooms, and shallot mixture over the sliced tenderloin. Garnish with chopped flat leaf parsley and serve immediately.

# Main

The pictured seafood stew is from an elegant dinner party I catered in Rochester Hills, Michigan. This bouillabaisse made with New Orleans andouille sausage, tomatoes, red wine, and fresh herbs took my guests' breaths away (because it was so good, not because of the abundance of spices, thank you)! It is a simple, yet classy dish, that pairs nicely with my herbed and cheesy garlic bread (page 129). As you can see, I use it as a "dramatic" garnish.

## Ingredients:

- 3 pounds andouille sausage (about 4 large links), cut into ½ inch thick slices
- 3 pounds large uncooked shrimp (16-20 count per pound), peeled and deveined
- 3 pounds any firm fish (e.g. sea bass, red snapper, or monkfish), cut into 2 inch pieces
- 4 tablespoons olive oil, divided
- 3 Vidalia onions, peeled and chopped coarsely
- 5 large celery stalks, chopped into 1 inch slices
- 5 large carrots, peeled and sliced into nickel-sized pieces
- 1 (32 ounce) can chopped tomatoes, with juice
- 1 (small) can tomato paste
- ½ cup fresh basil leaves, chopped finely
- 1 package rosemary (about 2 tablespoons), chopped finely
- 1 package thyme (about 2 tablespoons), chopped finely
- 2 bay leaves
- Juice from 2 whole lemons
- A few good shakes any hot sauce (such as Tabasco or Frank's)
- 3 tablespoons garlic (about 6 large cloves), minced
- 2 heaping tablespoons Old Bay seasoning
- 2 cups any good red wine (such as a Merlot or Cabernet)
- 4 cups seafood stock (p. 91)
- A pinch or two of Kosher salt and lots of freshly cracked black pepper, to taste
- Green onions, chopped (for garnish)
- ½ head fresh cilantro, chopped finely (for garnish)
- Optional: cheesy garlic bread (p. 129)

# Andouille Sausage

# and

# Seafood Stew

## Directions:

♦ In a medium sized pot or Dutch oven, over medium-high heat, add 2 tablespoons of olive oil and the andouille sausage slices, browning them for 10 minutes. Do not burn. Remove the sausages with a slotted spoon and allow them to drain on paper towels.

♦ Add to the Dutch oven the other 2 tablespoons of olive oil and the onions, celery, and carrots. Sauté for 8 minutes. The vegetables will begin to caramelize slightly.

♦ Add in the chopped tomatoes, tomato paste, basil, rosemary, thyme, bay leaves, juice from 2 lemons, hot sauce, minced garlic, Old Bay seasoning, red wine, and 4 cups of seafood stock. Add Kosher salt and freshly cracked pepper, to taste. Stir everything well. Bring the mixture to a full boil and then immediately reduce to a low simmer. Simmer, uncovered, for 1 hour. During this time, the sauce will begin to reduce and darken.

♦ Add the uncooked shrimp, cut-up fish pieces, and reserved andouille sausage. Raise the heat to medium and cook for no more than 8 minutes. The shrimp are fully cooked when they turn opaque or pink in color. The fish will be cooked through when the pieces become white and flaky but are not falling apart.

♦ Using a ladle, serve the stew in large, decorative soup bowls with long strips of cheesy garlic bread (p, 129) on the side. Garnish with chopped green onions and cilantro on top.

# Main

This fun and delicious recipe is dedicated to my younger son, Jameson Mortimer (affectionately referred to as, "Jamie"). I will try my best not to embarrass him, but he just so happens to also be one of my idols. His sheer intelligence, quiet demeanor, and God-given talent to work as a Software Engineer in New York City often leaves me speechless and quite humbled. I am a father filled with immense and total pride for both of my sons! Jamie is also a very good judge of gourmet food and he and his wife have traveled the world to enjoy many different cuisines. When he was about 7 or 8 years old, he was upstairs playing Nintendo with some of his closest friends. I told the boys that I was going to make my beer-battered shrimp and scallops to their enthusiastic approval. However, as I started cooking, I detected a rather foul scent in the air. Upon closer examination, I realized there might be a freshness problem with the scallops. I had just purchased them at the market, so they had to be fresh, right? Wrong! About 10 minutes into my cooking, Jamie entered the kitchen. He was staring at me with cold, beaded, and steely eyes. I tried not to "notice" him right away, but he would not move an inch. I asked, "Son, anything wrong?" Without missing a beat, Jamie answered, "Dad? What smells like ass?" It was then that I knew I could no longer continue with this dinner! Jamie was right! The entire house reeked of rotten scallops! I learned a valuable lesson once and for all that day. You cannot skimp on freshness, especially when it comes to your seafood! Many weeks later, I gained redemption by cooking this fabulous meal for the boys. The story had a very happy ending for sure! Make this wonderful dish for your own "idols" and enjoy!

## Beer-Battered Shrimp & Scallops Ingredients:

♦ 2 pounds fresh sea scallops, abductor muscle on the side removed from each scallop

♦ 2 pounds large shrimp, peeled completely and deveined

♦ 5 cups canola oil (for deep frying) (see Chef's Note)

♦ 2 large eggs, beaten well

♦ 2 cups all-purpose flour

♦ 2½ cups any beer

♦ 1 teaspoon baking powder

♦ 1 teaspoon baking soda

♦ 3 heaping tablespoons Old Bay seasoning

♦ 2 tablespoons garlic powder

♦ A few good shakes any hot sauce (such as Tabasco or Frank's)

♦ Plenty of freshly cracked black pepper, to taste

♦ Lemon slices (for garnish)

## Tartar Sauce Ingredients:

♦ 1½ cups mayonnaise

♦ 2 teaspoons Old Bay seasoning

♦ ½ cup dill pickles, chopped finely

♦ 3 tablespoons fresh parsley, minced

♦ 2 tablespoons onion, minced finely

♦ 1 tablespoon prepared yellow mustard

♦ Juice from 1 whole lemon

♦ Freshly cracked black pepper, to taste

# Beer-Battered Shrimp and Scallops with Homemade Tartar Sauce

YIELD: SERVES ABOUT 8

## Beer-Battered Shrimp and Scallops Directions:

♦ In a large, 4 quart Dutch oven, over medium-high heat, heat 5 cups of canola oil to 350 degrees Fahrenheit.

*Chef's Note: You will need a good candy thermometer for this recipe. This is an inexpensive tool that is required for making anything deep fried. Also, be sure to keep children away while deep frying with hot oil.*

♦ In a large mixing bowl, combine all of the listed ingredients (**except for** the uncooked seafood). Mix everything well with a wire whisk until a smooth batter is achieved.

♦ Dip each piece of seafood into the batter, coating them well. Set them on a serving platter to take to be fried. Very gently and carefully, add the seafood to the preheated oil. Do not overcrowd the Dutch oven. You should be able to comfortably fit about 4 or 5 pieces at a time. Cook each piece of seafood for 2-3 minutes, or until golden brown. Remove the seafood with a slotted spoon and place them on paper towels to drain.

♦ Place the cooked scallops and shrimp onto a clean serving platter. Garnish with sliced lemons. Serve with homemade tartar sauce (recipe follows).

## Tartar Sauce Directions:

♦ Whisk together the listed ingredients in a mixing bowl. Chill for at least 1 hour before serving. The tartar sauce will thicken slightly when chilled completely.

*Chef's Note: If you would also like a "kicked-up" red sauce for dipping, please refer to the shrimp cocktail recipe in the "Appetizer" section (p. 33).*

# Main

This is another emotional recipe for me. I dedicate this dish to my first cousin and "big brother," Mr. Charles Elder. Although he now resides in Houston, Texas with his lovely wife, my parents "adopted" Charles as a third son early on in his life and he lived with my family for much of the 1970's, where we created so many wonderful memories together. My mother, Bette, especially loved cooking shrimp curry for dinner parties and as I recall, she once telephoned Charles in Texas to tell him that she would be making his favorite dish. Lo and behold, Sarge (as we affectionately called him for short), took the next plane to New Jersey because he was not going to miss out on this special meal for anything! My mother's delightful and flavorful curry was something to behold and cherish. After many attempts, I think I have come pretty darn close to recreating her traditional dish. I know that my mom is smiling down from Heaven because this amazing recipe and her endless love will endure forever!

## Ingredients:

- 3 pounds jumbo shrimp (16-20 count per pound), peeled and deveined
- 2 tablespoons olive oil
- 2 large Vidalia onions, chopped finely
- 4 garlic cloves, minced finely
- 2 teaspoons ginger, ground
- 2 teaspoons cumin, ground
- 3 teaspoons turmeric, ground
- 2 teaspoons paprika
- 2 teaspoons chili powder
- 2 (14½ ounce) cans chopped tomatoes, with juice
- 2 (14 ounce) cans coconut milk
- A few good shakes Tabasco sauce or Bermudian sherry pepper sauce
- 4 cups white rice, steamed (cooked according to box directions)
- Kosher salt and freshly cracked black pepper, to taste

## Toppings:

- 2 cups pineapple (fresh or canned), chopped
- 2 cups Vidalia onion, chopped finely
- 2 cups unsalted cashews, chopped finely (be mindful of allergies)
- 2 cups coconut, shredded
- ½ cup green onions, chopped
- ½ cup fresh cilantro, chopped finely

# Bette's
# Shrimp Curry
# with Toppings

## Directions:

♦ In a large and deep skillet pan or an electric fryer, over medium-high heat, sauté the onions in the olive oil until translucent, about 8 minutes. Add the garlic and all of the other listed spices. Stir with the onions until well combined, about 2 additional minutes.

♦ Pour the chopped tomatoes (including their juice), and coconut milk into the pan. Season with a pinch of Kosher salt and some freshly cracked black pepper. Add a few good dashes of Tabasco sauce *or* some Bermudian sherry pepper sauce, to taste. Cook the mixture on a medium-low simmer for about 30 minutes, stirring often. Tend to your rice.

*Chef's Note: Bermudian sherry pepper sauce can be purchased online and used in so many recipes. My mom always served and kept her sherry pepper sauce on her dining room table for anyone who wanted to "kick it up" a few more notches.*

♦ Add the uncooked shrimp to the mixture and increase the stovetop heat to medium. The shrimp will be done when they turn opaque or pinkish in color, about 10-12 minutes.

♦ To serve, place the cooked white rice in the center of a pretty dinner plate. Spoon the hot shrimp curry over the rice and garnish with any of the toppings listed.

# Main

Oh my goodness! Is your mouth watering like mine is right now? If I was only granted one final meal to eat before the Good Lord took me away, this would probably be the one! I simply love Atlantic Ocean lobster tails with drawn garlic butter on the side and as you can see, I had mine with blanched broccoli just the other night! I admit, it is an expensive meal, but it is a most worthwhile indulgence, particularly for special occasions and for special people. To the romantics out there, this makes for a delightful and decadent dinner for your significant other on Valentine's Day! Do not forget to include the Godiva chocolates and long-stemmed rose for dessert!

## Ingredients:

- 4 (10 ounce) Atlantic lobster tails, frozen
- ½ cup unsalted butter (1 stick)
- 6 large garlic cloves, minced finely
- Juice from 1 whole lemon
- ¼ cup drinkable white wine
- 2 heaping tablespoons Old Bay seasoning
- 1 heaping tablespoon Dijon mustard
- 2 good shakes any hot sauce (such as Tabasco or Frank's)
- Plenty of freshly cracked black pepper, to taste
- Optional: fresh flat leaf parsley sprigs, chopped finely (for garnish)

# Broiled Lobster Tails with Garlic Butter and Old Bay Seasoning

YIELD: MAKES 4

10 OUNCE LOBSTER TAILS

## Directions:

♦ 1 hour before cooking, place your frozen lobster tails in a large, metal mixing bowl and add enough cold water to cover them. Set aside until the lobster thaws completely. Once thawed, dry off each tail with a clean kitchen towel. Using either good kitchen shears or a very sharp chef's knife, cut the back shell of each tail lengthwise to expose the meat. **Do not** cut all the way through the tail itself. Using your hands, carefully pull the meat away from the shell (without breaking or tearing the meat or shell), and mound the meat on top of the outer shell. Place each lobster tail in a broiler oven pan and set aside.

♦ Place your oven on the broiler setting.

♦ In a small Dutch oven or large saucepan, over medium heat, melt the 1 stick of unsalted butter. Add in the minced garlic, juice from 1 lemon, white wine, Old Bay seasoning, tablespoon of Dijon mustard, and a few good shakes of your favorite hot sauce. Season with plenty of freshly cracked black pepper. Whisk or stir together well and then remove the saucepan from the heat.

♦ Using a pastry brush, "paint" each lobster tail with some of the melted garlic butter mixture until they are well-coated.

♦ Place the lobster tails into the broiler and cook for 10 minutes. After this time, carefully remove the tails from the oven and "paint" them again with more garlic butter. Return to the broiler for an additional 8 minutes. Once done, set them on top of the stovetop to cool slightly, about another 10 minutes.

> *Chef's Note: Depending on the size of your broiler pan, the 4 lobster tails may need to be cooked in two batches.*

♦ When ready to serve, pour some of the remaining butter sauce into 4 individual, 6 ounce ramekins. Place a lobster tail in the center of each pretty plate and serve with your favorite vegetable(s) on the side.

> *Chef's Note: Please feel free to garnish your lobster tails with chopped, flat leaf parsley if you so desire.*

# Main

When I was 12 and 13 years old, I attended The Malcom Gordon School, an upscale boarding school situated directly across the Hudson River from the West Point Military Academy in Garrison, New York. I spent two years on the army campus training, playing ice hockey, praying in their beautiful cathedral, and doing a lot of marching with the Plebes. Every other Tuesday night, we attended a cafeteria-style dinner that they called, "KINCIP." Do you get it? That is the incorrect and backwards spelling of the word, "PICNIC!" Anyway, on those nights, we were served gamey and tough beef liver paired with acrid tasting onions and mushy vegetables on the side. It certainly did not provide the best of culinary memories for me. However, when I was on "home leave" for a week during the Christmas holiday, I watched my mother make herself a very small pan of calf's liver, bacon, and onions. She asked if I wanted to try a bite, so I just had to tell her about KINCIP. She laughed for a minute at my negativity and then held out a fork full of her creation for me to sample. I swear, from that day on, I was hooked! Her dish was so tender, so delicious, and it was not off-tasting in any way. Today, I try to make calf's liver for myself once a week because it is just that delicious (and quite healthy). Please do not thumb your nose at this wonderful recipe. You will not be disappointed one single bit!

## Ingredients:

- 8 large pieces fresh calf's liver (butcher cut), trimmed of any fat or "silver skin"
- 10 slices any good smoky bacon
- 6 tablespoons unsalted butter, divided
- 2 large Vidalia onions, peeled and chopped
- ½ cup all-purpose flour
- 2 heaping tablespoons Emeril's Bayou Blast spice
- 6 large garlic cloves, minced
- ¼ cup any good white wine (for deglazing)
- ¼ cup chicken stock (p. 89)
- 1 tablespoon Worcestershire sauce
- A few good shakes any hot sauce (such as Tabasco or Frank's)
- Freshly cracked black pepper, to taste
- Fresh flat leaf parsley, chopped (for garnish)

# Calf's Liver with Smoky Bacon and Sweet Onions

## Directions:

♦ In a large sauté pan, over medium heat, cook 10 slices of smoky bacon until both sides are "rendered" and crispy, about 10 minutes. Remove the bacon from the pan and drain them on paper towels. Set aside. Discard all but 2 tablespoons of bacon fat from the sauté pan.

♦ Along with the remaining bacon fat in the pan, over medium heat, melt 2 tablespoons of unsalted butter. Add and sauté the chopped onions for 10 minutes, or until they have begun to brown. Transfer the cooked onions to a bowl and set them aside.

♦ Spread the flour onto a large dinner plate or platter and, using a fork or spoon, mix with 2 heaping tablespoons of Emeril's Bayou Blast spice. Dredge each piece of calf's liver in the seasoned flour and shake off any excess.

♦ Reposition your large sauté pan over medium heat. Add in 2 tablespoons of unsalted butter and the minced garlic, stirring them together for 1 minute. Place your calf's liver fillets into the hot pan and cook undisturbed for 3 minutes. Turn them over and cook for an additional 3 minutes without touching them. Carefully transfer the liver fillets to a small platter. You may have to cook the liver in two batches to prevent the pan from being overcrowded.

*Chef's Note: It is imperative that you do not overcook calf's liver. Anything more than medium-rare will result in a "gamey" taste.*

♦ Deglaze the pan by pouring in ¼ cup of white wine. Using a wooden spoon, scrape up all of the food particles that have formed in the bottom of the pan. Pour in and whisk together the ¼ cup of chicken stock, Worcestershire sauce, a few shakes of hot sauce, and plenty of freshly cracked black pepper. Complete the sauce by whisking in 2 additional tablespoons of cold, unsalted butter. Swirl the pan in a circular motion to finalize and combine all of the elements of your sauce. Pour the sauce over the reserved calf's liver and garnish the top with the reserved onions, bacon, and a bit of chopped, flat leaf parsley. Serve immediately.

*Chef's Note: I love pairing my calf's liver dinner with garlic smashed potatoes and sweet corn-on-the-cob. The recipes are on pages 135 and 117, respectively.*

# Main

This recipe is dedicated to a wonderful friend and incredibly talented Executive Chef named, Chef Karla Williams. Actually, she is now married to a great man with the last name, "Angel," so I guess I have found another "true angel" in my life! We met in South Carolina during the summer of 2017 at the famous health and wellness resort, "Hilton Head Health." Chef Karla did a few, fabulous culinary demos while I stayed there and her talents and recipes inspired me in many ways. This is my own take on one of the beautifully prepared and healthy dishes that I had the pleasure of watching her make in person. Do you know how good fresh salmon is for your health? Ask any doctor about the benefits of eating fresh salmon weekly and you will be amazed by what they say! Thank you Karla and everyone at Hilton Head Health! You will forever have a place in my heart!

## Ingredients:

- 4 (8 ounce) freshly caught farm-raised salmon *or* meaty red Alaskan salmon
- 2 tablespoons fresh garlic (about 4 large cloves), minced finely
- 2 good shakes any hot sauce (such as Tabasco or Frank's)
- ½ cup fresh Parmesan Reggiano cheese, grated
- ¼ cup Dijon mustard
- ½ cup red onion, minced finely
- ¼ cup good olive oil
- 4 tablespoons Old Bay seasoning
- ¼ cup pecans, chopped finely (be mindful of potential allergies)
- Plenty of freshly cracked black pepper, to taste
- Green onions, chopped (for garnish)

CHEF CARDIE'S

# Chef Karla's
# Salmon with Pecan and
# Parmesan Dijon Mustard Crust

### YIELD: SERVES 6-8

## Directions:

- Preheat oven to 450 degrees Fahrenheit.

- In a medium sized mixing bowl, combine the minced garlic, hot sauce, parmesan cheese, Dijon mustard, and minced red onion. Slowly whisk in ¼ cup of olive oil to form an emulsion.

- Place the salmon fillets skin-side down on a cookie sheet that has been lined with aluminum foil and sprayed with non-stick butter spray. Sprinkle the fillets with ½ tablespoon of Old Bay seasoning per side and add lots of freshly cracked black pepper to both sides as well.

- With clean hands or a tablespoon, "mound" the garlic, red onion, and parmesan mixture across each salmon's entire length. Distributing the ¼ cup of chopped pecans evenly, gently, yet firmly, press the pecans into the tops of the covered salmon so they adhere to each fillet.

- Place the spice-coated salmon fillets onto the middle rack of the preheated oven to cook for exactly 10 minutes. Keep a watchful eye on this process. You want your salmon to be medium -rare with the top browned and crusty.

- Remove the salmon fillets from the oven and, using a rubber spatula, carefully transfer them to a pretty serving tray or white plate. Garnish the salmon fillets with some freshly chopped green onions and serve immediately.

# Main

The pictured Chicken Murphy is from a surprise Italian birthday party I catered several years ago. The hosts requested this classic, Italian-inspired main dish from my "Cardie Cooks" catering menu. Truthfully, I was scared and even a bit apprehensive about presenting this culinary creation to a large contingent of authentic Italians. I am not the finest of Italian cooks but I still wanted to prepare something special with a distinct Italian flair that I could call my own. Ultimately, I think I accomplished my goal! I remember serving this dinner like it was yesterday. The guests could not stop hugging me or singing my praises so I guess they approved! This recipe will feed a lot of people, especially when served with pasta. Do not forget some crusty Italian bread on the side!

## Ingredients:

♦ 4 pounds chicken thighs, boneless and skinless, cut into 2 inch chunks

♦ 4 pounds sweet and hot Italian sausage (combined), cut into 1 inch slices

♦ 4 tablespoons olive oil, divided

♦ 3 tablespoons unsalted butter

♦ 3 pounds golden baby golden russet potatoes, halved

♦ 2 large Vidalia onions, chopped into 1 inch pieces

♦ 2 red bell peppers, seeded and chopped into 1 inch pieces

♦ 2 green bell peppers, seeded and chopped into 1 inch pieces

♦ ½ cup banana peppers *or* hot Italian peppers, jarred (with their brine), chopped

♦ 2 cups cremini *or* button mushrooms, quartered

♦ 1 tablespoon dried oregano

♦ 1 tablespoon dried thyme

♦ 1 tablespoon dried basil

♦ 6 garlic cloves, minced finely

♦ 4 tablespoons all-purpose flour (for dredging chicken)

♦ 2 tablespoons Emeril's Bayou Blast spice

♦ 2 cups rich chicken stock (p. 89)

♦ 1 cup good white wine

♦ 1 box of linguini or spaghetti (cooked according to box directions)

♦ Freshly cracked black pepper

♦ Fresh flat leaf parsley, chopped (for garnish)

♦ Optional: fresh Italian bread

167

# Chicken
# Murphy

YIELD: SERVES 8-10

## Directions:

♦ Preheat oven to 350 degrees Fahrenheit.

♦ In a large sauté pan, over medium-high heat, add 2 tablespoons of olive oil. Add and cook the sausage slices until browned on all sides, about 8-10 minutes. With a slotted spoon, remove the sausage pieces and set them on paper towels to drain.

♦ In the same sauté pan, over medium-high heat, melt 3 tablespoons of unsalted butter. Add the halved golden russet potatoes; chopped onions; red and green bell peppers; hot Italian peppers (and their brine); quartered cremini mushrooms; dried oregano, thyme, and basil; and minced garlic. Sauté the vegetables until they are well browned and caramelized, about 12 minutes. Remove the vegetables from the pan and using a spatula, spread them out in a large aluminum pan or large Pyrex baking dish.

♦ In a large mixing bowl, dredge the chicken thigh pieces with 4 tablespoons of all-purpose flour mixed with 2 tablespoons of Emeril's Bayou Blast spice. Add plenty of freshly cracked black pepper, to taste. Using the same sauté pan from the directions above, add another 2 tablespoons of olive oil to the pan and cook the chicken thighs until they are well browned on all sides, about 12 minutes.

♦ Add the cooked sausage to the sauté pan and stir for 1 minute to combine with the chicken. Transfer the chicken and sausage to the casserole dish. Mix well with the cooked vegetables.

♦ Pour 2 cups of rich chicken stock and 1 cup of white wine over the chicken, potatoes, and vegetable mixture. Place the casserole, uncovered, in the preheated oven. Bake for 35 minutes, undisturbed. Cook your pasta.

♦ Place in large soup bowls or on decorative plates, a good amount of cooked linguini or spaghetti. Using a ladle or large spoon, serve a helping of Chicken Murphy right over the top of the pasta. Do not forget to include some of the rich sauce. Garnish with chopped flat leaf parsley. Serve immediately.

# Main

As you have probably realized by now, I have wonderful memories of my cooking demos at Kings Cooking Studios in Short Hills, New Jersey. One of my culinary classes was called, "A Taste of Paris," so naturally, each of the dishes had a French theme to it. This recipe is my take on their rich and delightful seafood stunner! You can buy inexpensive scallop shell dishes at most department stores (in their gourmet section), or online to give this classic recipe a well-deserved dramatic effect.

## Ingredients:

- 32 large and fresh sea scallops (4 to a person), abductor muscle on the side removed from each scallop
- 1 large white onion, sliced or chopped coarsely
- 2 lemons, quartered
- 3 large celery stalks, chopped coarsely
- 2 bay leaves
- 3 tablespoons Old Bay seasoning, divided
- 1½ cups white wine
- ½ cup seafood stock (p. 91)
- 10 tablespoons unsalted butter (1 stick and 2 tablespoons), divided
- 3 packages mixed fresh mushrooms (combination of wild, button, and cremini)
- 4 garlic cloves, minced
- ½ cup all-purpose flour
- 1 cup heavy cream
- 1 cup whole milk
- 1 tablespoon Emeril's Bayou Blast spice
- ½ head fresh flat leaf parsley, chopped
- ¼ cup green onions, sliced
- 2½ cups Gruyere cheese, shredded
- 1½ cups breadcrumbs, unseasoned
- ¼ cup olive oil
- 1 cup parmesan cheese, grated
- A pinch of Kosher salt and freshly cracked black pepper, to taste

- Fresh flat leaf parsley (for garnish)
- 1 small package tarragon, chopped (for garnish)

# Coquille Saint Jacques
# (Scallops in Cheese Sauce)

YIELD: SERVES 8

## Directions:

- In a 4 quart Dutch oven or pot, over medium heat, add the sliced onions, lemon quarters, chopped celery, bay leaves, 2 tablespoons of Old Bay seasoning, white wine, and seafood stock. Bring the mixture to a simmer. Add the scallops and poach them for approximately 8 minutes. Do not overcook fresh scallops. Remove the scallops with a slotted spoon and set them aside in a bowl. Reserve ¼ cup of poaching liquid for the sauce.

- In a large sauté pan, over medium heat, melt 2 tablespoons of butter. Add and cook the mushrooms for about 8 minutes. Add the minced garlic during the final minute. Using a slotted spoon, transfer the mushrooms to a platter and set aside.

- In the same 4 quart Dutch oven used for poaching, over medium heat, melt 1 stick of unsalted butter and sprinkle in ½ cup of all-purpose flour. Stir together to form a light or "blonde" roux, about 10 minutes. Slowly whisk in the 1 cup of heavy cream, 1 cup of whole milk, ¼ cup of scallop poaching liquid, 1 tablespoon of Emeril's Bayou Blast spice, a pinch of Kosher salt, and some freshly cracked black pepper. Blend until all ingredients have been well incorporated. Bring the mixture to a very light boil and watch carefully to prevent the milk from expanding or overflowing. Immediately turn the stovetop heat off as soon as the milk and cream come to a boil, or "reach temperature."

- Stir in the parsley, green onions, Gruyere cheese, and 1 more tablespoon of Old Bay seasoning. Mix well to combine everything. Gently fold in the reserved scallops and add the reserved cooked mushrooms to the mixture. Spoon everything into 6 ounce, greased ramekins or broiler safe "seashell" dishes greased with non-stick cooking spray.

- In a medium sized mixing bowl, mix the breadcrumbs with ¼ cup of olive oil. Sprinkle the breadcrumbs over the top of the scallop mixture and top each shell with enough grated parmesan cheese to cover it. On a large cookie sheet, place the shells or ramekins under a preheated broiler for about 3 minutes, or until the tops are golden brown and bubbly. Be very careful not to burn the mixture.

    *Chef's Note: If making for 8 people, the broiling process must be done in two batches to cook properly.*

- Garnish each shell or individual plate with freshly chopped tarragon leaves or flat leaf parsley. Serve immediately alongside my asparagus recipe (p. 115).

# Main

How can you tell someone is Irish? Because they are always craving a baked potato and a six pack! True to my Irish and English heritage, I love anything that has to do with corned beef! As a young boy, my mother would make us these incredible, corned beef Reuben sandwiches, especially for Sunday football games. Her creation was simply to-die-for and one reason was because of her delicious and spicy Russian dressing. This recipe can be enjoyed throughout the entire year but please get out these directions especially on Saint Patrick's Day!

## Corned Beef Ingredients:

♦ 1 (5 pound) uncooked corned beef
♦ 6 bottles beer (I use Irish Guinness)
♦ 3 cups cold water
♦ 2 onions, chopped
♦ 2 bay leaves
♦ 2 tablespoons apple cider vinegar
♦ 2 tablespoons mustard seed
♦ 2 tablespoons coriander seed

## Sandwich Ingredients:

♦ 2 packages rye bread (I use Levy's Jewish)
♦ ½ inch slices from the round of corned beef
♦ 1 (16 ounce) package any good sauerkraut (cooked according to package instructions)
♦ 2 packages Swiss cheese, sliced thinly (I use Irish imported)
♦ Unsalted butter (for frying) (see Chef's Note)

## Russian Dressing Ingredients:

♦ ½ cup any good catsup (additional catsup may be needed)
♦ 1 cup mayonnaise (I use Hellman's)
♦ 3 fresh dill pickles, chopped finely
♦ 1 tablespoon Worcestershire sauce
♦ 1 teaspoon onion powder
♦ 1 teaspoon garlic powder
♦ A few shakes any hot sauce (such as Tabasco or Frank's)
♦ Freshly cracked black pepper, to taste

# Corned Beef Reuben
# with "Kicked-Up"
# Russian Dressing

YIELD: SERVES 8-10

## Corned Beef Directions:

◆ Rinse the corned beef well in a clean sink to ensure that the salt brine has been removed.

◆ Lay the corned beef flat in a large pot or 6 quart Dutch oven. Pour the beer over it and add 3 cups of cold water so the meat is fully submerged. Add the onions, bay leaves, vinegar, and spices listed. Bring the mixture to a full boil and then reduce the heat to medium-low.

◆ Cover the pot with a lid and cook for 4 hours, skimming the fat that has risen to the top every 30 minutes or so. Add water, as necessary, to keep the meat submerged.

## Russian Dressing Directions:

◆ In a large metal bowl, whisk together the catsup, mayonnaise, dill pickles, Worcestershire sauce, onion powder, garlic powder, and a few good shakes of hot sauce. Add plenty of freshly cracked black pepper, to taste. Blend thoroughly and taste the dressing to see what extras it might need. Adjust accordingly. Cover the bowl with plastic wrap and place it in the refrigerator for at least 1 hour to chill before using.

## Sandwich Directions:

◆ Place the slices of fresh rye bread onto a large sheet pan. Using a culinary "paint brush," smear one side of each slice of bread with the Russian dressing. Place the sliced corned beef on one slice of bread. Be generous. Top with a good amount of cooked, drained sauerkraut. Top that with very thin slices of Irish Swiss cheese. Place another slice of rye bread, dressing-side down, on top of the mound. Using a rubber spatula, press firmly, without breaking the bread, to slightly compress the sandwich. Repeat this process for each sandwich.

◆ Using a preheated sauté pan or stovetop grill pan, over medium heat, melt 2 tablespoons of unsalted butter. Carefully place two sandwiches at a time on the grill pan and fry for about 2 minutes. Flip the Reubens over and repeat the process on the other side. The sandwiches should turn a beautiful golden brown (similar to how French toast would appear). Do not burn the bread!

*Chef's Note: You will need at least 2 tablespoons of unsalted butter to fry 2 sandwiches at a time in your sauté pan. Do not overcrowd the pan while making the sandwiches.*

◆ Place the sandwiches on a decorative platter garnished with flat leaf parsley and serve! As the picture shows, serve with my Jersey Shore coleslaw and maple syrup sweet potatoes. The recipes are found on pp. 61 and 123, respectively.

# Main

I could not publish this cookbook without offering my famous and to-die-for, Super Bowl chili recipe! I know that there are many good home cooks out there who make their own slow-cooked chili for their football parties. But a chili with dark beer and some dark chocolate in it? All I can say is, "Wow!" Three years ago, I made this dish for my own Super Bowl party. I had prepared my brined chicken wings (page 11), my wife made her delicious Mexican tortilla dip, and our guests brought other fun and tasty appetizers. However, when this chili was ready, the aromas made everyone run over with their bowls in hand and tongues wagging. From that point on, it was "survival of the fittest." I witnessed pure savagery as both men and women hip-checked each other out of the way to get a big spoonful! I tried to get a bite of my own chili, but to no avail. I had to rely on my guests' positive reviews because when this "little doggie" finally did reach the pot, the cupboard was bare!

## Ingredients:

- ♦ 3 pounds lean ground beef
- ♦ 3 tablespoons olive oil
- ♦ 3 medium Vidalia onions, chopped finely
- ♦ 5 garlic cloves, chopped finely
- ♦ 1 tablespoon ancho chili powder
- ♦ 3 chipotle peppers in adobo sauce (canned), drained and chopped
- ♦ 2 teaspoons dry oregano
- ♦ 2 teaspoons cumin powder
- ♦ 2 tablespoons tomato paste (from 1 small can)
- ♦ 2 dark chocolate candy bars, broken by hand or chopped into chunks
- ♦ 1 (28 ounce) can red kidney beans, drained and rinsed
- ♦ 4 (12 ounce) bottles dark stout (I use Irish Guinness)
- ♦ 4 cups rich beef stock (p. 87)
- ♦ A few good shakes any hot sauce (such as Tabasco or Frank's)
- ♦ 1 (28 ounce) can diced tomatoes, with juice
- ♦ Plenty of freshly cracked black pepper, to taste
- ♦ Optional: aged cheddar cheese, grated (for topping)
- ♦ Optional: dollops of sour cream (for topping)
- ♦ Optional: flat leaf parsley, chopped finely (for topping)
- ♦ Optional: ½ large red onion, chopped finely (for topping)

# Dark Chocolate and Guinness Stout "Super Bowl" Chili

YIELD: SERVES 8-10

## Directions:

- In a large pot or 4 quart Dutch oven, over medium heat, add 3 tablespoons of olive oil and stir in the 3 pounds of ground beef. Cook until the meat is well browned, about 10 minutes.

- In the same pot, still over medium heat, add the chopped onions, garlic, chipotle peppers, and ancho chili powder. Sauté for about 5 minutes, or until the onions begin to glisten and the garlic and spices become fragrant. Add to the pot the dry oregano, cumin powder, and tomato paste. Stir to combine for another 2 minutes.

- Add the dark chocolate chunks, red kidney beans, diced tomatoes (and their juices), 4 dark Guinness stout beers, and 4 cups of rich beef stock. Season the mixture with plenty of freshly cracked black pepper and a few shakes of your favorite hot sauce. Reduce the heat to medium-low and simmer slowly, uncovered, for 2-2½ hours.

- Using a ladle, scoop the chili into decorative soup bowls once done. Garnish with any of the listed toppings. Serve immediately.

*Chef's Note: I place the toppings in separate bowls next to the big pot of chili and let my guests garnish their bowls to their hearts' content.*

# Main

I worked alongside a wonderfully talented woman for many years while I ran my private catering company, "Cardie Cooks." Her name was Patricia Hansen and she really knew how to cook up a storm! "Recia," as we called her affectionately, had natural talents and uncanny expertise when it came to Italian cooking. Since I was not "formally trained" as an Italian chef, I sat back with my mouth shut and learned a lot of different culinary techniques and recipes from her! This picture is of our Dijon-crusted pork chops over a bed of garlic broccoli rabe that we made together. Is your mouth watering like mine is right now? After we happily "tested" this dish on each other, we placed it on our catering menu, where it was frequently ordered to rave review every single time! Try this special dish in your own home. It is easy to prepare and I guarantee that you will receive the same kudos Recia and I did from our appreciative guests!

## Ingredients:

- 8 pork chops (about 4 pounds total), bone in, 1 inch thick
- 2 bunches broccoli rabe *or* 3 bunches broccolini, thick stems trimmed
- ½ cup Dijon mustard
- 2 teaspoons paprika
- 2 tablespoons Emeril's Original Creole Essence spice
- 2 cups breadcrumbs (I use Panko)
- 2 tablespoons olive oil
- 6 large garlic cloves, minced finely
- 2 teaspoons red pepper flakes
- ½ cup rich chicken stock (p. 89)
- ½ cup good white wine
- 3 tablespoons freshly squeezed lemon juice (about 1 large lemon)
- A few pinches of Kosher salt and plenty of freshly cracked black pepper, to taste
- 1 lemon, sliced (for garnish)
- Optional: Fresh flat leaf parsley, chopped finely (for garnish)

# Dijon-Encrusted Pork Chops with Garlic Broccoli Rabe

## YIELD: SERVES 8

### Directions:

- Preheat oven to 375 degrees Fahrenheit.

- In a mixing bowl, whisk together the Dijon mustard, paprika, and Emeril's Creole Essence spice. Using a spatula or your clean hands, smear both sides of the pork chops with the seasoned mustard mixture. Coat the chops with the Panko breadcrumbs, pressing down gently to help them adhere to the meat.

  *Chef's Note: Pork chops can be prepared for roasting hours in advance. Once coated, you can put the chops into the refrigerator for holding. Let them return to room temperature, about 30 minutes, before you place them in the oven.*

- Transfer the pork chops to a large baking sheet and place them on the top rack of the oven. Roast the meat for 15 minutes on that side and 15 minutes on the other side, or until an instant-read thermometer, inserted into the thickest part of the pork chops, registers 145 degrees Fahrenheit. Do not burn the pork chops!

- While the pork chops are cooking, pour 2 tablespoons of olive oil into a large sauté pan over medium-high heat. Toss in the broccoli rabe, minced garlic, and 2 teaspoons of red pepper flakes. Season the mixture with a pinch or two of Kosher salt and lots of freshly cracked black pepper. Sauté and stir the broccoli rabe for 5 more minutes.

- Pour into the pan the ½ cup of chicken stock, ½ cup of white wine and 3 tablespoons of lemon juice. Raise the stovetop heat to high and let the mixture reach a full boil. Immediately, reduce the heat to medium-low and simmer the broccoli rabe for 25 minutes, undisturbed.

- Remove the broccoli rabe with a slotted spoon and create a "bed" of broccoli on a nice serving platter. Place the pork chops on top of the broccoli rabe and then pour the pan sauce over the pork and broccoli.

- Garnish the platter with lemon slices and finely chopped flat leaf parsley. Serve immediately.

# Main

My late father, affectionately named "Duke" by others, absolutely loved my mother's slow-cooked lamb! My mother sadly passed away in 1997 but I would prepare his favorite dish for him every time he came to our home for the next eighteen years. As a simple gourmand, Dad only requested a side of cooked vegetables (baby peas in particular), and some oven roasted red potatoes which cooked alongside the lamb. Oh, and a stunning lamb gravy that he could sop up with homemade biscuits was a must! I can see his approving smile and the happy gleam in his eyes just remembering those great days. I loved spoiling the man as both his "private chef" and adoring son. I will forever dedicate this wonderful recipe to my dad's loving memory!

## Ingredients:

- 1 (10 pound) leg of lamb, on the bone (from butcher)
- ¼ cup Dijon mustard
- 2 cups plain Greek yogurt
- 2½ cups red wine (I use a Merlot), divided
- ½ cup fresh mint leaves (2 full packages), chopped finely
- 3 tablespoons fresh rosemary leaves, chopped finely
- 3 tablespoons fresh thyme leaves, chopped finely
- 5 tablespoons garlic (about 8 cloves), minced
- 4 pounds baby red or golden russet potatoes, rinsed well and dried slightly
- 8 large carrots, chopped into ½ inch chunks
- 8 large celery stalks, chopped
- 4 large Vidalia onions, chopped
- 2 heaping teaspoons Emeril's Bayou Blast spice
- 2 tablespoons good olive oil
- 1½ cups rich beef stock (p. 87) (for gravy)
- ½ cup all-purpose flour (for gravy)
- Kosher salt and freshly cracked black pepper, to taste

177

# Duke's
# Signature 24 Hour Marinated,
# Roast Leg of Lamb with Pan Gravy

## Roast Leg of Lamb Directions:

♦ In a large mixing bowl, combine the Dijon mustard, yogurt, 1½ cups of the red wine, chopped mint, rosemary leaves, thyme leaves, and minced garlic. Whisk everything well to form a "paste" of sorts. Rub the mixture all over the lamb, completely coating its outside. Place the herb-coated lamb in a zip-lock bag and seal tightly. Place the package in the refrigerator for 24 hours.

*Chef's Note: Using a very sharp knife, you can make a series of tiny slits in the lamb so the marinade will permeate the meat.*

♦ When ready to roast, preheat the oven to 425 degrees Fahrenheit. Remove the lamb from the marinade and clean off any excess marinade using paper towels. Set the lamb into a large roasting pan fitted with a rack. Place the lamb in the oven for 20 minutes to roast and brown slightly and then carefully remove from the oven.

♦ Lower the temperature to 350 degrees Fahrenheit. Season the potatoes, carrots, celery, and onions with 2 heaping teaspoons of Emeril's Bayou Blast, 2 tablespoons of olive oil, and cracked black pepper. Position the vegetables around the lamb in the roasting pan.

♦ Return the lamb to the oven to roast for approximately 1 hour and 15 minutes. You want an instant meat thermometer to read between 140 and 145 degrees Fahrenheit. Once ready, remove the lamb and wrap it in heavy-duty aluminum foil. Set aside.

♦ Remove the carrots, celery, and onions from the roasting pan and set them aside in a bowl for serving. While the lamb rests for 15 minutes, return the potatoes to the oven to brown some more. In the meantime, make your gravy.

## Lamb Gravy Directions:

♦ Return your roasting pan with lamb particles and vegetable drippings to the stovetop over high heat. Add the remaining 1 cup of wine and, using a wooden spoon or wire whisk, scrape the particles at the bottom of the pan. This process is called, "deglazing." Add 1½ cups of beef broth and sprinkle in ½ cup of all-purpose flour. Stir or whisk constantly to prevent the flour from clumping. Reduce the heat to medium and let the gravy simmer, reduce, and thicken for approximately 10 minutes. Add salt and freshly cracked black pepper, to taste. Whisk occasionally to prevent scorching or burning.

*Chef's Note: If desired, the gravy may be strained through a fine, mesh sieve once you have finished cooking it but it is not necessary.*

# Main

In 2012, I did a sold-out culinary demo called, "Are You Hungry Tonight?" at Kings Cooking Studios honoring "The King" himself, Mr. Elvis Presley. We cooked everything from Memphis-style baby back ribs to slow-cooked kale (found on pages 225 and 111, respectively). We also included these peanut butter and banana sandwiches, named after Elvis because he was known to eat several a day. They are still served in many Memphis restaurants and when bacon is added, they are also known as "The Memphis." If you ever get the chance, please book a trip to Memphis so you can taste and see for yourself all of the great, culinary and historic places this city has to offer!

## Ingredients:

- ♦ 12 slices white bread *or* whole wheat bread, crusts removed
- ♦ 8 tablespoons creamy and smooth peanut butter (half a jar)
- ♦ 6 large ripe bananas, mashed in a bowl
- ♦ 12 slices any good bacon, fried until slightly crispy (but not burnt or overcooked)
- ♦ 2 tablespoons unsalted butter (see Chef's Note)
- ♦ 1 teaspoon cinnamon (for garnish)
- ♦ 1 ripe banana (for garnish)

# Elvis Presley's
# Peanut Butter, Banana,
# and Bacon Sandwich

◆─────────────────────────────◆
### YIELD: SERVES 6
◆─────────────────────────────◆

## Directions:

◆ Spread some mashed banana on one slice of bread. Spread the peanut butter on another slice of bread. Place a few slices of bacon on whichever side you choose. Fold the two pieces over to form a sandwich.

◆ In a sauté pan, over medium-high heat or the "fry" setting, melt 2 tablespoons of unsalted butter. Fry two sandwiches at a time for about a minute on each side, or until golden brown. Do not overcrowd your pan during this process.

   *Chef's Note: Additional butter may be needed for frying subsequent batches.*

◆ Remove the sandwiches from the pan and let them cool slightly. Slice on a diagonal and serve. Garnish each individual plate with a few slices of banana and a sprinkling of cinnamon.

   *Chef's Note: This recipe is very tasty, but it is definitely not "diet-friendly." However, it makes for a fun little meal for your child's birthday party. The bacon can be omitted if you so desire.*

# Main

This cookbook mentions, on several occasions, the importance of purchasing the freshest seafood possible when planning an unforgettable dinner. I have a wonderful seafood store within a few miles of my home and they only sell the freshest products. In fact, the owner gets up at 2:00 am every morning and drives to the world-famous, Fulton Fish Market in New York City. He brings back to his store an abundance of wonderful, never frozen, food from the deep blue sea. That is where I buy my fresh flounder and large shrimp for this dish. The seafood there smells so sweet and inviting! The flounder fillets are perfectly white and firm to the touch. The shrimp are plump and juicy. You cannot ask for anything more but you also should not ask for anything less. Your family and friends will love you for this meal because it is two popular seafood dinners combined into one!

## Ingredients:

- 16 (6 ounce) pieces fresh sole or flounder fillets (6 pounds total), 2 inches wide (cut by fish monger)
- 2 pounds medium shrimp, peeled completely, deveined, and cut once in half
- 1 tablespoon Emeril's Bayou Blast spice
- 2 shakes any good hot sauce (such as Tabasco or Frank's)
- 2 tablespoons olive oil
- 6 tablespoons unsalted butter, divided
- 8 large garlic cloves, minced very finely
- ¼ cup freshly squeezed lemon juice (about 2 lemons)
- ½ cup good white wine
- ¼ cup flat leaf parsley, chopped
- 5 heaping tablespoons Old Bay seasoning (1 teaspoon per fillet)
- 2 medium Vidalia onions, chopped finely
- 4 large celery stalks, chopped into ½ inch pieces
- 2 bunches green onions, sliced into ½ inch pieces
- ½ cup Italian breadcrumbs, seasoned
- Freshly cracked black pepper, to taste
- Fresh flat leaf parsley, chopped (for garnish)
- 2 lemons, sliced (for garnish)

# Flounder

# Stuffed with

# Shrimp Scampi

## Shrimp Scampi Directions:

♦ In a mixing bowl, combine the shrimp with 1 tablespoon of Emeril's Bayou Blast spice and 2 good shakes of your favorite hot sauce. Pour 2 tablespoons of olive oil into the bowl and mix the shrimp and spice with your hands.

♦ Heat a large sauté pan over medium-high heat. Add the shrimp with the spiced oil. Cook for 2 minutes, or until the shrimp begin to turn opaque. Add 3 of the tablespoons of unsalted butter and the minced garlic, lemon juice, white wine, and ¼ cup of chopped parsley. Add plenty of freshly cracked black pepper, to taste. Stir the mixture and cook until the wine reduces a bit, about 5 minutes. Remove the pan from the heat and allow it to cool slightly. Set aside.

## Stuffed Flounder Directions:

♦ Preheat oven to 350 degrees Fahrenheit. Lightly spray or grease a 9 x 11 inch Pyrex dish.

♦ On a cutting board, lay out each 6 ounce flounder fillet. Sprinkle each side of the fillets with ½ teaspoon of Old Bay Seasoning. Add some freshly cracked black pepper to both sides of each fillet as well. Set the fillets aside for a moment.

♦ In another sauté pan, over medium-high heat, melt the other 3 tablespoons of unsalted butter. Add the chopped onions, chopped celery, and sliced green onions. Stir the vegetables for 3 minutes, or until they are slightly wilted. Add the seasoned breadcrumbs and stir the mixture for an additional 1 minute.

♦ Stir into the vegetable sauté pan the reserved shrimp scampi mixture. With a spoon or spatula, make sure that all of the ingredients are well combined. Immediately remove the sauté pan from the heat and let it cool for 5 minutes.

♦ Place 2 tablespoons of the shrimp, vegetable, and breadcrumb mixture on the first ¼ portion of each flounder fillet. Then, in jellyroll-like fashion, roll up the flounder and stuffing into a dome-like shape. Secure each flounder fillet with 2 or 3 wooden toothpicks.

♦ Position the rolled-up flounder pieces in the baking dish side by side. Do not stack them on top of each other. Place the baking dish into the preheated oven and bake for 30 minutes, or until the fish has browned. Remove from the oven. Garnish the dish with chopped flat leaf parsley and some sliced lemons on the side. Serve immediately.

# Main

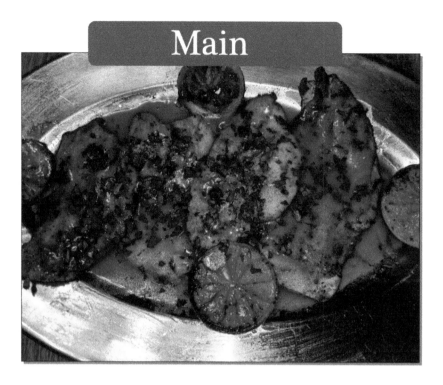

Who said that Chicken Francaise has to be dipped into flour, eggs, breadcrumbs, and then sautéed in hot oil on the stovetop? Not me! That may be the traditional way of creating this dish, but I have my very own style. This recipe is dedicated to my wife's wonderful cousin, Peggy Potenza, who lives in Florida. While visiting her and her husband, Ed, in their beautiful home in May 2019, I asked Peggy about her favorite food and she mentioned this particular chicken recipe. When I told her that I do my version of Chicken Francaise on the grill, her eyes lit up. With the enthusiasm of a little girl on Christmas Day, she asked me to make sure that this recipe was included in my cookbook. Well, here it is, Peggy! I hope you enjoy it half as much as I enjoyed writing it for you!

## Ingredients:

- 4 pounds chicken thighs, boneless and skinless *or* chicken breasts
- 2 tablespoons lemon pepper
- 2 tablespoons garlic powder
- 2 tablespoons Emeril's Original Essence seasoning
- 3 tablespoons olive oil (see Chef's Note)
- 2 tablespoons canola oil (for brushing grill) (see Chef's Note)
- 1 cup chicken stock (p. 89)
- ¼ cup freshly squeezed lemon juice (juice from about 2 large lemons)
- ½ cup any good white wine
- 3 tablespoons cornstarch
- ¼ cup water
- 3 tablespoons unsalted butter
- 3 additional lemons, halved and grilled (for garnish)
- Fresh flat leaf parsley, chopped finely (for garnish)

# Grilled
# Chicken Francaise

YIELD: SERVES ABOUT 8

## Grilled Chicken Francaise Directions:

♦ On a clean cutting board reserved for chicken use only (or plastic throwaway board), lightly pound the chicken pieces out using a metal or wooden mallet or the back of a cast iron pan. You want to flatten the fillets to about ½ inch thick. Do not pound the chicken too hard or tear the meat.

♦ In a mixing bowl, whisk together the lemon pepper, garlic powder, Emeril's Original Essence seasoning, and 3 tablespoons of olive oil. Place the skinless chicken thighs (or breasts), in the bowl and coat them in the mixture. Cover the mixing bowl with plastic wrap and let the chicken marinate for at least 3 hours (I marinate my chicken overnight).

♦ Brush an outdoor grill with a bit of canola oil and set to medium-high heat. Remove the chicken from the marinade and grill the first side of each piece for 3 minutes. Flip the chicken over and repeat the process. Make sure to get nice grill lines on each piece. Transfer the cooked chicken to a platter.

*Chef's Note: At this point, you can bring the grilled chicken inside. While you make the sauce, the chicken pieces can sit in a pre-heated oven set to 250 degrees Fahrenheit until you are ready to serve.*

*Chef's Note: I made this recipe for my family the other night and instead of going outside in the cold weather, I used a cast iron grill pan inside and cooked the chicken in batches. This worked just as well! If you use this method, I recommend cooking about 2 chicken pieces at a time and using an extra tablespoon of olive oil to sauté the chicken.*

## Chicken Francaise Sauce Directions:

♦ In a medium saucepan, combine the 1 cup of chicken stock with the ¼ cup of fresh lemon juice and ½ cup of white wine. Bring the mixture up to a simmer. Do not boil or burn the sauce. Stir 3 tablespoons of cornstarch with ¼ cup of cold water together to form a "slurry." Slowly add this slurry to the sauce until it begins to thicken. Whisk in 3 tablespoons of cold, unsalted butter.

♦ When ready to serve, remove the chicken platter from the oven. Spoon or ladle the reserved lemon sauce over the grilled chicken pieces. Garnish with grilled lemon halves and some finely chopped flat leaf parsley. Serve immediately.

# Main

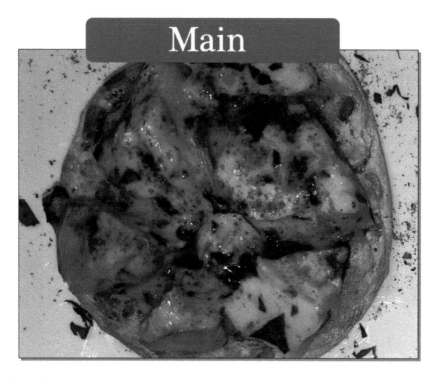

This is another classic seafood dish that I enjoyed so much during my younger days. I fondly remember my mom and dad coming to visit me while I lived at my boarding/military school near West Point Military Academy for two years. The brass had granted them permission to take me out to a local restaurant that happened to specialize in making Lobster Newburg. That restaurant served it over two English muffins and it was incredible! When I think of dishes like this one, I am greeted with full memories of those past encounters. I love honoring them by bringing "old time" recipes to the present for others to have their own experiences. In other words, you must try this Lobster Newburg! No, you do not have to buy live Maine lobsters and stress about plunging them into boiling water. The recipe can be made with a large can of lobster meat from your local fish monger or three, 10 ounce frozen and thawed lobster tails. There will be enough for all and you will be a local hero with your family and guests!

## Ingredients:

- 3 large (10 ounce) lobster tails, frozen and then thawed, halved lengthwise, and poached (recipe follows)
- 1 cup cold water
- 1 large Vidalia onion, chopped
- 3 large celery stalks, chopped
- Juice from 2 lemons
- 2 bay leaves
- 2 tablespoons Old Bay seasoning
- 1 cup white wine
- 3 egg yolks, beaten
- ½ cup heavy cream
- ½ cup unsalted butter (1 stick)
- ½ cup dry sherry or Madeira wine
- 1 heaping tablespoon Emeril's Bayou Blast spice
- 1 teaspoon fresh nutmeg, grated
- 1 package English muffins, sliced, toasted, and buttered
- Paprika (for garnish)
- Fresh, flat leaf parsley, chopped finely (for garnish)

# Lobster Newburg

## Directions:

♦ In a medium sized pot or Dutch oven, over medium heat, add the cold water, onion, celery, lemon juice, bay leaves, Old Bay seasoning, and white wine. Bring the mixture up to a simmer. Do not let it reach the boiling point. Add the halved lobster tails, meat-side down, and poach them for approximately 20 minutes. Do not overcook the lobster meat. Remove the lobster tails with a slotted spoon and let them cool for 10 minutes. Remove the meat from the shells and cut the tails into 1 inch chunks. Set aside.

♦ In a mixing bowl, whisk the egg yolks and heavy cream together until well blended.

♦ In a 4 quart Dutch oven, over medium-low heat, melt 1 stick of unsalted butter. Add the egg yolk mixture and dry sherry while whisking vigorously to prevent the eggs from scrambling. Cook until the mixture begins to thicken, about 5 or 6 minutes.

♦ Stir in the reserved lobster meat, 1 heaping tablespoon of Emeril's Bayou Blast spice, and the grated nutmeg. Continue to cook until everything is piping hot.

> *Chef's Note: If you are using canned lobster, gently heat it in the Newburg sauce on the stovetop over medium-low heat for about 10 minutes.*

♦ Place a toasted and buttered English muffin slice on each plate and spoon the lobster mixture over both slices. Garnish each serving with a sprinkling of paprika and some chopped fresh flat leaf parsley. Serve immediately.

# Main

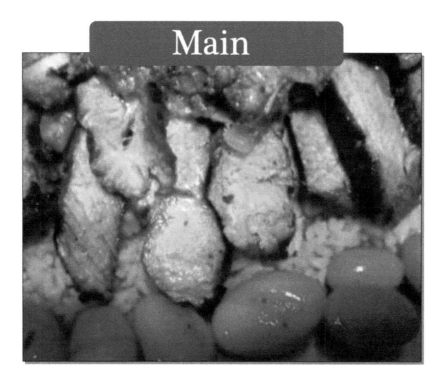

Many ladies may love petite fillet mignons and some men may like to dig into Brontosaurus-sized Porterhouse steaks but rib eye is, by far and away, my favorite steak on this good Earth. The extra "marbling" or fat content sends me to "Seventh Heaven!" I grilled a bunch of these rib eyes at a Kings Cooking Studios class called, "A View to a Grill." As you can see, the meat slices were served over yellow saffron rice and grilled baby tomatoes and the audience enjoyed my Mexican-styled grilled corn (page 117) on the side. They could not shove the food into their mouths fast enough!

## Rib Eye Steak Ingredients:

- ♦ 4 large Rib Eye steaks (with good "marbling" and vibrant color)
- ♦ 4 tablespoons dry steak spice rub
- ♦ ¼ cup canola oil

## Marinade Ingredients:

- ♦ 1 cup dark brown sugar, packed
- ♦ 6 garlic cloves, minced and diced
- ♦ 2 tablespoons fresh oregano leaves (1 package), chopped finely
- ♦ 2 tablespoons fresh thyme leaves (1 package), chopped finely
- ♦ 2 cups red wine (such as a Cabernet or Merlot)
- ♦ Freshly cracked black pepper

# Marinated and Grilled
# Rib Eye Steak

YIELD: SERVES 10-12

## Directions:

♦ Combine ¼ cup of canola oil with the dry steak spice rub in a bowl. Mix together well and rub the mixture all over the front and back of your rib eye steaks.

♦ In a large mixing bowl, add the dry marinade ingredients and then whisk in 2 cups of any good red wine. Mix well to combine. Put the rib eye steaks into a large oven roasting pan or several large marinating bags. Pour the marinade over the steaks to cover them. Marinate the steaks for at least 3 hours (overnight is even better).

♦ Preheat an outside grill to medium-high. Place the rib eye steaks on the grill at a 45 degree angle facing the 9 o'clock position. Cook for 3 minutes without turning. Then move your steak, without turning, to the 3 o'clock position. This will give you those beautiful grill lines that you see when ordering steak at a restaurant.

♦ Flip the steak and repeat this process two more times to ensure a nice medium-rare for your steak. Please do not overcook very good and expensive cuts of meat. For those of you who require your steak to be medium or medium-well, leave it on the grill for another minute or two but that is about it. Overcooked steak tastes like shoe leather.

*Chef's Note: Serve this steak dinner with my mushrooms in wine, garlic, and breadcrumbs (p. 119).*

# Main

Doesn't this picture of my dinner buffet just say it all? Are your mouths watering yet? Believe me, I have cooked a lot of Southern fried chicken in my day and this is, by far and away, my favorite recipe. Instead of deep frying the chicken thighs and legs in hot and dangerous cooking oil, they are marinated in buttermilk, seasoned with various spices, breaded lightly, and placed in a preheated oven to cook. This chicken comes out so tender and moist that the juices will run down your chin while you eat it!

## Ingredients:

- 5 pounds chicken thighs and legs, bone in and skin on
- 3 cups buttermilk, divided
- 4 tablespoons garlic, minced finely, divided
- 6 heaping tablespoons Emeril's Bayou Blast spice, divided
- 4 sprigs fresh thyme, leaves removed and chopped finely, divided
- 4 sprigs fresh rosemary, leaves removed and chopped finely, divided
- 4 cups broken-up Ritz crackers
- ¼ cup cold water (for egg wash)
- 4 eggs (for egg wash)
- 3 cups all-purpose flour
- Kosher salt and freshly cracked black pepper, to taste
- 2 tablespoons paprika (for garnish)
- Either: flat leaf parsley, chopped *or* Romaine lettuce leaves (for garnish)

# Marinated and Oven-Baked Fried Chicken

## Marinade Directions:

♦ Divide the chicken legs and thighs evenly and place them into two, 1 gallon zip-lock bags. Pour into each bag: 1½ cups of the buttermilk, 2 tablespoons of minced garlic, 2 tablespoons of Emeril's Bayou Blast spice, and the leaves from 2 sprigs each of thyme and rosemary. Seal the bags tightly and marinate the chicken for at least 12 hours (overnight is preferable). The next day, drain the chicken with a colander over the sink but do not wash the chicken off with cold water. Simply dab the excess liquid lightly with a paper towel. Set the marinated chicken aside.

## Oven-Baked Fried Chicken Directions:

♦ In a food processor fitted with a steel blade, chop 4 cups of broken Ritz crackers to make coarse breadcrumbs. Scatter the breadcrumbs onto a large plate or platter and set aside.

♦ Preheat oven to 400 degrees Fahrenheit.

♦ In a bowl, add the water and eggs, whisking together to form an egg wash. In another bowl, blend the all-purpose flour with 2 tablespoons of Emeril's Bayou Blast spice. Stir well to combine and set aside.

♦ Using your clean hands or kitchen tongs, dredge each piece of chicken thigh (or leg), first in the flour, then the egg wash, and finally in the breadcrumbs (covering all sides). Repeat this process until all of the chicken has been coated.

♦ Place the chicken pieces onto a non-stick sprayed, aluminum foil-covered cookie sheet or roasting pan. If possible, chill the chicken in the refrigerator for 45 minutes. This will prevent the coating from falling off of the chicken. Do not stack the chicken pieces on top of one another. They should all lie flat at the bottom of the pan or on the cookie sheet.

♦ Remove the pieces from the refrigerator and let them return to room temperature, about 20 minutes. Return the chicken pieces to the preheated oven and cook them for 30 minutes. Remove the chicken pieces from the oven and turn them over once. Return them to the oven for an additional 30 minutes to finish cooking.

♦ Remove the chicken from the oven and place the thighs and legs onto a pretty, metal serving platter. Re-season with a pinch or two of Kosher salt and freshly cracked black pepper, to taste. Sprinkle the chicken with 2 tablespoons of paprika and some chopped, flat leaf parsley *or* place them over Romaine lettuce leaves, as pictured.

# Main

Here is a little touch of South American cuisine for the cookbook. I have not yet been to that part of the world, but I would love to visit Brazil and Argentina someday. I hear that the sights, sounds, and food they offer are simply incredible! Many years ago, I was asked to prepare a traditional, stuffed beef dish for a dinner party with a distinct Spanish "theme" to it. During our pre-interview with the clients, they told me about this delicious dish from their native Argentina and I knew I had to create my own. My local butcher helped make this easy-to-prepare meal even simpler and more importantly, the guests were very pleased with the beautiful dish. I love learning the rich stories and fun facts behind dishes and while I was diligently researching matambre, I learned that the Spanish "matar," means "to kill" and "hambre" means "hunger" so together, matambre means "hunger killer!" It can be cooked in the oven or on an outdoor grill but either way, I know you and your hungry "gauchos" will love this delicious and different main course!

## Ingredients:

- ◆ 1 (3 pound) flank steak, "butterflied" by butcher
- ◆ ¼ cup good olive oil
- ◆ ¼ cup cilantro, chopped coarsely
- ◆ ¼ cup flat leaf parsley, chopped coarsely
- ◆ 6 large garlic cloves, minced finely
- ◆ 2 teaspoons Kosher salt
- ◆ 1 teaspoon red pepper flakes
- ◆ 3 hardboiled eggs, quartered (see recipe for deviled eggs on p. 39)
- ◆ 1 large red pepper, seeds removed, sliced lengthwise, and then into thin, long strips
- ◆ 1 large green pepper, seeds removed, sliced lengthwise, and then into thin, long strips
- ◆ ¼ cup green olives, pitted and halved
- ◆ ¼ cup black olives, pitted and halved
- ◆ 2 heaping tablespoons Emeril's Original Essence
- ◆ Plenty of freshly cracked black pepper

# Matambre

# (Argentinian Stuffed Flank Steak)

YIELD: SERVES ABOUT 6-8

## Directions:

♦ Preheat your oven to 425 degrees Fahrenheit.

♦ As mentioned in the ingredient section, have your butcher "butterfly" a 3 pound flank steak for you. Once sliced open, it will resemble a large, open book. If you prefer the meat a bit thinner and flatter, you can pound it out on a cutting board when you get home using a metal mallet or the back of a cast iron pan.

♦ In a large mixing bowl, combine the olive oil, chopped cilantro, chopped parsley, minced garlic, 2 teaspoons of Kosher salt, red pepper flakes, and plenty of freshly cracked black pepper. Whisk together well and set the bowl aside for a few moments. What you have just made is a traditional Spanish chimichurri.

♦ Spread out the flank steak on a large cutting board. Using a spoon or rubber spatula, spread the chimichurri over the steak's entire surface. Arrange the quartered eggs in 3 rows across the middle of the flank steak. Similarly position the long, thin slices of the red and green peppers in rows around and between the egg layers. Sprinkle on the sliced olives.

♦ Carefully, roll up the flank steak from left to right like you are making a jelly roll. Tuck the rolled seams in tightly with your hands to hold in the stuffing. Once completely rolled, using 5 or 6 pieces of butcher's twine, tie up the stuffed flank steak at 1½ inch increments.

♦ Season the outside of the meat with 2 heaping tablespoons of Emeril's Original Essence and some more freshly cracked black pepper, to taste. Place the rolled-up steak seam-side down in a large roasting pan. Bake for 15 minutes and then immediately reduce the temperature to 350 degrees Fahrenheit, roasting the steak for 50 additional minutes. You want the meat thermometer to register 120 degrees Fahrenheit for medium-rare.

♦ Remove the meat from the oven and let it rest for 15 minutes before carving into 1½ inch thick slices. Serve over some brown Spanish rice with a chosen vegetable on the side.

*Chef's Note: As mentioned, the matambre can also be grilled outdoors over medium-high heat. Grill for 5-6 minutes per side for a total grilling time of 20 minutes. Then place it in a roasting pan and finish cooking it in an oven at 375 degrees Fahrenheit for an additional 20 minutes.*

# Main

A few years back, my wife and I had the privilege of traveling to Memphis, Tennessee and I really had the time of my life. We did the typical tourist thing and even said a heartfelt prayer over Elvis Presley's grave at Graceland! One of the main reasons we went to Memphis was to experience and savor their wonderful barbecued chicken, baby back ribs (page 225), and melt-in-your-mouth brisket. We were not disappointed in any way! Here is my take on their delicious and easy to make barbecue sauce. I know that you and your guests will truly enjoy it!

## Ingredients:

- 2 medium Vidalia onions, diced finely
- 6 large garlic cloves, crushed and minced
- 4 tablespoons unsalted butter
- 2 cups any good tomato sauce
- ½ cup dark molasses (I use Steen's)
- ¼ cup apple cider vinegar
- ¼ cup rice wine vinegar
- 4 good shakes Worcestershire sauce (about 4 tablespoons)
- 2 cups dark brown sugar, packed
- 2 tablespoons dry mustard (I use Colman's)
- A few good shakes any hot sauce (such as Tabasco or Frank's)
- A pinch or two of Kosher salt and freshly cracked black pepper, to taste

CHEF CARDIE'S

# Memphis-Style
# Barbecue Sauce

YIELD: 2 CUPS OR MORE

## Directions:

♦ In a large saucepan, over medium heat, melt 4 tablespoons of butter. Add and cook the diced onions until softened or translucent, about 8 minutes.

♦ Add the garlic and cook for another 2 minutes or so, being careful to stir often to prevent the garlic from burning. Add the remaining listed ingredients and let mixture reach a full boil.

♦ Reduce the heat to a low simmer and cook, uncovered, for approximately 1 hour, or until the mixture thickens slightly. This sauce will keep in an airtight jar, refrigerated, for two months.

# Main

I have prepared this recipe countless times, both as a chef working in the deep South and with my private catering company, "Cardie Cooks." In June 2019, we served my Jambalaya to over 80 hungry guests at a beautiful and successful benefit dinner that raised funds for the Tennessee Valley Coalition for the Homeless. It was an incredibly special evening in every way possible and the crowd just loved this main course and staple of New Orleans cuisine. You can find it on almost any New Orleans restaurant menu or you can make it yourself with the help of this recipe. It is a real crowd pleaser and your guests will truly enjoy the fruits of your labor. Do not forget to include some crusty French bread on the side or better yet, make the cheesy garlic bread on page 129!

## Ingredients:

- 3 pounds andouille sausage, sliced into ¼ inch thick, nickel-size rounds
- 4 pounds chicken thighs, boneless and skinless, cut into 2 inch chunks
- 4 tablespoons olive oil, divided (see Chef's Note)
- 5 tablespoons unsalted butter, divided (see Chef's Note)
- 3 tablespoons Emeril's Bayou Blast spice, divided
- 2 large Vidalia onions, chopped
- 2 green bell peppers, chopped
- 6 celery stalks, chopped
- 2 large leeks, cleaned of their sand, chopped (use mostly the white parts)
- 3 tablespoons garlic cloves (from 1 whole head), chopped
- 2 tablespoons any hot sauce (such as Tabasco or Frank's)
- 3 cups long grain rice
- 6 cups chicken stock (p. 89)
- 1 (14½ ounce) can diced tomatoes, with juice
- 1 (small) can tomato paste
- Kosher salt and freshly cracked black pepper, to taste
- Green onions, chopped (for garnish)
- Flat leaf parsley, chopped (for garnish)

CHEF CARDIE'S
# New Orleans Chicken, Vegetable, and Andouille Jambalaya

YIELD: SERVES 8-10

## Directions:

♦ In a large, heavy-bottomed Dutch oven, over medium-high heat, add 2 tablespoons of olive oil and 3 tablespoons of unsalted butter. Add the chicken and sausage. Season lightly with salt, pepper, and 2 tablespoons of Emeril's Bayou Blast spice. Brown the meat on all sides, working in small batches if necessary. Set the browned chicken and cooked sausage on a platter.

   *Chef's Note: Using your discretion, you may add butter or olive oil to finish browning the chicken and sausage as needed.*

♦ Add the remaining 2 tablespoons of olive oil and 2 tablespoons of unsalted butter to the Dutch oven. Add the onions, bell peppers, celery, and leeks, cooking until the vegetables soften, about 12 minutes. Add the chopped garlic, 1 more tablespoon of Emeril's Bayou Blast spice, hot sauce, and some Kosher salt and freshly cracked black pepper, to taste.

♦ Add 3 cups of long grain rice. Stir the rice in the vegetable mixture for 3 minutes.

♦ Return the cooked chicken and sausage to the pot. Pour in the chicken broth and add the tomatoes and tomato paste. Stir well to combine. Bring the mixture to a full boil, cover the pot with a tight lid, and reduce the heat to medium-low. Cook until the rice has absorbed most of the liquid, about 40 minutes.

♦ Serve the jambalaya in bowls garnished with chopped flat leaf parsley and green onions.

# Main

In my most humble opinion, the best city in the world for eating is, "The Big Easy," better known as New Orleans, Louisiana. Culinary delights from this fabulous and historic city are limitless. The dishes are defined by the influx of many different cultures from around the world and there are tastes that you will not find anywhere else. I went to culinary school there in the late 1970's and even then, New Orleans was bursting with new restaurants and exciting recipes. The best Crab Imperial I have ever tasted was at Commander's Palace, a restaurant in the Garden District that is still owned by the world-famous Brennan family. Many years ago, Commander's Palace hired a relatively unknown chef from Fall River, Massachusetts and gave him his start in the business. His name was Emeril Lagasse. The rest is history!

## Ingredients:

- ♦ 2 pounds jumbo lump fresh crabmeat (I use 2 cans of Phillips brand)
- ♦ 4 garlic cloves, minced finely
- ♦ ½ medium red onion, minced finely
- ♦ 2 medium green bell peppers (about ½ cup), chopped finely
- ♦ 2 egg yolks, beaten lightly
- ♦ 2 heaping tablespoons Old Bay seasoning
- ♦ 2 teaspoons dry mustard powder (I use Colman's)
- ♦ 1 can artichoke hearts, drained and then chopped coarsely
- ♦ ¾ cup mayonnaise (I use Hellman's)
- ♦ ½ cup fresh parmesan cheese, grated
- ♦ ½ cup Italian breadcrumbs, seasoned
- ♦ Kosher salt and plenty of freshly cracked black pepper, to taste
- ♦ 4 green onion stalks (white and light green parts only), sliced finely (for garnish)

# New Orleans
# Crabmeat Imperial

YIELD: 6 LARGE SERVINGS

OR 8 SMALL SERVINGS

## Directions:

♦ Preheat oven to 375 degrees Fahrenheit.

♦ In a large mixing bowl, combine the crabmeat, minced garlic, red onion, green bell peppers, egg yolks, Old Bay seasoning, mustard powder, artichoke hearts, and ¾ cup of mayonnaise. Fold in all ingredients until well blended (see Chef's Note). Season with freshly cracked black pepper, to taste.

> *Chef's Note: You must not break up your expensive, jumbo lump crabmeat. The culinary term, "folding," refers to the technique of blending one ingredient into another. In a slow, circular fashion and using a rubber spatula, gently shift the ingredients from the bottom of the mixing bowl to the top until all ingredients have been thoroughly blended (or folded), together.*

♦ Spoon the crabmeat mixture into greased, 8 ounce ramekins or culinary seashells (see Chef's Note). Then sprinkle about 1½ tablespoons of seasoned breadcrumbs and 1½ tablespoons of parmesan cheese on top of each serving. Place the individual crabmeats onto a cookie sheet that has been lined with aluminum foil.

> *Chef's Note: Personally and professionally, I find that large, white scallop shell dishes work beautifully with this recipe. You can purchase these online or at certain gourmet stores in the area. Just make sure that the purchased shells can be used in a hot oven or under the broiler.*

♦ Place them in the oven and bake until heated through and bubbly on top, about 25 minutes.

♦ Carefully remove the sheet from the oven and switch your oven to the broiler setting. Once at temperature, return the shells to the oven to broil for 2 minutes, or until the mixture has turned golden brown. Do not burn them! Garnish each shell with a sprinkling of sliced green onions and serve immediately.

# Main

I absolutely love tasting and sampling good food from cultures and cities all over the world, especially if they have a rich and interesting history. Red beans and rice is one such dish. It has been a Creole staple of New Orleans cooking since the late 1700's, at least. In New Orleans, the beans were traditionally soaked in a pot on a Sunday and cooked on the Monday. "Why?" you might ask? Because, many years ago, Monday was when ladies did their heavy loads of laundry. They would toil for hours on end doing their washing but they also had to prepare a complete dinner for their families. So, they threw red beans, sausage, and water into a large pot and cooked it for hours without worrying about it one bit. Of course, that washing custom does not really exist anymore, but slow-cooking rice and beans sure does! This dish was also legendary musician, Louis Armstrong's, favorite meal and he often celebrated the joy of eating it while playing his trumpet to the song, "When the Saints Go Marching In!" You will be marching down your very own "Bourbon Street" soon after your first bite of this classic recipe!

## Ingredients:

- 1 pound red kidney beans
- 2 pounds andouille sausage (about 5 links), cut into 1 inch slices
- 1 large and meaty ham hock bone (purchased from butcher)
- 4 cups long grain rice (cooked according to box instructions)
- 10 cups rich chicken stock (p. 89) (plus stock for cooking rice and thinning sauce)
- 2 tablespoons unsalted butter
- 2 tablespoons olive oil
- 2 large onions, chopped finely
- 2 green peppers, chopped finely
- 4 celery stalks, chopped finely
- 2 tablespoons Emeril's Bayou Blast spice
- A few shakes any hot sauce (such as Tabasco or Frank's)
- 4 large thyme sprigs
- 2 bay leaves
- 5 large garlic cloves, chopped finely
- Freshly cracked black pepper
- Green onions, chopped or sliced (for garnish)

# New Orleans
# Red Beans and Rice

YIELD: SERVES 8

## Directions:

♦ The day before you make this dish, place 1 pound of red beans into a large colander and rinse them completely under cold, running water. Discard, or "sort," any broken or discolored beans. Fill a stock pot (that has a tight lid), with cold water. Add the rinsed and sorted beans to the pot to soak, covered, overnight. The next day, before you begin to cook, drain the beans with the colander and set them aside.

*Chef's Note: Following the directions on your bag or box of rice, start cooking the long grain rice before you begin making the rest of the dish. The rule of thumb when preparing white rice is to use 2 cups of liquid for every 1 cup of rice. For extra flavor, I use white wine or chicken stock instead of water.*

♦ In a 4 quart stockpot or Dutch oven, over medium-high heat, melt 2 tablespoons of unsalted butter and combine it with 2 tablespoons of olive oil. Sauté the onions, bell peppers, celery, and Emeril's Bayou Blast spice. Add in a few dashes of hot sauce and the thyme sprigs. Cook the entire mixture for 8-10 minutes, stirring constantly.

♦ Add the 2 bay leaves and andouille sausage. Sauté for an additional 6 minutes, stirring continuously until the sausage browns a bit. Season with plenty of cracked black pepper.

♦ Add the reserved red beans, large ham hock, and chopped garlic. Pour 10 cups of rich chicken stock into the pot. Bring up to a full boil and then immediately reduce the heat to medium. Simmer uncovered, stirring often, for about 3 hours. If the mixture becomes too thick or "reduced," add cold water or some more chicken stock to the simmering pot.

♦ Once ready, remove the ham hock bone, bay leaves, and thyme sprigs. Ladle the red beans, sausage, and some of the cooked stock over the cooked rice that you have placed in a pretty serving bowl. Garnish with chopped or sliced green onions. Serve immediately.

*Chef's Note: Scrape or cut any remaining meat off the ham hock bone with a sharp kitchen knife. Cut into chunks and add the meat right into the rice and bean mixture. Delicious!*

# Main

I just love the rich history of jolly ol' England and I love dining on their traditional fish and chips. But fresh cooked cod and slow-roasted tomato confit? My, oh my, give it a try! I was first inspired to make this dish by a New Jersey company that prepares traditional, deep-fried fish and chips for various charitable events. The recipe became a menu staple for my catering company, "Cardie Cooks." I was delighted when hungry guests inhaled this dish and women in fancy formal dresses raved about the food with their mouths fully open! I think your kids will love this main entrée as well! It sure beats those frozen fish stick dinners!

## Tomato Confit Ingredients:

- 25 on-the-vine ripe plum tomatoes
- 2 tablespoons extra virgin olive oil
- 3 tablespoons granulated sugar
- 8 large garlic cloves (about 2 full heads of garlic), sliced in half
- 1 package fresh thyme sprigs
- 12 large basil leaves, torn in half (by hand)
- Freshly cracked black pepper, to taste

## Cod Ingredients:

- 10 (6 ounce) fresh cod fillets
- 3 cups Saltine crackers
- 2 cups fresh parmesan cheese, grated
- 2 cups all-purpose flour
- 2 tablespoons Old Bay seasoning
- 2 tablespoons garlic powder
- 2 tablespoons dry oregano
- 2 eggs, beaten
- ¼ cup cold water
- 2 large lemons, sliced (for garnish)
- Freshly cracked black pepper, to taste

# Oven-Baked,
# Parmesan-Crusted
# Cod with Tomato Confit

## Tomato Confit Directions:

◆ Preheat oven to 200 degrees Fahrenheit.

◆ Line a large baking sheet with aluminum foil and spray with non-stick cooking spray.

◆ Cut each plum tomato in half lengthwise. With your fingers or a small spoon, remove and discard any seeds. Toss the tomatoes in a mixing bowl along with the 2 tablespoons of olive oil, 3 tablespoons of granulated sugar, halved garlic cloves, and plenty of freshly cracked black pepper, to taste. Mix well so the tomato halves are coated on all sides.

◆ On the aluminum covered cookie sheet, make a "bed" using thyme sprigs and basil leaves. Lay each tomato half over the fresh herbs, cut-side down.

◆ Place the cookie sheet on the center rack of your oven for 3 hours. After 90 minutes, remove the cookie sheet from the oven, flip over the tomatoes, and return them to the oven to bake for the final 90 minutes.

◆ The tomatoes are done cooking when they shrivel up slightly but still retain their shape. Allow them to cool.

## Cod Directions:

◆ Preheat oven to 375 degrees Fahrenheit. Line a large cookie sheet with aluminum foil.

◆ Process the Saltine crackers in a food processor until smooth cracker crumbs have been achieved. Add the parmesan cheese to the crumb mixture and mix well. Set aside in a bowl.

◆ Combine the all-purpose flour, Old Bay seasoning, garlic powder, dried oregano, and freshly cracked black pepper in a separate bowl. Mix well with a spoon or spatula

◆ In another separate bowl, whisk the 2 eggs with ¼ cup of cold water to form an egg wash.

◆ Dip and coat each cod fillet first into the flour mixture, then the egg mixture, and finally the cracker mixture. Place each breaded fillet onto a wire rack over the cookie sheet. Make sure the fillets are lying flat on the wire rack and are not overlapping or touching one another.

◆ Bake the cod fillets, without turning, for 15 minutes, or until the fish sets up or is slightly firm to the touch. Do not overcook the fish or it will fall apart when you try to remove it.

◆ Place the cooked fillets onto a pretty serving platter. Place the reserved tomato confit on top of the fish. Garnish with fresh lemon slices on the side and serve immediately.

# Main

Many people have asked me what my all-time favorite restaurant is for dining. I actually have a pretty long list of places. It depends on the food group. However, when it comes to traditional, delicious, and freshly prepared seafood, one place immediately comes to mind. Don Pepe's is an authentic, Portuguese restaurant that has several locations across northern New Jersey and I have been dining at them for over 45 years. My wife, Lynne, and I love their garlic shrimp and saffron rice dish. The nice thing is that when she orders it, I know that I will be able to enjoy the remaining half the next day in front of a football game on the big-screen because the portions are so large! If you cannot enjoy Don Pepe's in person, try this easy-to-prepare and authentic Portuguese shrimp dish. It will have your family and friends doing the lively Fandango dance (enjoyed in Spain and Portugal), all around the house!

## Ingredients:

- 3 pounds extra-large fresh shrimp from local fish market (not frozen), shells removed (except around the tail), and shrimp cleaned and deveined
- Cloves from 2 large garlic heads, minced finely
- ½ cup unsalted butter (1 stick)
- 1 cup Vidalia onions (about 3 medium or 2 large onions), chopped finely
- 1½ cups long grain rice
- 3 cups rich chicken stock (p. 89)
- 3 pinches saffron threads
- Juice from 2 limes
- Juice from 1 lemon
- ¼ cup good olive oil
- A few good shakes any hot sauce (such as Tabasco or Frank's)
- 2 tablespoons Old Bay seasoning
- Plenty of freshly cracked black pepper, to taste
- Curly parsley, stems removed and chopped finely (for rice garnish)
- Optional: crusty Portuguese bread

# Oven-Baked, Portuguese Citrus and Garlic Shrimp over Saffron Rice

## Saffron Rice Directions:

♦ In a 4 quart Dutch oven or large sauté pan, over medium-high heat, add the ½ cup of unsalted butter. Stir in the 1 cup of chopped onions until they have softened and turned translucent, about 6 minutes. Reduce the heat to medium-low and continue cooking, stirring until the onions turn very tender and dark brown, about 15 to 20 minutes.

♦ Add the long grain rice and stir to blend well with the onions. Slowly pour in the chicken stock and 3 pinches of saffron threads. Keep the stovetop on medium-low heat and cover the pan or pot with a lid. Simmer until the liquid absorbs about 30 minutes. Fluff the rice with a fork, mix in the finely chopped curly parsley, and set the rice aside while you cook your garlic shrimp.

*Chef's Note: Once cooked, spoon the rice into a Pyrex dish or baking pan. Cover tightly with aluminum foil to keep warm until you have finished the shrimp.*

## Garlic Shrimp Directions:

♦ Preheat oven to 425 degrees Fahrenheit.

♦ Place the large shrimp into a resealable, 1 gallon bag. Pour in the juice from 2 limes, juice from 1 lemon, and ¼ cup of good olive oil. Add a few good shakes of your favorite hot sauce, the finely minced garlic, 2 heaping tablespoons of Old Bay seasoning, and plenty of freshly cracked black pepper as well. Shake the bag vigorously to spread the marinade around the shrimp. Refrigerate the bag of shrimp for no more than 1 hour.

*Chef's Note: If you marinate your shrimp in citrus juices for too long they will begin to cook themselves and toughen. A well-known citrus cooked seafood dish is ceviche.*

♦ Transfer the marinated shrimp to a 9 x 13 inch Pyrex dish, positioning the shrimp in a flat, single layer. Reserve the liquid. Place the shrimp in the oven and cook for 15 minutes. There is no need to turn them. Once done, using a large serving spoon, spread the cooked garlic shrimp and garlic sauce over the bed of saffron rice. Serve immediately with crusty and delicious Portuguese bread on the side!

This is an exotic, delicious, and delectable rice dish that can be served year-round as either a side course or as a complete dinner. Of course, making this recipe around Halloween gives it a dramatic and wonderful effect! Please, do not be scared of making risotto. It is really, no big deal and there are no "tricks" involved! In fact, you will stir and move your hips so much while making it that you will be able to skip a day at the gym! I cooked this risotto in front of 30 very happy guests at a Kings Cooking Studios demo called, "The Pumpkin Patch." It was a real "thrill" for everyone in attendance and I can assure you that your little "goblins" at home will love you for making this special treat!

## Ingredients:

- 6 cups rich chicken *or* vegetable stock (pp. 89 and 99, respectively)
- 6 links good Italian sausage (sweet, hot, or a combination), sliced into 1 inch pieces
- 5 tablespoons olive oil, divided
- 1½ cups wild mushrooms (e.g. button, cremini, or portobello), chopped coarsely
- 1½ medium Vidalia onions, chopped coarsely
- 6 garlic cloves, peeled and chopped finely
- 1 cup bell peppers (I use 1 red and 1 green bell pepper), chopped finely
- 3 tablespoons unsalted butter
- 3 cups Arborio (or short grain) rice
- 1½ cups dry white wine
- 1½ tablespoons dried thyme *or* fresh thyme leaves, chopped finely
- 1½ tablespoons dried rosemary *or* fresh rosemary leaves, chopped finely
- 3 large bay leaves
- ½ cup half-and-half
- ¼ cup pure maple syrup (not the commercial one used on pancakes)
- A few good shakes any hot sauce (such as Tabasco or Frank's)
- 3 cups canned pumpkin puree
- 1 full teaspoon cinnamon, ground
- ½ teaspoon nutmeg, grated
- A pinch of Kosher salt and plenty of freshly cracked black pepper, to taste
- ½ cup fresh Parmesan Reggiano cheese, grated (for topping)
- Fresh flat leaf parsley, chopped (for garnish)

# Pumpkin Risotto
# with Parmesan, Wild
# Mushrooms, and Sausage

◆————————————◆

YIELD: SERVES 8-10

◆————————————◆

## Directions:

♦ Pour the chicken or vegetable stock into a 3 quart Dutch oven. Bring to a full boil. Then reduce the heat to a low simmer and hold it aside. It is crucial that the stock is hot and remains hot while making this recipe.

♦ In another Dutch oven or a large sauté pan, over medium heat, add 3 tablespoons of olive oil and brown the sliced sausage pieces, about 6-8 minutes. Drain the sausages on a sheet pan lined with paper towels and set them aside in a bowl. Drain most of the sausage fat from your Dutch oven. Continuing over medium heat, add 2 more tablespoons of olive oil and sauté the chopped mushrooms, onions, garlic, and bell peppers for another 6-8 minutes. Combine the cooked vegetables mixture with the reserved sausage in the bowl. Set aside.

♦ In the same Dutch oven, over medium heat, add the 3 tablespoons of unsalted butter and 3 cups of Arborio rice. Gently sauté until the rice begins to brown, about 6-7 minutes. You will start smelling the "nutty" flavor emanating from the rice. Do not let the rice burn or stick.

♦ Add the 1½ cups of dry white wine, finely chopped thyme and rosemary, and 3 bay leaves. Stir vigorously until the rice has absorbed most of the wine, about 6 minutes. Scrape the sides and bottom of the pot to prevent sticking. When the wine has almost evaporated, using a small ladle, add ¼ cup at a time of the hot chicken or vegetable stock. Stir constantly until the stock has mostly been absorbed into the rice. You will need to repeat this process about 5 or 6 times, or for about 25-30 minutes total.

♦ After these 25-30 minutes, add the reserved sausage and mushroom mixture to the rice pot. Stir and mix to combine well. At this point, taste the rice. It is only finished when the rice is tender but not overly soggy or watery. It should be cooked al dente (or "to the tooth").

*Chef's Note: Add lesser amounts of hot liquid as the risotto nears completion.*

♦ Remove the Dutch oven from the heat and gently stir in the half-and-half, pure maple syrup, a few shakes of your favorite hot sauce, the pumpkin puree, 1 teaspoon of cinnamon, some grated nutmeg, and a pinch of Kosher salt with plenty of freshly cracked black pepper, to taste. Return the pot to medium-low heat and simmer the mixture for another 5 minutes, or until it is creamy and hot. During this time, locate and discard the 3 bay leaves.

*Chef's Note: Once the risotto is cooked through, you can place a lid over it and let it sit until you are ready to serve. Then, gently reheat the risotto over medium -low heat for about 15 minutes, stirring constantly so that it will not burn or stick to the bottom of the pot.*

♦ Once ready to plate, top the pot of warm risotto with ½ cup of freshly grated Parmesan Reggiano cheese. Garnish with freshly chopped flat parsley. Serve immediately.

*Chef's Note: The risotto can be served and brought to the table in the Dutch oven in which you cooked it.*

# Main

I came up with this delicious dish while I was a chef working in the deep South. Our Southern friends just love their chicken and they most certainly love a garlicky broth that they can use as a dip for warm biscuits (page 137). This is a recipe that you can make ahead of time and simply warm up in the oven when your guests or family arrive for dinner. I am a real garlic lover myself and I can promise you that you will need a few breath mints after you finish this incredible chicken!

## Ingredients:

♦ 8 whole chicken legs (with thighs attached) *or* 8 chicken thighs (bone in) and 8 chicken legs

♦ 3 tablespoons olive oil (additional oil may be needed for second chicken batch)

♦ 2 heaping tablespoons Emeril's Bayou Blast spice

♦ 40 garlic cloves (about 6 large garlic heads), peeled and garlic left whole

♦ 2 tablespoons fresh rosemary (1 full package), chopped finely (plus uncut sprigs for garnish)

♦ 2 tablespoons fresh thyme leaves (1 full package), chopped finely (plus uncut sprigs for garnish)

♦ Juice and zest from 2 lemons (both lemons for each)

♦ 3 tablespoons all-purpose flour

♦ ½ cup dry white wine

♦ 2 cups rich chicken stock (p. 89)

♦ 3 tablespoons unsalted butter, cold

♦ Kosher salt and freshly cracked black pepper, to taste

♦ Fresh flat leaf parsley, chopped (for garnish)

♦ Optional: crusty French bread or Southern biscuits (p. 137)

# Roasted and Herbed Chicken Legs and Thighs with 40 Cloves of Garlic

YIELD: SERVES 8-10

## Directions:

♦ Preheat oven to 350 degrees Fahrenheit.

♦ Season the chicken pieces with 2 heaping tablespoons of Emeril's Bayou Blast spice. In a large Dutch oven or pot, over medium-high heat, heat the olive oil, but not to the smoking point. Cook the chicken pieces in batches, turning the chicken often to caramelize, or brown, the outside. Transfer the pieces to a platter and set aside.

♦ In the same pot, over medium heat, add the garlic cloves and cook, stirring for about 3 minutes. Do not burn the garlic. Remove the pot from the heat and add the rosemary, thyme, lemon zest, and lemon juice. Add a pinch of Kosher salt and freshly cracked black pepper, to taste. Cover the pot with a tight lid and roast in the oven for 30 minutes without peeking.

♦ After the first 30 minutes of cooking, remove the lid of the pot. Baste the chicken pieces with their juices and continue roasting for an additional 30 minutes. Transfer the cooked chicken to a warm platter.

♦ Set the pot over medium-high heat. Add and slightly mash the garlic cloves with the back of a wooden spoon. Sprinkle in 3 tablespoons of all-purpose flour and stir to mix. Pour in the white wine and chicken broth and stir until the sauce thickens, about 6 minutes. Vigorously whisk in 3 tablespoons of cold, unsalted butter.

♦ Pour the garlic sauce over the top of the reserved chicken. Garnish with freshly chopped flat leaf parsley and some thyme and rosemary sprigs. Serve with crusty French bread or hot Southern biscuits (p. 137), on the side for dipping.

# Main

I did a sold-out crepe cooking class at the prestigious Adult School in Montclair, New Jersey a few years ago and we had more fun making sweet and savory crepes than a barrel of monkeys! So many wonderful people have asked me for these recipes, so I am now sharing them with all of you. It may take some practice before you get the knack of making the perfect crepe, but then again, who said a crepe had to be perfect in the first place? The essential thing is to buy an inexpensive, yet durable crepe pan. You will use it time and again to make these delicious French pancakes!

## Ingredients:

♦ 1 cup all-purpose flour *or* flour of choice (such as whole wheat). **Do not use** self-rising flour. Sift the flour through a wire mesh to remove any impurities.

♦ 2 eggs

♦ ½ cup whole milk

♦ ½ cup water

♦ 2 tablespoons unsalted butter, melted (plus 1 tablespoon for pan)

♦ A pinch of Kosher salt

♦ <u>Savory Crepes:</u> To "kick up" your crepes to "notches unknown," you can add 2 tablespoons of fresh (not dried), finely chopped herbs of your choice (e.g. fresh basil, rosemary, oregano, parsley, or dill), or even chopped sun-dried tomatoes, to your batter. Have fun experimenting because you really cannot go wrong!

♦ <u>Sweet Crepes:</u> To make sweet crepes follow the listed directions but **do not** add any fresh herbs to your batter. Instead, add 1 tablespoon of vanilla extract, ¼ cup of granulated sugar, and 2 good tablespoons of your favorite sweet liqueur (I use Amaretto, Chambord, or Grand Marnier).

# Savory and Sweet
# French Crepes

YIELD: ABOUT 12 CREPES

## Directions:

♦ Using an electric blender or handheld whisk, mix together the flour and eggs. Slowly whisk in the milk, water, melted butter, and a pinch of salt. Continue to whisk until you have a smooth batter which slightly covers the back of a wooden spoon. Cover the bowl with plastic wrap and place it in the refrigerator to chill for at least 2 hours.

♦ In a 9 inch non-stick skillet or crepe pan, over medium-high heat, melt 1 tablespoon of butter or spray the pan lightly with non-stick butter spray (I find the latter easier).

♦ Using a small ladle or measuring cup, pour about 6 ounces of batter into the pan. Remove the pan from the heat and tilt and swirl it so that the batter completely covers the bottom of the pan thinly and evenly. Try not to leave any large holes. After the first few crepes, you will know exactly how much batter your pan will hold.

♦ Cook the crepe until the edges turn brown, about 1 minute and 30 seconds. Carefully flip the crepe using a spatula or even your fingers! Cook the crepe on the second side for only 30 more seconds. Remove the pan from the heat and invert the crepe onto a warm plate. Stack each crepe between a small layer of wax or parchment paper.

*Chef's Note: Crepes may be sealed and kept in freezable storage bags for up to 2 months. You can also add sweet or savory fillings to your crepes. I have made Peking duck crepes, spinach and cheese crepes, and fruit-filled lemon curd crepes. Let your imagination run wild as you come up with crepe "fillings" you can truly call your own. The sky is the limit!*

# Main

During my last summer of culinary school (in 1978 New Orleans), my mother purchased for me two of the largest and most beautiful non-stick, professional sauté pans imaginable. She would not let me have my "gift" until Christmas rolled around that year. However, somehow, I managed to "sweet talk" her into giving them to me a little bit earlier! I still own those two pans to this day and I use them to make my own version of this classic dish. Paella is an exciting and very colorful, Portuguese and Spanish recipe. All of the ingredients are cooked and served in one pan and the meal is meant to be shared with the family and friends that you so dearly love. There are many different versions of paella and just about any ingredient can go into making it. I think you and your family will truly enjoy this traditional and historic dish. Pair the recipe with some crusty Portuguese bread and a few glasses of hearty Spanish sangria and you will have a most unforgettable dining experience!

## Ingredients:

- ◆ 4 tablespoons good olive oil, divided
- ◆ 2 pounds large shrimp, peeled and deveined, tails left intact
- ◆ 2 pounds andouille sausage *or* Spanish chorizo sausage (about 5 links), sliced into ½ inch pieces
- ◆ 1 pound monkfish, cubed into 1 inch pieces
- ◆ 1 pound fresh red snapper, cubed into 1 inch pieces
- ◆ 2 teaspoons sweet Spanish-smoked paprika
- ◆ 2 tablespoons Emeril's Bayou Blast spice
- ◆ 2 cups Vidalia onion (about 4 onions), chopped
- ◆ 1 cup red bell pepper (about 2 large red peppers), chopped
- ◆ 1 cup green bell pepper (about 2 large green peppers), chopped
- ◆ 4 tablespoons garlic (about 8 large cloves), minced
- ◆ 2 teaspoons saffron threads (about 3 sprigs), crumbled
- ◆ 3 cups short grain Arborio rice (do not use long grain rice for this recipe)
- ◆ 5 cups rich seafood stock (p. 91)
- ◆ 2 cups green peas (fresh or frozen)
- ◆ 1 jar red pimentos, left whole
- ◆ Fresh flat leaf parsley, chopped finely (for garnish)
- ◆ Green onions, chopped finely (for garnish)

# Shrimp, Andouille, and Seafood Paella

YIELD: SERVES 8-10

## Directions:

♦ Preheat oven to 325 degrees Fahrenheit.

♦ Season all of the shrimp with 2 tablespoons of Emeril's Bayou Blast. In a large, ovenproof sauté pan, over medium-high heat, add 2 tablespoons of olive oil. Once the oil is hot, sear the shrimp for about 2 minutes per side. Remove the shrimp from the pan and set aside.

♦ Add another 2 tablespoons of olive oil and the andouille sausage. Sear the meat, stirring occasionally, until the sausage is browned all over, about 8 minutes.

♦ Add the chopped onions, bell peppers, minced garlic, and saffron threads and sauté, stirring often, until caramelized, about 7 minutes. Add the rice and stir for an additional 3 minutes. Add the seafood stock and bring to a boil. Reduce the heat to a simmer and cook, undisturbed, until the rice has absorbed most of the liquid, about 25-30 minutes.

♦ Add the monkfish and red snapper fish cubes. Add the peas, pimentos, and 2 teaspoons of smoked paprika, continuing to cook for another 6 minutes. Do not overcook the seafood. Return the reserved cooked shrimp to the pan.

♦ Cover the pan with aluminum foil and place in the preheated oven. You want all of the liquid to evaporate into the rice, vegetables, and seafood. The pan can remain in the oven for a maximum of 20 minutes.

♦ Remove the pan from the oven and let it sit for another 10 minutes before serving. Garnish the paella with chopped green onions and flat leaf parsley. Present the pan of paella to your family or guests at the dinner table.

# Main

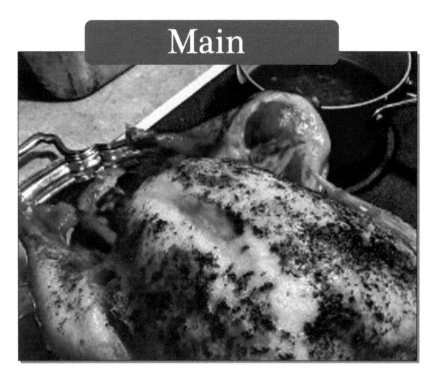

If you purchased this cookbook for no other reason, I can tell you, without a doubt, that this recipe will make your investment worthwhile and holidays incredibly special. Chef Cardie is going to alleviate the stress and worry when it comes to cooking your next Thanksgiving or Christmas turkey. While my dad was still alive, I was the one in charge of roasting a nice, fat turkey for my entire family (brother, sisters, wives, husbands, and grandkids). We all celebrated and dined each year at his historic and picturesque Westfall Farm in Montague, New Jersey. I will admit that I cooked a few "clunkers" in my day and the turkeys ended up tasting dry and overcooked! Then I learned how to brine a turkey overnight. I cannot begin to tell you the difference this will make to your meal! Your bird will come out so tender and juicy that you will be singing my praises from the highest mountaintop! This classic, holiday recipe does require a bit of grunt work on your part so have someone with strong muscles on hand in case you need them! Please cook your next holiday turkey this way because the recipe is so easy and fun to prepare that even a "bird brain" will not be able to screw it up!

## Turkey Brine Ingredients:

- ◆ 1 (18-20 pound) fresh non-frozen turkey (ordered 2 days ahead from butcher)
- ◆ 16 cups ice water (1 gallon)
- ◆ 1 bunch fresh thyme
- ◆ 1 bunch fresh rosemary
- ◆ 1 bunch fresh sage
- ◆ 6 (12 ounce) bottles dark beer (I use Guinness)
- ◆ 16 cups vegetable stock (p. 99)
- ◆ 4 cups light brown sugar
- ◆ 5 cups Kosher salt

## Roasted Turkey Ingredients:

- ◆ 1 bunch fresh thyme
- ◆ 1 bunch fresh rosemary
- ◆ 1 bunch fresh sage
- ◆ 4 large celery stalks
- ◆ 2 small Vidalia onions, quartered
- ◆ 2 large carrots, chopped
- ◆ ¼ cup Kosher salt (for rub)
- ◆ ¼ cup freshly cracked black pepper (for rub)
- ◆ ½ cup canola oil (for rub)

Turn Page Over for Turkey Gravy Ingredients (p. 215)

# Signature Brined,
# Holiday Roasted Turkey
# with Pan Gravy

YIELD: SERVES 10-12

## Turkey Brine Directions:

♦ You will need to purchase a large brining bag for the turkey. These bags can be found in gourmet stores and most supermarkets (especially during the holidays).

♦ On the morning prior to the day you begin cooking, in a very large stockpot or large Dutch oven, over medium heat, combine all of the brine ingredients **except for** the gallon of iced water and the turkey itself. Bring the vegetable stock mixture up to a full boil, stirring the ingredients often. Immediately remove the pot from the burner to allow the mixture to cool to room temperature, about 1 hour.

♦ Place your thawed turkey into the brining bag. Over the sink, pour the cooled brining mixture over the turkey. Then pour in 1 gallon (16 cups), of ice water. Seal the bag tightly with zip ties and make sure the liquid covers the turkey completely. Add additional vegetable stock, beer, or water as needed.

♦ If you do not have enough refrigerator room for the brined turkey, simply place the brining bag into a large ice chest (like the ones used for a tailgate party). Cover the turkey with ice or ice bags to stay cool. Shut the lid tightly and brine the turkey for at least 12 hours. Overnight is preferable.

♦ The next morning and over the sink, carefully remove the turkey from the brining liquid. Using a lot of paper towels, dry the turkey entirely from the inside to the outside. You want the turkey to be completely dry before seasoning and roasting.

*Chef's Note: Before you begin the brining process, make sure you have removed the inner organs from the turkey cavity. They can be used to make a giblet gravy, but I discard them.*

## Roasted Turkey Directions:

♦ Preheat oven to 475 degrees Fahrenheit. Remove all racks **except for** the bottom one.

♦ Stuff the inner cavity of the turkey with the fresh spices, celery, onions, and carrots. Place the turkey onto the rack of a large roasting pan. Fold the wings under the turkey's breast. Season the outside of the turkey with Kosher salt and freshly cracked black pepper. With clean hands, rub the turkey all over with canola oil.

♦ Place the turkey breast-side-up on the bottom rack of your oven and cook for 30 minutes without opening the oven door. After 30 minutes, immediately reduce the temperature to 350 degrees Fahrenheit. Carefully remove the hot turkey pan from the oven momentarily and insert a digital meat thermometer into the thickest part of the turkey breast. Do not let the probe touch any bones of the meat. Cut out a piece of aluminum foil just large enough to fit over the breast area of the turkey and drape it over to prevent the breast from scorching or burning.

♦ Return the turkey roasting pan to the oven and cook until your digital meat thermometer registers 180 degrees Fahrenheit. This should take about 2 hours and 15 minutes.

Turn Page to Continue and for Turkey Gravy Directions

# Main

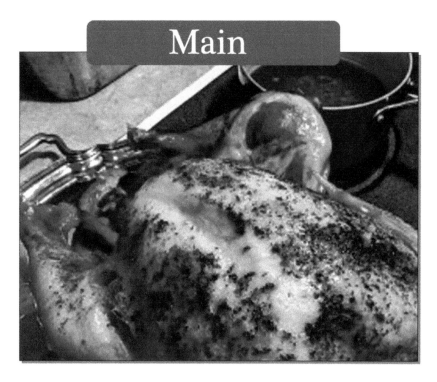

If you purchased this cookbook for no other reason, I can tell you, without a doubt, that this recipe will make your investment worthwhile and holidays incredibly special. Chef Cardie is going to alleviate the stress and worry when it comes to cooking your next Thanksgiving or Christmas turkey. While my dad was still alive, I was the one in charge of roasting a nice, fat turkey for my entire family (brother, sisters, wives, husbands, and grandkids). We all celebrated and dined each year at his historic and picturesque Westfall Farm in Montague, New Jersey. I will admit that I cooked a few "clunkers" in my day and the turkeys ended up tasting dry and overcooked! Then I learned how to brine a turkey overnight. I cannot begin to tell you the difference this will make to your meal! Your bird will come out so tender and juicy that you will be singing my praises from the highest mountaintop! This classic, holiday recipe does require a bit of grunt work on your part so have someone with strong muscles on hand in case you need them! Please cook your next holiday turkey this way because the recipe is so easy and fun to prepare that even a "bird brain" will not be able to screw it up!

(Continued)

## Roasted Turkey Ingredients:

- 1 bunch fresh thyme
- 1 bunch fresh rosemary
- 1 bunch fresh sage
- 4 large celery stalks
- 2 small Vidalia onions, quartered
- 2 large carrots, chopped
- ¼ cup Kosher salt (for rub)
- ¼ cup freshly cracked black pepper (for rub)
- ½ cup canola oil (for rub)

## Turkey Gravy Ingredients:

- 1 cup red wine (such as a Merlot or Burgundy)
- 2 cups chicken stock (p. 89)
- 2 sprigs fresh thyme
- 2 sprigs fresh rosemary
- ½ cup all-purpose flour
- Kosher salt and freshly cracked black pepper

# Signature Brined,
# Holiday Roasted Turkey
# with Pan Gravy

(Continued)

### Roasted Turkey Directions:

♦ Once at temperature, remove the bird from the oven and place it onto a large cutting board. Drape the turkey loosely with aluminum foil while you make the gravy. Let the turkey rest for at least 30 minutes before carving.

### Turkey Gravy Directions:

♦ Place the roasting pan on the stovetop, over two burners at medium high-heat. Pour in 1 cup of red wine and scrape up any food particles that have formed at the bottom of the roasting pan. Pour in 2 cups of chicken stock and add the fresh sprigs of herbs. Sprinkle in ½ cup of all-purpose flour and whisk vigorously to prevent the flour from clumping.

♦ Lower the heat to medium-low and simmer the gravy for about 15 minutes, stirring often. Taste the gravy to see if you need to add a pinch of Kosher salt or extra black pepper. Once reduced and smooth, strain the gravy through a fine mesh sieve into a small soup pot. Discard the herb sprigs. Keep the gravy warm on very low heat while you carve the turkey.

# Main

A few years back, I had the wonderful opportunity to cook and teach at the prestigious Adult School of Montclair, New Jersey. Since I had already taught a French-inspired culinary class at King's Cooking Studios, I needed to think of new, creative and exciting recipes to include. This is one of the dishes that amazed and stunned the minds and taste buds of the sold-out class, "A Taste of Paris." Since I was young, I loved the custardy dessert the French call, a "Napoleon," so I asked myself, "Why not create a savory dish using chicken or veal and layers of delicious cheeses and some prosciutto ham?" As you can see, I topped it off with a classic French Velouté sauce (recipe follows) and some haricot verts filets extra-fins (steamed French baby string beans). This is a meal that even the notorious emperor would be extremely proud to eat!

## Chicken Napoleon Ingredients:

- 12 large chicken breasts, skinless and boneless (purchased from butcher)
- 2 cups all-purpose flour
- 4 tablespoons Emeril's Bayou Blast spice, divided
- 3 eggs (for egg wash)
- 5 tablespoons water, divided (for egg wash and steaming spinach)
- 2 cups breadcrumbs (I use Panko)
- 8 tablespoons unsalted butter (1 stick), divided (for frying chicken)
- 8 tablespoons olive oil, divided (for frying chicken)
- ½ cup white wine (for steaming spinach)
- 2 packages baby spinach leaves, stems trimmed or removed
- 36 slices from a large round of Brie cheese, sliced

## Velouté Sauce Ingredients:

- ½ cup all-purpose flour
- ½ cup unsalted butter (1 stick)
- 4 cups chicken stock (p. 89), heated in a pan
- 1 tablespoon thyme leaves, minced finely
- 2 tablespoons Dijon mustard
- Kosher salt and freshly cracked black pepper

# Signature
# Chicken Napoleons
# with Velouté Sauce

◆────────────── YIELD: 12 NAPOLEONS ──────────────◆

## Napoleon Directions:

- Preheat oven to 350 degrees Fahrenheit.

- Create flour, egg, and breadcrumb dredging containers or "stations." The 2 cups of flour should be seasoned with 2 tablespoons of Emeril's Bayou Blast spice. The 3 eggs should be mixed with 1 tablespoon of cold water to create an egg wash. The breadcrumbs should be seasoned with the remaining 2 tablespoons of Emeril's Bayou Blast spice.

- On a clean cutting board and using a heavy meat pounder (or back of an iron skillet), flatten each chicken breast to ¼ inch thick. Cut each breast in half crosswise and then halve again crosswise. Trim the edges of each piece to create four equal rectangles per chicken breast. Dredge each piece in the flour, followed by the egg wash, and finish with the breadcrumbs. Set the chicken on a large plate and refrigerate for at least 15 minutes.

- In a large sauté pan, over medium-high heat, melt 2 tablespoons of unsalted butter and heat 2 tablespoons of olive oil. Place about 6 of the chicken pieces in the pan. The pan should not be overcrowded; the chicken will be cooked in several batches. Brown each set of chicken for 3 minutes per side. Once golden, transfer to a large platter or roasting pan. They can be pat dry with paper towels, but this is not necessary.

  *Chef's Note: Before browning each new batch of chicken, remember to melt another 2 tablespoons of unsalted butter and heat 2 tablespoons of oil.*

- In a small Dutch oven or pot, over the stovetop, add ½ cup of white wine and ¼ cup of cold water. Add the bunches of trimmed spinach leaves and some Kosher salt and freshly cracked black pepper, to taste. Cover the pot with a tight lid and steam the spinach (without peeking), for 6 minutes. Drain the spinach with a colander and allow it to cool. Using a clean dish towel or large coffee filter, drain as much of the water as possible.

- Using another clean cutting board, line up the Napoleon ingredients: the cooked chicken breasts; cooked spinach; thin slices of Brie and Fontina cheese; and thin, halved ham slices. Lay down 1 piece of chicken and top it with 2 spinach leaves, 1 slice of Brie, 1 slice of Fontina, and ½ slice of prosciutto ham. Add another piece of chicken on top, press together, and repeat the process 2 more times. You will have a stack of 4 pieces of chicken per serving. Secure the chicken Napoleon stacks with 2 long wooden toothpicks.

- Place the 12 chicken Napoleons onto a large cookie sheet or roasting pan. Bake uncovered for 15 minutes, or until the cheese has melted. While the chicken is baking, make your Velouté sauce.

- Top each Napoleon with a dollop or two of Velouté sauce. Garnish each with a sprinkling of flat leaf parsley.

## Velouté Sauce Directions:

- In a medium saucepan or small Dutch oven, over medium heat, add and whisk the flour and butter together for 3 minutes to form a roux. Add the heated chicken stock to the roux, whisking constantly until the mixture begins to thicken, about 5 minutes. Add the minced thyme leaves and mustard. Season with Kosher salt and freshly cracked black pepper. Mix well. Taste the sauce and adjust accordingly.

# Main

New Orleans has many famous and historical dishes, but this might be the best known one of all! Gumbo is popular because it does not cost an arm and leg to make and it feeds an entire family. When you take a bite of this delicious concoction, you are tasting its many influential cultures and countries. The word for the green and slimy vegetable we call, "okra," derives from West African languages, where many refer to it as, "Gombo." Well, I am quite sure you get the reference. For this recipe, you must cook an authentic roux very slowly. Do not worry, I will take you through this process. Please prepare this dish for your family while paying homage to a beautiful city that has endured so much heartache in recent years. New Orleans is bigger and better than ever before so get down there and enjoy! I can assure you that its great people will welcome you with open arms!

## Roux & Gumbo Ingredients:

- 2 pounds chicken thighs, skinless and boneless, cut into 1 inch cubes
- 2 pounds andouille sausage, cut crosswise into ½ inch thick slices
- 1 (16 ounce) package frozen okra, thawed but left whole, sliced
- 2 pounds large shrimp, peeled completely and deveined
- 1 cup vegetable oil
- 1 cup all-purpose flour
- 5 tablespoons olive oil, divided
- 3 large Vidalia onions, chopped
- 2 red bell peppers, seeded and chopped
- 2 green peppers, seeded and chopped
- 8 celery stalks, chopped
- 8 large garlic cloves, minced finely
- 2 tablespoons Emeril's Bayou Blast spice
- 1 cup dry white wine
- 1 full bunch fresh thyme, leaves removed and chopped
- 3 large bay leaves
- 4 cups homemade rich chicken stock (p. 89) *or* store-bought low sodium stock
- 1 (28 ounce) can diced tomatoes, with juice
- A few shakes any hot sauce (such as Tabasco or Frank's)
- 4 cups white long grain rice, steamed (cooked according to box directions)

- Kosher salt and freshly cracked black pepper, to taste
- Fresh flat leaf parsley, minced (for garnish)
- Green onions, chopped (for garnish)
- Optional: crusty French bread (for dipping)

# Signature New Orleans Chicken, Andouille, and Shrimp Gumbo

## YIELD: SERVES 8-10

## Roux Directions:

*Chef's Note: There are four primary "colors," or variations, of a properly cooked roux. The first color is the "blonde" stage, followed by "peanut butter," "brunette," and finally, the "chocolate" stage. You must be a highly trained chef to create a "chocolate" roux without burning it. This recipe will help you attain a "peanut butter" or "brunette" roux.*

♦ In a very heavy cast iron pan or an iron Dutch oven, over medium-low heat, add 1 cup of vegetable oil and whisk it together with 1 cup of all-purpose flour. Begin the process of stirring non-stop in a slow, circular (or "figure 8"), motion. It is vital that you continually whisk your roux to prevent little black specks from appearing. These spots indicate that the roux has been burnt and must be discarded.

♦ Continue to whisk the roux over medium-low heat for at least 30 minutes. To attain a darker roux, this process must last 45 minutes to an hour. Please be careful. A cooked roux can burn your skin badly. Keep children out of the way during this time.

♦ When you have achieved a nice, dark color, remove the roux from the stovetop and set it aside to cool slightly.

## Gumbo Directions:

♦ In a large sauté pan or Dutch oven, over medium-high heat, add 2 tablespoons of olive oil, the sliced sausage, and cut-up chicken thighs. Brown both meats, on all sides, for 10-12 minutes. Remove the sauté pan from the stovetop and let the meat mixture cool.

♦ In a 6 quart Dutch oven, over medium-high heat, add 3 tablespoons of olive oil. Add the chopped onions, bell peppers, and celery (commonly known in New Orleans as, "The Holy Trinity"). Stirring frequently, cook until the vegetables are soft and brown, about 10 minutes. Add the minced garlic and Emeril's Bayou Blast spice, stirring for an additional 2 minutes. Add the white wine, thyme leaves, bay leaves, chicken stock, and reserved cooked roux. Whisk vigorously to incorporate everything well. Bring the entire mixture up to a full boil, stirring often. Immediately reduce the stovetop heat to medium-low.

♦ Add the diced tomatoes (with their juice), cooked chicken thigh pieces, andouille sausage, and thawed okra pieces. Simmer until the chicken is completely cooked, about 10 minutes.

♦ Add the uncooked shrimp to the pot and cook them until they are just opaque, stirring often, about 5 more minutes. Season your gumbo with a pinch of Kosher salt, some freshly cracked black pepper, and a few good dashes of your favorite hot sauce, to taste.

♦ In large, individual soup bowls, place an ice cream scoop full of white rice into the center of the bowl. Ladle or spoon the gumbo around the mound of rice. Garnish each bowl with minced flat leaf parsley and some chopped green onions on top. Serve immediately.

*Chef's Note: I like to serve my gumbo with plenty of sliced French bread on the side for dipping into the rich sauce. Do not forget the Sangria or Chianti! Cheers!*

# Main

These slow-cooked short ribs could be considered by many, as my signature dish. People begin asking for second helpings before they even fully finish their first bite! This recipe may demand some time and patience on your part but I can promise you that it is worth the effort. Prepare these short ribs for your next dinner party and get ready for some rave reviews!

## Ingredients:

- 14 large and meaty short ribs, bone in
- 4 tablespoons canola oil
- 4 tablespoons Emeril's Cajun Essence
- 3 Vidalia onions, peeled and chopped coarsely
- 8 large celery stalks, chopped into ½ inch pieces
- 8 large carrots, peeled and sliced into ½ inch cubes
- 8 large garlic cloves, chopped finely
- 4 tablespoons all-purpose flour
- 4 cups sweet tawny port wine
- 2 cups wine (I use a Burgundy or Pinot Noir)
- 4 cups rich beef stock (p. 87)
- 1 (29 ounce) can chopped tomatoes, seeded
- 1 (small) can tomato paste
- 1 package fresh oregano, left whole
- 1 package fresh thyme sprigs, left whole
- 1 package fresh rosemary sprigs, left whole
- ½ cup fresh flat leaf parsley, chopped
- 3 bay leaves
- Freshly cracked black pepper, to taste
- Fresh flat leaf parsley, chopped finely (for garnish)
- Green onions, chopped finely (for garnish)
- Optional: crusty French bread

CHEF CARDIE'S
# Signature Slow-Cooked
# Beef Short Ribs in
# Tawny Port

YIELD: SERVES 10-12

## Directions:

♦ Preheat oven to 275 degrees Fahrenheit.

♦ In a large Dutch oven, over medium-high heat, add 4 tablespoons of canola oil. Season all of the short ribs with about 4 heaping tablespoons of Emeril's Cajun Essence and lots of freshly cracked black pepper. When the oil is hot, cook about 6 short ribs at a time until they caramelize and brown on all sides, approximately 12 minutes per batch. Transfer the ribs to a platter and repeat the process with the remaining short ribs. When done, remove all but 2 tablespoons of fat from the Dutch oven and reduce the heat to medium.

> *Chef's Note: As mentioned above, the short ribs will have to be seared and browned in several batches. If needed, add a little extra canola oil as required.*

♦ Add in the onions, celery, and carrots, cooking until the vegetables begin to caramelize, about 10 minutes. Add the chopped garlic and sprinkle the vegetables with 4 tablespoons of all-purpose flour and continue to cook, stirring constantly for another 5 minutes. Make sure all of the flour has been "cooked out."

♦ Add the port wine, burgundy wine (or Pinot Noir), beef stock, chopped tomatoes, tomato paste, oregano, thyme, rosemary, ½ cup of chopped parsley, and 3 bay leaves. With a wooden spoon, scrape the bottom of the Dutch oven to release any browned bits that may have accumulated at the bottom. Bring mixture to a full boil and then shut off the heat.

♦ Return the browned short ribs and their juices to the Dutch oven. Cover with a tight-fitting lid or heavy-duty aluminum foil and place ribs in the oven. Cook until the meat is fork-tender and beginning to pull away from the bones, basting the ribs from time to time with the braising liquid. This should take 3½-4 hours.

♦ Transfer the ribs to a large platter, discarding any loose bones. Cover the ribs to keep them warm but still let them cool slightly. Skim the fat that has risen to the top of the braising liquid (I do this step the following day). Transfer the vegetables from the pot to a platter. Discard the thyme and rosemary sprigs as well as the bay leaves.

> *Chef's Note: The onions, celery, and carrots cook down quite a bit during the slow-cooking process but they do not have to be discarded. Instead, add them to the sauce when you go to serve the meal.*

♦ Transfer the braising liquid to a pot or small Dutch oven over medium heat. Simmer until the liquid has reduced to a sauce consistency and is just thick enough to coat the back of a spoon.

♦ Pour the sauce directly over the ribs and garnish them with chopped flat leaf parsley, chopped green onions, or both! Do not forget to include some crusty French bread on the side to sop up the delicious sauce!

> *Chef's Note: You can also serve the ribs over a bed of grilled vegetables or my creamy, garlic smashed potatoes (p. 135).*

# Main

Without getting too descriptive, a lamb shank comes from the lower, more muscular part of the animal's leg so it is considered a "tougher cut." However, when cooked slowly and properly, it is a delicacy which can be found on any good restaurant's menu. I have a total affinity for low and slow-cooking. Maybe it is because I used to cook smoked briskets for 15 hours or pork bellies for 10 hours while I worked in the deep South. This recipe reminds me of those good times. Thankfully, this recipe does not take too long to make and it is relatively inexpensive. Good lamb shanks purchased from the butcher are about half the cost (per pound) as a roast leg of lamb. Try these lamb shanks for your next formal and intimate dinner party. Your guests will show you lots of love, that is for sure!

## Ingredients:

- 8 (10 ounce) large and meaty leg shanks (from butcher)
- 4 tablespoons Emeril's Bayou Blast spice
- 1 cup all-purpose flour
- 4 tablespoons olive oil (see Chef's Note)
- 4 large Vidalia onions, chopped into 2 inch chunks
- 8 large carrots, cut into 2 inch chunks
- 8 large celery stalks, chopped
- 3 tablespoons garlic (about 8 large cloves), minced
- 4 bay leaves
- 2 tablespoons fresh thyme leaves (1 package), chopped finely
- 2 tablespoons fresh rosemary (1 package), chopped finely
- 2 cups any good red wine (I use a nice Merlot or Burgundy)
- 1 quart beef stock (p. 87) (see Chef's Note)
- 1 quart chicken stock (p. 89) (see Chef's Note)
- 3 pounds baby red potatoes
- Kosher salt and freshly cracked black pepper, to taste
- Flat leaf parsley, chopped (for garnish)

# Slow-Cooked Lamb Shanks

---

## YIELD: SERVES ABOUT 8

---

### Directions:

- In a roasting pan or large mixing bowl, season each lamb shank with a pinch of Kosher salt and some freshly cracked black pepper along with ½ tablespoon of Emeril's Bayou Blast spice. Rub the spice blend into the meat well, pressing in with your fingers.

- Dredge each seasoned lamb shank into the all-purpose flour, completely coating each side. Shake off any excess flour. In a 6 quart metal pot or large Dutch oven (preferable), over medium-high heat, add 4 tablespoons of olive oil. When the oil is hot enough, add and sear the shanks for 3 minutes per side, or until all sides have browned completely. This will have to be done in at least two batches to prevent overcrowding. Transfer the browned lamb shanks to a platter and set aside.

  *Chef's Note:  An extra tablespoon or two of olive oil may be needed to brown the remaining lamb shanks in batches. Add as needed.*

- Still using medium-high heat, add the chopped onions and sauté them for 6 minutes. Add the chopped carrots and celery and let these cook for 3-4 minutes. Season with a little Kosher salt and freshly cracked black pepper. Stir in the minced garlic, bay leaves, thyme, and rosemary. Continue to stir and cook for another 1 minute.

- Deglaze the Dutch oven with 2 cups of red wine, scraping the bottom and sides to loosen any browned particles that have formed. Pour in the beef and chicken stocks. Bring the liquid to a boil and then immediately reduce the heat to a low simmer.

- Add the reserved, browned lamb shanks and continue to cook for 2½ hours, or until the sauce has thickened slightly and the lamb meat has started to peel away from the bone. During the final hour of simmering the lamb shanks, add the baby red potatoes to the mixture and cook until tender.

  *Chef's Note: You want your lamb shanks and vegetables to be pretty much submerged in the simmering liquid throughout this process. If you do not have enough liquid, simply add some cold water or more chicken or beef stock to cover the food.*

- Remove the shanks from the liquid and set them onto a warm platter. With a slotted spoon, remove the potatoes, carrots, and onions from the liquid and position them in a circle around the lamb shanks, for serving.

- At this point, you can strain the remaining gravy through a fine mesh sieve into a small soup pot or saucepan. Reheat the gravy, over medium heat, to thicken it a bit more and then spoon it over the vegetables and lamb shanks. Garnish individual servings with some chopped flat leaf parsley.

# Main

Memphis-style baby back ribs are one of my favorite foods to eat and I prepared the marinated ribs, shown here, several years ago for a sold-out Kings Cooking Studio class we called, "Are You Hungry Tonight?" Yes, we were honoring "The King" himself, Mr. Elvis Presley. Every person in attendance claimed these were the best ribs they had ever tasted in their lives. They are easy to prepare and I promise, you will not get "all shook up!"

## Baby Back Ribs Ingredients:

- ♦ 8 pounds baby back pork ribs
- ♦ 1 cup (minimum) Memphis-style barbecue sauce (p. 193 or use Sweet Baby Rays)
- ♦ ¼ cup (minimum) Memphis dry rub spice (recipe follows)

## Dry Rub Ingredients (For 8 Pounds of Ribs):

- ♦ ½ cup paprika (not smoked)
- ♦ 1 cup dark brown sugar, packed
- ♦ ½ cup white sugar
- ♦ 2 tablespoons salt
- ♦ 2 tablespoons celery salt
- ♦ 2 tablespoons freshly cracked black pepper
- ♦ 2 tablespoons Emeril's Bayou Blast Cajun seasoning
- ♦ 2 tablespoons dry mustard
- ♦ 2 tablespoons roasted garlic powder
- ♦ 2 tablespoons onion powder

# Slow-Cooked

# Memphis-Style

# Baby Back Ribs and Dry Rub

## Baby Back Ribs Directions:

♦ Tear off 4 or 5 large pieces of heavy-duty aluminum foil and set aside.

♦ Rub the sets of baby back rack ribs liberally with at least ¼ cup of dry rub. The white membranes on the back of the ribs do not need to be removed (it is purely optional), but poke some knife holes in the membrane so the dry rub will permeate. Place the ribs meat-side down on pieces of aluminum foil and carefully fold up the ribs like you are wrapping a gift. Place the ribs inside the refrigerator and let them marinate in the dry rub overnight.

♦ The following day, preheat your oven to 300 degrees Fahrenheit. Spray a large cooking sheet with non-stick buttered cooking spray. Place each aluminum foil-covered rib package on the cooking sheet and bake for 3 hours. Remove from the oven and carefully open the foil to expose the ribs. Reset the oven temperature to 400 degrees Fahrenheit. Liberally brush the ribs with at least 1 cup of Memphis-style barbecue sauce and return them to the oven, uncovered, for 25 minutes.

*Chef's Note: If you want your ribs richly caramelized, place them under a broiler for about 3 minutes (meat-side up). Do not leave them unattended as the barbecue sauce will burn quite rapidly.*

## Dry Rub Directions:

♦ Place all ingredients in the bowl and mix well with a wooden spoon or rubber spatula. This mixture can be put into an airtight jar. It will keep fresh for up to 3 months.

# Main

Here is another meal I just loved to eat as a young man and very much enjoyed making for guests as a professional chef because of the wonderful memories it evoked. Why *did* tasty pot roast dinners disappear from the menus of most fancy restaurants? I know that it is a rather inexpensive piece of meat, but when it is slow-cooked for hours on end in a rich beef stock (page 87), Merlot wine, root vegetables, and delicious spices, it is one of the best tasting dishes on Earth! You will thank me for including this recipe when you make this dish for you and your family. It has had a part in many memories and is one that will provide memories for a lifetime. On many occasions, my mother cooked it for our Sunday night family dinners, which were full of their own stories. But they all began the same. From all around the house, my father, two sisters, brother, and I would smell her wonderful pot roast slowly simmering in the oven and begin to get restless. By the time dinner rolled around, we were starved and ready to dig into this beautiful and succulent, one-pot masterpiece!

## Ingredients:

♦ 1 (5 pound) chuck roast *or* beef round, boneless, trimmed of excess fat
♦ ½ cup all-purpose flour
♦ 3 heaping tablespoons Emeril's Original Essence spice
♦ 3 tablespoons olive oil
♦ 4 tablespoons unsalted butter
♦ 2 large Vidalia onions, peeled and chopped into 2 inch chunks
♦ 6 large celery stalks, cut diagonally into 2 inch pieces
♦ 6 large carrots, peeled and cut diagonally into 2 inch pieces
♦ 2 cups wine (I use a Merlot)
♦ 6 fresh thyme sprigs (1 full package)
♦ 6 fresh rosemary sprigs (1 full package)
♦ 6 large garlic cloves, chopped coarsely
♦ 3 cups rich beef stock (p. 87)
♦ 3 bay leaves
♦ 2½ pounds large Yukon Gold potatoes, quartered *or* 1 bag baby Yukon Gold potatoes, left whole
♦ 2 tablespoons cornstarch and ¼ cup water mixed together to form a "slurry" (for thickening)
♦ Freshly cracked black pepper, to taste
♦ Fresh flat leaf parsley, chopped finely (for garnish)

CHEF CARDIE'S

# Slow-Cooked

# Pot Roast with

# Vegetables

YIELD: SERVES 6-8

## Directions:

♦ Preheat oven to 325 degrees Fahrenheit.

♦ In a large, metal mixing bowl or an oven pan, whisk together the ½ cup of flour and 3 tablespoons of Emeril's Original Essence. Add plenty of freshly cracked black pepper. Roll the chuck roast in the spice and flour mixture so it coats the meat on all sides.

♦ In a large pot or Dutch oven, over medium-high heat, add 3 tablespoons of olive oil. Add the roast and, using tongs, sear the meat for 15 minutes, or until it has browned on all sides. Place the roast onto a platter and set it aside.

♦ In the Dutch oven, over medium-high heat, melt 4 tablespoons of unsalted butter. Add the chopped onions, celery, and carrots. Cook your vegetables for 10 minutes, stirring constantly.

♦ Return your browned roast to the Dutch oven. Pour in the Merlot wine and add the thyme sprigs, rosemary sprigs, chopped garlic, rich beef stock, and 3 bay leaves. Raise the heat to high and bring the mixture to a full boil. Immediately, turn off the heat. Cover the Dutch oven with a tight lid and place in the oven to bake for 4½ hours.

♦ After the first 2½ hours of cooking, open the oven door, slightly slide out the pot, and add the Yukon Gold potatoes. Cover again with a lid and cook for an additional 2 hours. Remove the pot from the oven and let it cool for about 20 minutes.

♦ Carefully, transfer the meat from the liquid to a large serving platter. Discard the thyme sprigs, rosemary sprigs, and 3 bay leaves. Remove all of the vegetables with a slotted spoon and place them in a circle around the roast. The meat should be ready to fall apart by this time. You can carve it into 1 inch slices or you can use a fork to pull it apart.

> *Chef's Note: The liquid in the Dutch oven may not need much thickening. However, if it does, over medium heat, slowly add the cornstarch and water "slurry" and stir this into the liquid to create a smooth and thicker gravy.*

♦ Pour the gravy over the top of the pot roast and garnish the meal with some finely chopped flat leaf parsley. Serve immediately and enjoy!

# Main

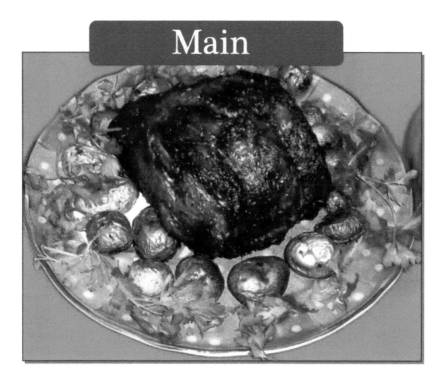

To all the meat lovers out there, please tell me, who does not enjoy a good slab of medium-rare prime rib smothered in an herbed au jus gravy? I also have a little riddle for you. "What do you get when you include side dishes of slow-roasted baby potatoes, baked sweet potato casserole, tomato and cucumber salad, and the famed English side dish, Yorkshire Pudding?" The answer? "A meal fit for a king!" I am not going to lie to you. Authentic prime rib is quite expensive, but it is also very friendly to cook. Furthermore, it is important to ask your local butcher to remove the chine bone of the prime rib when you purchase it. I make this meal at Christmas-time because there is no better time of year to spoil your loved ones!

## Prime Rib Ingredients:

- 1 (8-10 pound) beef rib roast, bone in
- ¼ cup good olive oil (plus 1 tablespoon for tossing potatoes)
- 2 tablespoons Kosher salt (plus salt for tossing potatoes)
- 2 tablespoons freshly cracked black pepper (plus pepper for tossing potatoes)
- 8 garlic cloves, halved
- 5 large carrots, chopped
- 3 large Vidalia onions, chopped
- 3 large celery stalks, chopped
- 1 package fresh thyme sprigs
- 1 package fresh rosemary sprigs
- 1 (5 pound) bag baby red potatoes, unpeeled
- Fresh flat leaf parsley, chopped finely (for garnish)

## Au Jus Ingredients:

- 1 cup red wine (such as a Merlot or Burgundy)
- 2 cups rich beef stock (p. 87)
- ½ cup all-purpose flour *or* Wondra flour
- A pinch of Kosher salt and freshly cracked black pepper, to taste

## Yorkshire Pudding Ingredients:

- ½ cup reserved drippings from the prime rib
- 1½ cups all-purpose flour
- 1 teaspoon Kosher salt
- 1 cup whole milk
- 4 large eggs, at room temperature, beaten well
- ¼ cup cold water

CHEF CARDIE'S

# Slow-Cooked Prime Rib

# with Au Jus and

# Yorkshire Pudding

YIELD: SERVES 8-10

## Prime Rib Directions:

♦ Preheat oven to 450 degrees Fahrenheit.

♦ Rub the prime rib all over with the olive oil, Kosher salt, and freshly cracked black pepper. Place the boned prime rib into a large roasting pan. Using a sharp paring knife, make a series of tiny incisions in the top of the meat and insert the garlic halves into each slit. Press the garlic into the meat firmly so the cloves will not slip out during the cooking process.

♦ Place the chopped carrots, onions, and celery, as well as the sprigs of fresh thyme and rosemary, around the meat in a semi-circle. Cook the meat, uncovered, for 30 minutes without opening the oven door. Carefully remove the meat from the oven and immediately lower the heat to 350 degrees Fahrenheit. In a mixing bowl, toss the potatoes in a little bit of Kosher salt and freshly cracked black pepper along with 1 tablespoon of olive oil. Spread the potatoes around the bottom of the roasting pan and return the pan to the oven for an additional hour or more (depending on the exact size of your roast).

♦ The prime rib will be ready to remove from the oven when the meat thermometer registers 140 degrees Fahrenheit. Once removed, drain ½ cup of the pan drippings into a mixing cup and reserve it to make the Yorkshire Pudding. Wrap the prime rib in heavy-duty aluminum foil and allow it to rest for 30 minutes. Transfer the vegetables to a large bowl. Discard the thyme and rosemary sprigs. Cover the bowl and keep warm.

## Au Jus Directions:

♦ Place the roasting pan on the stovetop, over two burners at medium-high heat. Pour in 1 cup of red wine and scrape up all of the food particles which have formed at the bottom of the roasting pan. Pour in the 2 cups of beef stock. Sprinkle in ½ cup of all-purpose flour and whisk vigorously to prevent the flour from clumping.

♦ Reduce the heat to medium-low and simmer the gravy for at least 15 minutes, stirring often. Taste the gravy to see if you need to add a pinch or two of Kosher salt or freshly cracked black pepper. Once reduced and smooth, strain the gravy through a fine mesh sieve into a small soup pot. Keep the gravy warm on a very low heat before serving.

## Yorkshire Pudding Directions:

♦ Preheat oven to 425 degrees Fahrenheit.

♦ Using non-stick butter spray, coat the bottoms of a large muffin tin. Divide the ½ cup of reserved prime rib pan drippings into each muffin insert. Place the muffin tin in the preheated oven for 10 minutes. Remove the pan only when the batter has been made.

♦ In a large mixing bowl, mix the flour and salt together. Make a small circle in the center of the flour and add the milk, eggs, and water. Whisk constantly until a smooth batter has been achieved. It will look and feel like pancake batter.

Turn Page to Continue and for Serving Directions

# Main

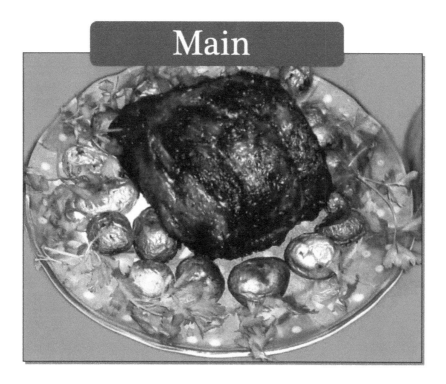

To all the meat lovers out there, please tell me, who does not enjoy a good slab of medium-rare prime rib smothered in an herbed au jus gravy? I also have a little riddle for you. "What do you get when you include side dishes of slow-roasted baby potatoes, baked sweet potato casserole, tomato and cucumber salad, and the famed English side dish, Yorkshire Pudding?" The answer? "A meal fit for a king!" I am not going to lie to you. Authentic prime rib is quite expensive, but it is also very friendly to cook. Furthermore, it is important to ask your local butcher to remove the chine bone of the prime rib when you purchase it. I make this meal at Christmas-time because there is no better time of year to spoil your loved ones!

(Continued)

## Prime Rib Ingredients:

- ♦ 1 (8-10 pound) beef rib roast, bone in
- ♦ ¼ cup good olive oil (plus 1 tablespoon for tossing potatoes)
- ♦ 2 tablespoons Kosher salt (plus salt for tossing potatoes)
- ♦ 2 tablespoons freshly cracked black pepper (plus pepper for tossing potatoes)
- ♦ 8 garlic cloves, halved
- ♦ 5 large carrots, chopped
- ♦ 3 large Vidalia onions, chopped
- ♦ 3 large celery stalks, chopped
- ♦ 1 package fresh thyme sprigs
- ♦ 1 package fresh rosemary sprigs
- ♦ 1 (5 pound) bag baby red potatoes, unpeeled
- ♦ Fresh flat leaf parsley, chopped finely (for garnish)

## Au Jus Ingredients:

- ♦ 1 cup red wine (such as a Merlot or Burgundy)
- ♦ 2 cups rich beef stock (p. 87)
- ♦ ½ cup all-purpose flour *or* Wondra flour
- ♦ A pinch of Kosher salt and freshly cracked black pepper, to taste

## Yorkshire Pudding Ingredients:

- ♦ ½ cup reserved drippings from the prime rib
- ♦ 1½ cups all-purpose flour
- ♦ 1 teaspoon Kosher salt
- ♦ 1 cup whole milk
- ♦ 4 large eggs, at room temperature, beaten well
- ♦ ¼ cup cold water

231

# Slow-Cooked Prime Rib

# with Au Jus and

# Yorkshire Pudding

(Continued)

### Yorkshire Pudding Directions:

♦ Carefully remove the muffin tin from the oven and set it on the stovetop. Using a spoon or small ladle, pour the flour and egg mixture right over the pan drippings. Immediately place the muffin tin into the preheated oven and bake for 25 minutes, or until the Yorkshire pudding has risen and turned golden brown.

### Serving Directions:

♦ Place a piece of medium-rare prime rib on a plate. Spoon the au jus gravy over the prime rib and garnish with finely chopped flat leaf parsley. Serve with the Yorkshire pudding, roasted baby potatoes, and cooked vegetables on the side.

*Chef's Note: To make life simpler, you can prepare the Yorkshire pudding base the day prior. Place the mixture in a metal mixing bowl, cover it, and refrigerate overnight. Let it come to room temperature before placing it in the heated muffin tins.*

# Main

I made this wonderful and decadent recipe when I visited the great state of Michigan back in 2018. While in the beautiful city of Rochester Hills, I catered a large cocktail party for students and friends of Michigan State University. The atmosphere was electric in every way possible and the guests could not wait to dig into the assortment of dishes that I had so lovingly prepared. I cannot say for certain which dish was enjoyed the most, but had they been handing out awards that evening, I think that this dish would have won first place! This is a relatively expensive recipe to make but it is one that is completely worth it in the end!

## Ingredients:

♦ 3 pounds elbow macaroni

♦ 3 pounds lobster meat (I use 3 or 4, 10-12 ounce frozen lobster tails), thawed, poached, and chopped into chunks

♦ 1 cup unsalted butter (2 sticks), divided

♦ 4 large garlic cloves, crushed and minced finely (for poaching)

♦ ½ cup any fresh herbs (e.g. parsley, tarragon, and thyme), chopped finely (for poaching)

♦ 2 cups white wine (for poaching)

♦ 3 tablespoons Old Bay seasoning (for poaching)

♦ ½ cup all-purpose flour

♦ 2 cups heavy cream

♦ 2 cups whole milk

♦ 2 cups Gruyere cheese, grated

♦ 2 cups aged white cheddar cheese, grated

♦ 2 cups Pepper Jack cheese, grated

♦ 2 cups breadcrumbs, seasoned (I use Panko)

♦ Kosher salt and freshly cracked black pepper, to taste

♦ Optional: 1 (small) white truffle (can find in gourmet supermarkets), diced finely or grated

CHEF CARDIE'S

# Three Cheese
# Macaroni and Cheese with
# Butter-Poached Lobster

## Butter-Poached Lobster Directions:

♦ In a 6 quart Dutch oven or heavy pot, over medium to low heat, melt 1 stick of unsalted butter and add the minced garlic and fresh herbs (I use a combination of chopped, not minced, parsley, tarragon, and thyme). Add the white wine and Old Bay seasoning. Do not let the mixture come to a boil. With kitchen scissors or a very sharp knife, halve the tail shells by cutting through the top shell and place them meat-side down in the pot.

♦ Cook the lobster for 15 minutes in the warm poaching liquid. Turn over the lobster halves and cook for an additional 10 minutes. Do not overcook. The lobster will be almost fully cooked through at this time but remember that it will further cook when it is baked in the oven with the other ingredients.

## Macaroni and Cheese with Butter-Poached Lobster Directions:

♦ Preheat oven to 375 degrees Fahrenheit.

♦ In 3 quarts of salted, boiling water, cook the elbow macaroni for 10 minutes, or until it is al dente (to the tooth). Drain the macaroni and set it aside in a bowl.

♦ In a Dutch oven, over medium heat, add the other 1 stick of unsalted butter and, using a wire whisk, slowly add ½ cup of flour to form a basic roux. Stir for 10 minutes and do not let it burn. Slowly add in 2 cups of heavy cream and 2 cups of whole milk, whisking often to keep the mixture smooth. Add the three cheeses and whisk until the entire mixture comes together and begins to thicken.

> *Chef's Note:* To "kick up" your macaroni and cheese to stratospheres unknown, add the optional truffle pieces to the milk and heavy cream mixture. They are unfortunately, expensive but the taste is so worth it.

♦ Add the macaroni and chopped lobster meat to the cheese and cream mixture. Season liberally with Kosher salt and freshly cracked black pepper. Place the mixture in buttered or sprayed 8 ounce ramekins and top with seasoned breadcrumbs. Cook the ramekins for about 20 minutes, or until the mixture is browned and bubbly on top.

# Main

Oh, I can hear you yelling at me right now! I can hear you saying, "Chef Cardie, please not another old-fashioned and boring recipe from your childhood days!" My three-word answer to you is "yes and no." Yes, it is an old recipe but no, it is far from boring or being the same kind of entrée you dined on as a child. This triple meatloaf comes out crunchy on the outside and moist and tender on the inside. Trust me, the flavors are simply incredible! The spicy tomato sauce that you brush on the outside of this meatloaf caramelizes while it cooks. I can almost promise you that this recipe will have your kids running *towards* the dinner table and not away from it!

## Ingredients:

- ½ pound lean ground beef (from butcher)
- ½ pound ground veal (from butcher)
- ½ pound ground pork (from butcher)
- 4 slices white *or* whole wheat bread, crusts removed and bread sliced into 1 inch cubes
- ¼ cup buttermilk
- 1 tablespoon olive oil (for sautéing vegetables)
- 2 tablespoons unsalted butter (for sautéing vegetables)
- 1 large Vidalia onion, chopped finely
- 1 cup celery (about 4 large stalks), washed and chopped into ½ inch pieces
- 2 tablespoons Emeril's Bayou Blast spice, divided
- 4 large garlic cloves, minced finely
- 3 large eggs, beaten well
- ½ cup ketchup
- 4 tablespoons brown sugar, packed
- 1 tablespoon apple cider vinegar
- Plenty of freshly cracked black pepper
- Fresh whole parsley sprigs (for garnish)
- Optional: a few good shakes any hot sauce (such as Tabasco or Frank's)

CHEF CARDIE'S

# Triple Meatloaf with Spicy Tomato Glaze

## YIELD: SERVES ABOUT 6

## Directions:

♦ Preheat oven to 375 degrees Fahrenheit.

♦ Pour ¼ cup of buttermilk into a mixing bowl and add the bread cubes. Using a handheld potato masher or your clean hands, press the bread into the buttermilk until you have formed a bit of a "paste." Set the mixture aside.

♦ In a large sauté pan, over medium-high heat, add the 1 tablespoon of olive oil and 2 tablespoons of unsalted butter. Add the chopped onion pieces, chopped celery, 1 of the tablespoons of Emeril's Bayou Blast spice, and minced garlic. Cook the mixture until the onions and celery become translucent, about 8 minutes. Remove the sauté pan from the heat and allow the mixture to cool for 10 minutes.

♦ In another large mixing bowl, add the ground beef, ground veal, ground pork, and 3 large beaten eggs. Season liberally with freshly cracked black pepper and the remaining 1 tablespoon of Emeril's Bayou Blast spice. Using your bare hands, combine the chopped onion, celery, and garlic mixture with the bread and buttermilk mixture. Mix everything well until most of the liquid has been absorbed.

♦ Using a bread loaf pan that has been liberally sprayed with non-stick butter spray, add the combined meat mixture to the pan. As you add the meatloaf, press down gently (but firmly), with your hands or a rubber spatula to compress and smooth the meat.

♦ Set the bread pan onto a cookie sheet that has been lined with aluminum foil and sprayed with non-stick cooking spray. Place in the preheated oven to cook for 35 minutes. While the meatloaf is cooking, make the spicy tomato sauce as follows:

♦ In a bowl, whisk together the ketchup, brown sugar, apple cider vinegar, and optional hot sauce, to taste. After 35 minutes, remove the meatloaf from the oven and allow it to cool, undisturbed, on the stovetop for 15 minutes. Then, invert the meatloaf pan onto the lined and sprayed cookie sheet. Using a pastry brush, "paint" the tomato sauce gently (yet evenly), over the top and surrounding sides of the meatloaf. Return the dish to the oven and bake for an additional 30 minutes, or until it is well-browned and crusty on all sides.

♦ Remove the meatloaf from the oven and let it cool for 15 minutes before cutting it into 1 inch slices. If desired, garnish with a few sprigs of whole parsley. Serve immediately.

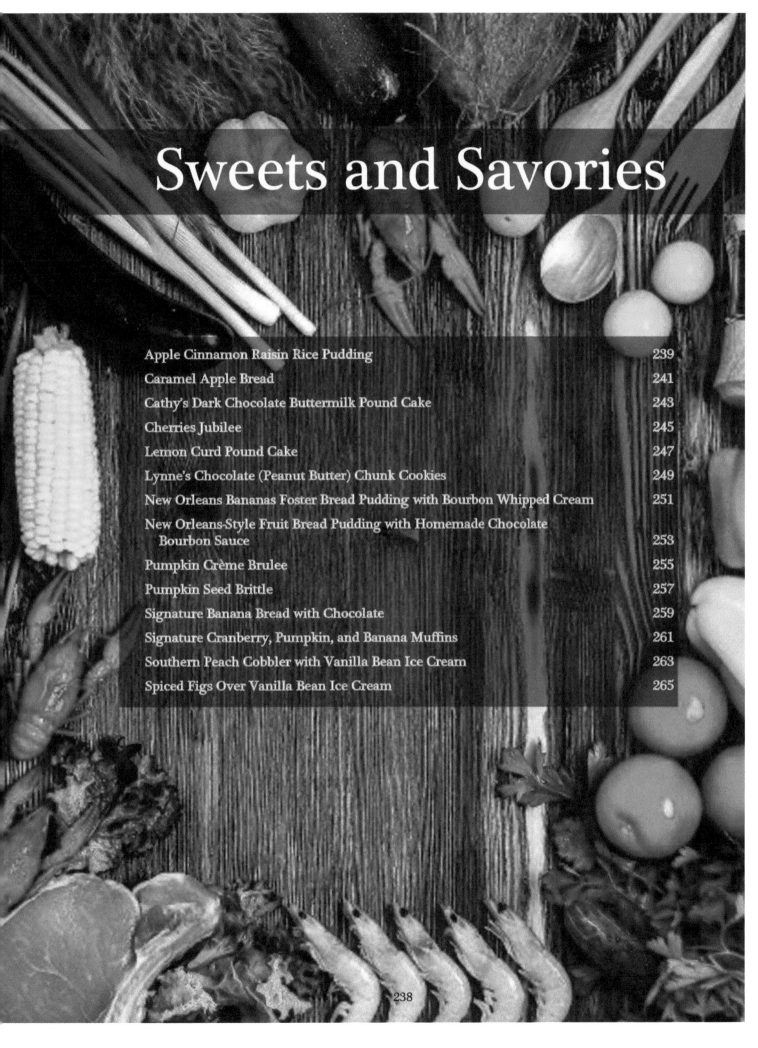

# Sweets and Savories

# Sweet & Savory

I grew up loving the taste and texture of a good rice pudding. As I recall, my high school cafeteria's version was pretty darn good! When I operated my catering company, "Cardie Cooks," I told my staff that I wanted to come up with a different style of rice pudding for people to enjoy. If our customer response was any indication, we had a lot of success with this tasty and unique creation! I think this is a dessert the entire family will enjoy. It is easy to make and can be eaten immediately but if you prepare it a day or two in advance, the flavors really get the chance to blend with one another beautifully.

## Ingredients:

- ◆ 4 large red apples (such as McIntosh), peeled, cored, and diced
- ◆ ½ cup raisins, soaked in warm water for 15 minutes
- ◆ 3 tablespoons unsalted butter
- ◆ ½ cup white granulated sugar, divided
- ◆ 2 teaspoons Saigon cinnamon, ground
- ◆ ½ teaspoon salt
- ◆ 1 cup Arborio short grain rice (see Chef's Note)
- ◆ 4 cups whole milk
- ◆ 2 tablespoons all-purpose flour
- ◆ 3 teaspoons vanilla extract
- ◆ Optional: unpeeled red apples, sliced (for garnish)
- ◆ Optional: whipped cream (for garnish)

# Apple Cinnamon
# Raisin Rice
# Pudding

YIELD: SERVES 8-10

## Directions:

♦ In a large saucepan or 3 quart Dutch oven, melt the unsalted butter over medium-high heat. Add in the peeled and diced apples, ¼ cup of the granulated sugar, 2 teaspoons of cinnamon, and ½ teaspoon of salt. Cook, stirring often, for about 5 minutes, or until the apples have softened. Remove from the heat and transfer the mixture to a large bowl.

♦ Return the saucepan to medium-high heat. Stir in the Arborio rice and other ¼ cup of granulated sugar. Pour in the milk and whisk in the 2 tablespoons of flour. Heat the mixture until tiny bubbles form on top. Do not burn or scorch the milk! Stir often to prevent anything from sticking to the bottom. Reduce the heat to low and cover the pot or saucepan. Let it simmer, stirring occasionally, for about 30 minutes, or until the rice is very tender.

*Chef's Note: Please, do not use long grain or Uncle Ben's converted rice for this dessert. Your local grocery store sells Arborio or Italian-style short grained rice.*

♦ Stir in the reserved apple mixture, plumped-up raisins, and vanilla extract. Combine well. Remove the saucepan or pot from the stovetop. Let cool for about 15 minutes.

♦ Garnish each serving with whipped cream and surround with sliced red apples. Sprinkle each serving with a little extra cinnamon as a final garnish. Serve at room temperature or chilled.

# Sweet & Savory

Do you remember eating caramel apples on a stick as a child? They were sold at nearly every amusement park or state fair that I visited. I loved caramel apples and cotton candy, even if they did put me into a "sugar coma." This recipe is great because it will provide sweet nostalgia without cracking your front teeth! Your kids will sing your praises for sure and it can even serve as a cute, little gift for your elderly next-door neighbor!

## Ingredients:

- 4 apples, cored, peeled, and chopped coarsely
- 3 large eggs, beaten
- 1½ cups all-purpose flour, sifted
- ½ teaspoon baking powder
- ½ teaspoon baking soda
- 1 heaping teaspoon Saigon cinnamon, ground
- ½ teaspoon nutmeg, ground
- 1 teaspoon vanilla extract
- ½ cup buttermilk
- ½ cup unsalted butter (1 stick)
- 1 cup light brown sugar, packed
- ¼ cup heavy cream
- Pinch of salt

# Caramel Apple Bread

## Directions:

♦ Preheat oven to 325 degrees Fahrenheit

♦ Spray a 9 x 13 inch bread pan well with non-stick, buttered cooking spray.

♦ In a large mixing bowl, combine the flour, baking powder, baking soda, cinnamon, and nutmeg. Mix well and set aside.

♦ In another mixing bowl, add and whisk the beaten eggs, vanilla extract, and buttermilk. Mix everything well with a rubber spatula

♦ In a large sauté pan, over medium heat, melt the 1 stick of unsalted butter. Add in the 1 cup of brown sugar and whisk together, stirring constantly for about 3 minutes. Add in the chopped apple pieces and continue to whisk until the mixture thickens a bit, another 2 minutes. Add in ¼ cup of heavy cream and stir well to combine. Let the mixture cool.

♦ After 10 minutes, fold the caramel mixture into the reserved, wet ingredient bowl. Stir well.

♦ Fold the dry ingredients into the wet ingredients until all of the flour has been completely incorporated. Do not over mix. Pour the batter into the prepared bread pan.

♦ Bake for 1 hour and 15 minutes, or until golden brown on top. Let the bread cool on a wire rack. Test for doneness by inserting a long toothpick into the center of the bread. If it comes out clean, you are good to go!

♦ Once cooled (about 15 minutes later), this bread should slip right out of the pan. Invert it onto a white plate, slice it, and serve. This bread can also be bundled in plastic wrap to keep fresh for at least 3 days.

# Sweet & Savory

I dedicate this recipe to my wonderful best friend, Cathy Van Hise, whom I have known for well over 45 years. Cathy is one courageous, beautiful, and caring woman. She has the same, indelible "fighting spirit" qualities that my late mother possessed and she loves chocolate. It seems that all of the "great ones" do! Anyway, do you remember the last scene from the hit show, "The Sopranos?" Of course you do! Who could possibly forget the scene when Tony took his family to the well-known, Holsten's Brookdale Confectionary in Bloomfield, New Jersey for ice cream? Well, Holsten's also has an assortment of amazing, homemade chocolates! I slowly melt some of their dark chocolate into a double boiler (but any good dark chocolate will suffice), and all I can say is, "OMG!" Pardon the pun, but with this recipe, you will have a real "hit" on your hands!

## Ingredients:

- 3 (4 ounce) bars good dark chocolate (for baking and melting)
- ½ cup unsweetened cocoa powder
- ¼ cup whole milk
- 3 cups all-purpose flour, sifted (plus ¼ cup for pan)
- 1 cup unsalted butter (2 sticks), softened and cut up
- 2 cups white granulated sugar
- 6 eggs
- 2 teaspoons vanilla extract
- 2 cups buttermilk
- 1 teaspoon salt
- 1 teaspoon baking powder
- Confectioner's sugar (for garnish)
- 1 pint fresh strawberries (for garnish)

CHEF CARDIE'S
# Cathy's
# Dark Chocolate
# Buttermilk Pound Cake

YIELD: SERVES 8-10

## Directions:

- Preheat oven to 325 degrees Fahrenheit.

- In a double boiler (or in a bowl over 2 cups of boiling water over a small Dutch oven), add the ¼ cup of milk and break the dark chocolate apart into chunks. Stir well and ensure mixture does not burn. Once the chocolate is completely melted, set the bowl aside to cool slightly.

- Spray a 10 inch Bundt pan with non-stick, buttered cooking spray. Sprinkle the pan with ¼ cup of flour. Set the greased and floured Bundt pan aside.

- In a large bowl, cream together the softened butter and sugar using a handheld mixer until light and fluffy. Slowly beat in one egg at a time and then beat in the vanilla extract.

- Using a wire whisk, slowly alternate adding to the bowl the 3 cups of flour and 2 cups of buttermilk at ½ cup increments. Add the salt and baking powder. Whisk or blend until the flour is completely integrated into the butter and cream.

- Using a large kitchen spoon or spatula, fold in the reserved, melted dark chocolate and cocoa powder. Fold the ingredients until everything is well blended.

- Place the mixture in the greased Bundt pan and fill it halfway up the sides of the pan. Bake for 1 hour and 15 minutes. Remove and check whether it is done by inserting a long toothpick into the cake. If it emerges clean, you are all set! Let the cake cool on a wire rack for 30 minutes. Remove it from the pan by inverting the cake onto either a plate or dessert platter.

- Dust the cooled cake with confectioner's sugar and serve with sliced or whole strawberries.

# Sweet & Savory

While I was attending cooking school in New Orleans during the late 1970s, it was required that students learn how to prepare three dishes tableside while working the "front of house" at various restaurants in the great city. Those meals were: Caesar Salad (page 53), Bananas Foster (page 251), and Flaming Cherries Jubilee served over vanilla bean ice cream. See how lucky you are? All three recipes are included in this cookbook! The restaurant patrons always thoroughly enjoyed our culinary demos and many of these entertaining "side shows" are still performed in upscale eateries such as Brennan's and Commander's Palace. Please make sure that any curious guests are not too close to you or the stovetop and that the little ones are under parental control and away from the flaming brandy. We want your kitchen festivities to be a "jubilation," not an "annihilation!"

## Ingredients:

♦ 3 tablespoons unsalted butter

♦ ¼ cup granulated sugar

♦ 2 tablespoons cornstarch

♦ ¼ cup orange juice

♦ 1 pound sweet cherries, pitted *or* 1 pound canned cherries (with juice) *or* frozen Bing cherries, pitted (thaw frozen cherries for 1 hour before using)

♦ 1 teaspoon orange zest

♦ 1 tablespoon fresh lemon juice (the juice from ½ lemon)

♦ 1 pint vanilla bean ice cream (can prepare and freeze servings beforehand)

♦ ¼ cup very good brandy

♦ Optional: 6 sprigs fresh mint (for garnish)

# Cherries Jubilee

## Directions:

♦ In a large sauté pan or skillet, over medium-high heat, melt the 3 tablespoons of unsalted butter. Whisk in ¼ cup of granulated sugar, 2 tablespoons of cornstarch, and ¼ cup of orange juice. Whisk everything together until slightly thickened, about 3 minutes. Slowly bring the mixture to a boil.

♦ Add in the 1 pound of pitted cherries, 1 teaspoon of orange zest, and 1 tablespoon of fresh lemon juice. Stir to combine well and then remove from the heat.

♦ Either place a large scoop (or more), of vanilla ice cream into each serving bowl *or* remove your pre-scooped ice cream bowls from the freezer.

♦ In a circular motion, pour into your skillet or sauté pan the ¼ cup of good brandy. Return the skillet to the stovetop and, using a long handled lighter or fireplace match, ignite the brandy. Wait for the flames completely subside, about 1 minute. Do not return the pan to the heat.

   *Chef's Note: When you return the skillet to the stovetop, you can also tilt your pan towards the open flame to ignite the brandy.*

♦ Using a large spoon or miniature ladle, top each bowl of vanilla bean ice cream with a serving of the hot Cherries Jubilee. Garnish the top of each bowl with 1 sprig of fresh mint. Serve immediately.

# Sweet & Savory

Cathy Van Hise is one of my dearest and closest friends, a courageous cancer survivor, and a serious lemon lover. When her doctor recommended that she incorporate more fruit into her daily diet, I knew I needed to create a delightful treat for her. This pound cake is layered with homemade lemon curd, making every bite moist and sweet! Needless to say, Cathy and her wonderful husband, Jim, went crazy for this recipe! You and your family will as well!

## Lemon Curd Ingredients:

♦ 1 cup freshly squeezed lemon juice (about 8 large lemons)

♦ 1 cup white granulated sugar

♦ 2 tablespoons lemon zest (about 3 large lemons)

♦ 3 eggs, beaten well

♦ ½ cup unsalted butter (1 stick)

## Pound Cake Ingredients:

♦ 3 cups all-purpose flour, sifted (plus ¼ cup for pan)

♦ 1 cup unsalted butter, softened (2 sticks)

♦ 3 cups white granulated sugar

♦ 6 eggs

♦ 1 teaspoon vanilla extract

♦ 2 cups buttermilk

♦ 1 teaspoon salt

♦ 1 teaspoon baking powder

♦ Confectioner's sugar (for garnish)

♦ Lemon slices (for garnish)

# Lemon Curd
# Pound Cake

## Lemon Curd Directions:

♦ In a 2 quart saucepan, over medium-low heat, add 1 cup of lemon juice, 1 cup of white sugar, the zest from 3 lemons, 3 beaten eggs, and 1 stick of unsalted butter. Stir constantly. It will begin to thicken as the mixture heats. Do not boil. Cook for 6-8 minutes, or until very small bubbles begin to appear. Remove from the heat and let cool.

## Lemon Pound Cake Directions:

♦ Preheat oven to 325 degrees Fahrenheit.

♦ Spray a 10 inch Bundt pan with non-stick, buttered cooking spray. Sprinkle the pan with ¼ cup of all-purpose flour. Set the greased and floured Bundt pan aside.

♦ In a large bowl, cream together the 1 cup of softened butter and 3 cups of white granulated sugar with a handheld mixer until light and fluffy. Slowly beat in one egg at a time and then beat in the 1 teaspoon of vanilla extract.

♦ Using a wire whisk, slowly alternate adding to the bowl the 3 cups of flour and 2 cups of buttermilk at ½ cup increments. Add the salt and baking powder. Whisk until the flour is completely mixed into the butter and cream.

♦ Place the mixture in the Bundt pan and fill it a quarter of the way up the sides. Take the reserved lemon curd and, using a tablespoon, in a circular motion, drizzle the curd around the entire batter. Repeat this process once more, or until you have reached halfway up the sides of the Bundt pan.

♦ Place the Bundt pan into the preheated oven. Bake for 1 hour and 15 minutes. Remove and check whether it is done by inserting a long toothpick into the cake. If it emerges clean, you are all set! Let the cake cool on a wire rack for 30 minutes. Remove it by from the pan by inverting the cake onto either a pretty plate or dessert platter.

♦ Once cooled, drizzle the pound cake with the remaining lemon curd. Dust the entire cake with confectioner's sugar and garnish each serving plate with lemon slices.

# Sweet & Savory

My lovely wife, Lynne, an excellent baker in her own right, turned me on to this recipe a long time ago. In fact, she just made a batch of these sweet and delectable treats for our immediate family and some of her closest friends. I tried my best to hide more cookies away for myself but it, unfortunately, did not work out that way! Oh well, better luck next time! Lynne also made these cookies for a teacher of the year party that we catered in Bergen County, New Jersey. They asked for something decadent and special in the form of a chocolate chip cookie and they sure got it! This is also a simple recipe that can be made year-round with your kids. After you do, give a batch of these cookies to an elderly neighbor, a local nursing home, or a medical rehab center. Just like the Grinch, your children's hearts will grow three times bigger that day!

## Ingredients:

- 2 cups all-purpose flour, sifted
- 1 teaspoon baking soda
- 1 teaspoon salt
- ½ cup unsalted butter (1 stick)
- ½ cup shortening (I use Crisco)
- ¾ cup light brown sugar, packed
- 1 teaspoon vanilla extract
- ½ cup granulated sugar
- 1 large egg
- 1½ cups semisweet chocolate (12 ounces) *or* 1½ cups Reese's Peanut Butter Cups, either chopped coarsely (be mindful of potential allergies)

# Lynne's Chocolate (Peanut Butter) Chunk Cookies

## YIELD: 2 DOZEN COOKIES

### Directions:

♦ Preheat oven to 375 degrees Fahrenheit.

♦ In a large bowl, sift together the flour, baking soda, and salt. Set aside.

♦ In a separate large bowl and using a handheld electric mixer or metal whisk, cream butter, shortening, brown sugar, vanilla extract, and granulated sugar together. Blend or whisk for 2 minutes at medium speed. Add in the 1 large egg and whisk or beat for another 30 seconds.

♦ Using a spatula, fold in the sifted dry ingredients. Add the 1½ cups of chocolate chunks or peanut butter chunks to the bowl and blend everything together well. Make sure you have incorporated all of the flour into the mixture.

♦ Using a tablespoon or small ice cream scooper, place 1½ tablespoons of the cookie dough onto baking sheets that have been greased with buttered cooking spray. This recipe should fit about 12 portions per pan. Space the dough mounds at least 2 inches apart from one another.

♦ Bake the cookies for 10-12 minutes, or until golden brown. Be careful not to burn them! Remove from the oven carefully and place the cookie sheets on a wire rack to cool for 10 minutes. Store cookies in an airtight container for up to two weeks.

# Sweet & Savory

This dish is entirely credited to Chef Emeril Lagasse, who, as a guest teacher at my culinary school in New Orleans, told us we would all eventually need to make Bananas Foster tableside. It turned out that we needed to make this dessert (as well as flaming Cherries Jubilee (page 245), and traditional Caesar salad (page 53)), at our restaurant placements to graduate, so he was totally correct! I lit one woman's hair on fire during one of my preparations (easy to do with all of her hairspray, in my defense), but I kept my job! I encourage you to make this historic, delicious, and epic dessert but please, keep small children or heavily hair-sprayed individuals away from the stove when you go to do the flambé!

## Ingredients:

♦   8 firm bananas, peeled and cut crosswise into ½ inch diagonal slices

♦   ¼ cup banana liqueur (I use Bols)

♦   ¾ cup dark rum (I use Myers dark rum blend)

♦   Juice from 1 lemon (to prevent bananas from browning)

♦   6 large eggs, lightly beaten (plus 2 egg yolks)

♦   1½ cups light brown sugar, packed, divided

♦   3 cups heavy cream

♦   2 cups milk

♦   2 teaspoons pure vanilla extract

♦   8 cups day-old French bread, baguettes, or croissants, cut into 1 inch cubes

♦   ½ cup unsalted butter (1 stick)

♦   2 tablespoons Saigon cinnamon, ground

♦   Confectioner's sugar (for garnish)

♦   Any good whipped cream, flavored (for garnish)

♦   Optional: 1 ounce good Kentucky bourbon (stirred into whipped cream)

# New Orleans Bananas Foster Bread Pudding with Bourbon Whipped Cream

### YIELD: SERVES 10-12

## Directions:

- Preheat oven to 350 degrees Fahrenheit. Butter or Pam spray a 10 by 14 inch baking dish.

- Peel and cut bananas into diagonal slices, ½ inch thick. Sprinkle with the juice from 1 lemon to prevent the bananas from oxidizing, or turning brown. Set the bananas aside.

- In a large bowl, whisk the 6 eggs and 2 egg yolks with ½ cup of brown sugar, 3 cups of heavy cream, 2 cups of milk, and the vanilla extract. Pour this mixture over your French bread and with clean hands, submerge the bread into the mixture. The longer the bread absorbs the milk mixture, the better your bread pudding. This process should last for at least 30 minutes

- While the bread is soaking, melt 1 stick of unsalted butter into a large metal skillet over medium-high heat. Add 1 cup of firmly packed brown sugar and 2 tablespoons of cinnamon and cook, stirring until the sugar dissolves or "caramelizes." This takes about 5 minutes. Add the banana slices and cook, turning them until the bananas start to soften and brown. This should take about 3 minutes.

- Remove the pan from the heat. Add the banana liqueur in a circular motion and stir to blend. Then, carefully pour in the dark rum, also in a circular motion. Place the pan back over medium-high heat and shake the pan back and forth to warm. This should ignite, or flambé, the pan.

    *Chef's Note: You can flambé your mixture by slightly tilting the pan towards the gas flame or using a handheld kitchen igniter. Let the flames die down and remove the pan from the heat. Let the mixture cool for at least 15 minutes.*

- Once the banana mixture has cooled, add it to the bread and milk mixture. Mix well and spread it to all sides of the cooking tray.

- Bake for 1 hour and 15 minutes, or until it sets with a golden-brown top. Serve individual servings of the bananas foster bread pudding with a small dollop of flavored whipped cream. Sprinkle your plate with some white confectioner's sugar for a dramatic effect. Hail New Orleans!

# Sweet & Savory

Bread pudding is a staple of New Orleans cuisine. It can feed a lot of hungry mouths without costing an arm and leg to do so and it is full of personality. There are many different recipes out there for various bread puddings. You can use the following instructions and make this dish as is or you can use these guidelines and then add some of your own flair! I made this recipe for my younger brother, Loren, a long time ago and he said it was one of the best tasting desserts he ever had. I will take his word for it because he is a great connoisseur of food and wine!

## Fruit Bread Pudding Ingredients:

♦ 5 cups any mixture fresh fruit (e.g. pears, strawberries, blackberries, blueberries, peaches, apples, pitted plums, or pitted cherries), cut into pieces. (drained, canned fruit, like Del Monte will suffice, but fresh fruit is always the better option)

♦ 3 (large) day-old French breads, torn into 1 inch pieces

♦ 2 cups heavy cream

♦ 1 stick unsalted butter, melted

♦ 1 cup whole milk

♦ 3 cups half-and-half

♦ 1 cup brown sugar

♦ 1 cup white granulated sugar

♦ 8 large eggs, beaten (plus 2 egg yolks)

♦ 2 teaspoons vanilla extract

♦ 2 teaspoons nutmeg, grated

♦ 2 tablespoons dry cinnamon

♦ ½ cup semi-sweet chocolate morsels

♦ Vanilla bean ice cream

♦ Optional: whipped cream or Cool Whip

## Chocolate Sauce Ingredients:

♦ 1 cup semi-sweet chocolate morsels

♦ ¼ cup whole milk

♦ ¼ cup heavy cream

♦ 2 heaping tablespoons brown sugar

♦ Pinch of cinnamon

♦ Optional: 1 tablespoon Kentucky bourbon

CHEF CARDIE'S

# New Orleans-Style Fruit Bread Pudding with Homemade Chocolate Bourbon Sauce

YIELD: SERVES 10-12

## Fruit Bread Pudding Directions:

♦ Preheat oven to 350 degrees Fahrenheit.

♦ Place the cubed croissants or bread in a medium, disposable aluminum pan (or 9 x 13 inch Pyrex dish), greased or sprayed with non-stick, butter cooking spray.

♦ In a Dutch oven, combine the cream, butter, milk, half-and-half, brown sugar, and white granulated sugar. Heat the mixture slowly and stir constantly until everything just reaches the simmer point. Turn off the heat and set aside.

♦ In a separate bowl, combine the eggs, egg yolks, vanilla extract, nutmeg, and cinnamon and whisk until smooth. Pour some of the hot milk mixture into the egg mixture and combine well. This process is called "tempering" (hot to cold, never cold to hot). Stir vigorously so eggs do not cook or scramble. Combine everything into one large mixing bowl and pour the entire cream mixture over the bread pieces. Stir to combine using your clean hands or a rubber spatula. Let the bread sit for 45 minutes at room temperature, or until the bread has absorbed most of the mixture.

♦ Add the fruit to the bread mixture and fold in the ½ cup of reserved chocolate morsels. Pour mixture into your buttered pan and smooth with a spatula. Bake, uncovered, for 1 hour and 15 minutes, or until the center is firm and the top has turned golden brown. Once baked, cool the bread pudding (without touching it), for 25 minutes on the stove top.

## Chocolate Sauce Directions:

♦ In a pot, combine ¼ cup of whole milk, ¼ cup of heavy cream, 2 heaping tablespoons of brown sugar, and a good pinch of cinnamon. Bring mixture to a light boil. Slowly add in the reserved 1 cup of chocolate morsels, stirring constantly until they have melted completely. Using a large spoon or spatula, drizzle the chocolate sauce over the top of the bread pudding, making long, lazy, and artistic lines back and forth.

> *Chef's Note: Bread pudding can be made hours ahead of time (or even the day prior), and then warmed in an oven at 300 degrees Fahrenheit for about 15 minutes. Do not burn or overcook the bread pudding.*

♦ Serve over vanilla bean ice cream and top with your favorite whipped cream or Cool Whip.

> *Chef's Note: In New Orleans, they add a tablespoon of good Kentucky bourbon to their chocolate sauce. Do not worry, the alcohol will evaporate out as it cooks so it is still very much "kid friendly."*

# Sweet & Savory

I began making crème brulee early into my culinary career. While I cannot remember exactly who taught me how to make this dessert, I do remember that once I got the hang of it, I was able to create wonderfully dramatic, and very tasty, dessert masterpieces. I demoed this recipe during my "Pumpkin Patch" cooking class in front of an approving crowd at Kings Cooking Studios in 2013. We all had a "screaming" good time eating these "spooky" culinary delights.

## Ingredients:

- 12 large egg yolks
- 1 cup granulated "sugar in the raw," divided
- 1 cup pumpkin puree
- 4½ cups heavy cream
- 1½ cups whole milk
- 1 heaping teaspoon vanilla extract
- 4 teaspoons cinnamon, ground, divided
- ¼ teaspoon fresh nutmeg, grated
- ¼ teaspoon ginger, ground
- ¼ teaspoon clove, ground
- Optional: whipped cream

# Pumpkin
# Crème Brulee

YIELD: SERVES 10-12

## Directions:

♦ Preheat oven to 325 degrees Fahrenheit.

♦ In a large saucepan, over medium heat, add the cream, milk, vanilla extract, 2 teaspoons of cinnamon, nutmeg, ginger, and ground clove. Stir until it reaches a slight boil. Do not burn or scorch. Immediately turn off the heat and set the pan aside for 15 minutes for flavors to infuse.

♦ In a large bowl, using a wire whisk, combine the egg yolks along with ½ cup of "sugar in the raw." Whisk until the eggs begin to turn pale-yellow, about 2 minutes. Using a ½ cup ladle, gradually pour the hot cream mixture into the cold mixture, whisking constantly, to prevent the eggs from scrambling. This process is called "tempering." Repeat this process once more. Now, pour the entire egg mixture into the warm milk mixture. Add the 1 cup of pumpkin puree and whisk well. Pour the mixture into 10, 8 ounce ramekins or 12, 6 ounce ramekins. Place them onto a kitchen towel-lined, large roasting pan. Add boiling or scalding water from a liquid measuring cup around the ramekins to form a water bath. The water itself should come about halfway up the sides of the ramekins. Be careful not to splash water into the custard mix.

♦ Bake until custards are almost set but still soft and "jiggly" in the center, approximately 1 hour. Custards solidify as they cool. Carefully remove from water bath and cool for 15 minutes.

♦ Tightly cover each ramekin with plastic wrap. Plastic should not touch custard surface. Refrigerate for at least 2 hours or up to 24 hours in advance.

♦ When ready to serve, preheat your oven broiler. Mix the remaining cinnamon into the reserved ½ cup of "sugar in the raw." Top each custard with at least one tablespoon of this mix.

♦ Twirl the ramekins in your hands using a tilted, circular motion and pour out any excess cinnamon sugar into the next custard. Place the ramekins onto a large sheet pan and broil (on the top rack), until the sugar has caramelized and darkened, about 2 minutes. Watch carefully and do not blacken the custards! Remove from the oven and let them cool for 2 minutes. Serve each custard with whipped cream and a slice of pumpkin seed brittle on the side (p. 257).

*Chef's Note: You can also buy (online or in any good culinary store), an inexpensive "chef's torch" or lighter. Instead of using the oven broiler, use your "torch" to brulee your custards' tops.*

# Sweet & Savory

A past employee of my catering company, "Cardie Cooks," taught me how to make this recipe. She was a fabulous pastry chef and dessert maker. She also assisted me when I did the "Pumpkin Patch" class at Kings Cooking Studios. We made this as a side dessert to accompany the Pumpkin Crème Brulee. Can you hear the "oohs" and "aahs" from where you are reading this? It is important to remember that a good candy thermometer is imperative to correctly prepare this recipe.

## Ingredients:

♦ 1 cup hulled pumpkin seeds, toasted (can buy at health food stores)

♦ 1 teaspoon baking soda

♦ 2 teaspoons vanilla extract

♦ ½ teaspoon salt

♦ 2 teaspoons cinnamon, ground

♦ 2½ cups granulated sugar

♦ ¾ cup light corn syrup

♦ ½ cup unsalted butter (1 stick), cut into chunks

# Pumpkin Seed
# Brittle

## Directions:

- Spray a large cookie sheet with non-stick butter spray. Do not use wax or parchment paper.

- In a small bowl, stir together the baking soda and vanilla extract. Combine well.

- In another bowl, stir together the pumpkin seeds, salt, and cinnamon.

- In a large saucepan or Dutch oven, over medium heat, stir together the sugar, corn syrup, and ½ cup of butter until the butter has melted and sugar has completely dissolved. Do not burn.

- Increase the heat slightly and boil the sugar and corn syrup mixture, stirring well until it turns a deep amber color and registers 293-295 degrees Fahrenheit on a candy thermometer. This should take about 10 minutes.

  *Chef's Note: Watch the caramelization of your sugar closely. Sugar cooks very quickly once it begins to turn color, so have all of your ingredients measured and ready beforehand.*

- Remove the sugar mixture from the heat and carefully stir in the vanilla extract and baking soda mixture. Stir in the pumpkin seeds, mixing well. Immediately pour onto the sheet pan. Using a spatula, slowly and evenly spread the mixture to fill most of the cookie sheet.

- Let the brittle cool to room temperature, about 30 minutes. Then chop or break the brittle into nice-sized pieces. Use them to garnish your pumpkin crème brulee.

  *Chef's Note: Brittle can be stored in an airtight container at room temperature for up to two weeks. This also makes for a great gift for someone special during the holidays.*

# Sweet & Savory

I have been making this delicious dessert bread for my family and friends for a very long time. Bananas and chocolate paired together creates a flavorful profile that will have you craving more. It is also a fun and easy recipe to make, so get your kids or grandkids involved. As you can see in the picture (and for the adults only), I like to serve this bread with a nice California tawny port wine on the side. Delish!

## Ingredients:

- ◆ 4 ripe bananas, mashed
- ◆ ½ cup semi-sweet chocolate morsels, crushed
- ◆ 1½ cups all-purpose flour, sifted
- ◆ 1½ cups granulated sugar
- ◆ ½ teaspoon baking powder
- ◆ ½ teaspoon baking soda
- ◆ 1 heaping teaspoon Saigon cinnamon, ground
- ◆ ½ teaspoon nutmeg, ground
- ◆ 3 large eggs, beaten
- ◆ 1 teaspoon vanilla extract
- ◆ ¼ cup vegetable oil
- ◆ ½ cup buttermilk
- ◆ Pinch of salt
- ◆ Optional: ½ cup crushed almonds or chopped pecans (be mindful of allergies)

CHEF CARDIE'S

# Signature
# Banana Bread with
# Chocolate

**YIELD: 2 SMALL LOAVES**

**OR 1 LARGE LOAF**

## Directions:

♦ Preheat oven to 325 degrees Fahrenheit.

♦ Spray a 9 x 13 inch bread pan well with non-stick, buttered cooking spray.

♦ In a large mixing bowl, combine the flour, granulated sugar, baking powder, baking soda, cinnamon, nutmeg, and chocolate morsels. Mix well and set aside.

♦ In another mixing bowl, mash your bananas with a fork or potato masher until smooth. Add the beaten eggs, vanilla extract, vegetable oil, and buttermilk. Mix well with a rubber spatula.

♦ Fold the dry ingredients into the wet ingredients until all of the flour has been completely incorporated. Do not overmix. Pour the batter into the prepared bread pan.

♦ Bake for 1 hour and 15 minutes, or until golden brown on top. Let the bread cool on a wire rack. Test for doneness by inserting a long toothpick into the center of the bread. If it comes out clean, you are good to go!

♦ Once cooled (about 15 minutes later), this bread should slip out of the pan. Invert it onto a white plate, slice it, and serve. It can be bundled in plastic wrap to keep fresh for up to 3 days.

*Chef's Note: On occasion, I have added ½ cup of crushed almonds or chopped pecans to this recipe. It made it even more delicious! However, be mindful about potential eaters having nut allergies, especially young children.*

# Sweet & Savory

I prepared this recipe on the nationally syndicated television program, "The Better Show," in New York City in 2014 where it was viewed by about 10 million people. The hosts and producers wanted me to prepare something healthy, fun, delicious, different, and with a distinct "Thanksgiving theme." I believe I delivered. They could not keep up with all of the requests for directions to make these delicious muffins. Now you have my special recipe all to yourself! Make some for family and friends and spread the joy!

## Ingredients:

- ½ cup dried cranberries, soaked in orange juice to plump
- 3 small bananas, mashed
- 2 cups pure pumpkin puree
- 4 cups all-purpose flour, sifted well
- 4 teaspoons baking powder
- 1 teaspoon baking soda
- 1 teaspoon salt
- 2 teaspoons cinnamon, ground
- 1 tablespoon ginger, ground
- ½ teaspoon fresh nutmeg, grated
- Zest from 1 large orange
- 1 cup unsalted butter (2 sticks), thawed to room temperature
- 1 cup white granulated sugar
- 1 cup light brown sugar, packed
- 4 large eggs, at room temperature
- 2 teaspoons vanilla extract
- ½ cup buttermilk
- Optional: ⅔ cup unsalted, raw sunflower seeds (for topping)
- Optional: turbinado sugar (for topping)

# Signature
# Cranberry, Pumpkin, and
# Banana Muffins

### Directions:

♦ Preheat oven to 375 degrees Fahrenheit and make sure the oven rack is in the center of the oven. Grease or spray two, 12 cup muffin pans, or use paper liners to hold the batter. Place the muffin tins on a cookie sheet.

♦ In a small saucepan, add the dried cranberries and enough water to cover them. Bring water to a boil, remove from the heat, and allow cranberries to sit for 15 minutes. Drain the cranberries and set them aside.

♦ In a medium bowl, combine the flour, baking powder, baking soda, salt, cinnamon, ginger, and nutmeg. Add the zest from 1 large orange (about 1 tablespoon). Mix well and set aside.

♦ In another small bowl, mash the bananas with a fork or potato masher and set aside. Using a hand-held mixer, in a larger bowl, beat 2 sticks of softened butter on medium speed. Add the white and brown sugars and beat for about 2 minutes. Add the 4 large eggs, one at a time, mixing after each addition. Scrape down the sides of the bowl. Add the bananas, pumpkin puree, vanilla extract, and buttermilk. Stir well with a large spoon or spatula.

♦ Fold in the reserved dry ingredients to your wet mixture until everything is well blended. Add the plumped cranberries and stir to combine.

♦ Using a tablespoon or small ice cream scooper, divide the batter evenly among the muffin cups and sprinkle with Turbinado sugar and sunflower seeds on top if you so desire.

♦ Bake the muffins for 30 minutes. Cool on a wire rack for at least 10 minutes. Carefully remove each muffin from its mold and serve.

# Sweet & Savory

I have had the great privilege to cook at several restaurants in the deep South over the course of my wonderful culinary career. One such location was in historic, fun, and exciting Savannah, Georgia. During my time there, I learned from some of the most talented chefs in the country and they taught me so much about Southern cooking and Southern living. This is one of their classic dessert recipes. Not only are you taking a bite out of history, but it is a cinch to make!

## Ingredients:

♦ 6 cups peeled and sliced peaches (fresh or canned but fresh is preferable)

♦ 1¼ cups white granulated sugar, divided

♦ 1 heaping teaspoon cinnamon

♦ ¼ teaspoon fresh nutmeg, grated

♦ Juice from 1 whole lemon

♦ ½ cup unsalted butter (1 stick)

♦ 1½ cups all-purpose flour, sifted through a fine mesh sieve

♦ 2 teaspoons baking powder

♦ 1½ cups whole milk

♦ Pinch of salt

♦ Vanilla bean ice cream (for serving)

CHEF CARDIE'S

# Southern Peach Cobbler with Vanilla Bean Ice Cream

YIELD: SERVES 10-12

## Directions:

♦ Preheat oven to 350 degrees Fahrenheit.

♦ In a large bowl, mix the sliced peaches with ¼ cup of sugar, 1 teaspoon of cinnamon, ¼ of a teaspoon of nutmeg, and juice from 1 lemon. Toss the peaches to coat well.

♦ Place a 9 x 13 inch Pyrex dish into the oven with only butter in it and let it melt completely, about 3 minutes. Once melted, remove the dish and set aside for a moment.

♦ In a separate bowl, add the flour, 1 cup of white sugar, baking powder, and a pinch of salt. Mix well with a whisk. Slowly add the milk and whisk until smooth and integrated with the flour. It should resemble pancake batter at this time.

♦ Spoon and spread the blended flour and milk mixture evenly over the melted butter. Do not stir, mix, or spread the batter with a spatula. Gently place your peaches on top of the mixture.

♦ Place the baking dish into the preheated oven and bake for 50 minutes to an hour. The cobbler is done when it turns golden brown on top and the peach mixture has started to bubble from the edges.

♦ To serve, spoon out some of the warm peach cobbler and put it in a nice dessert bowl. Garnish with a scoop of vanilla bean ice cream and enjoy!

# Sweet & Savory

I know that I allude to my childhood days quite a bit in this cookbook, but I make no apologies about it whatsoever. With special thanks to my mother, who was a fabulous cook in her own right, I was exposed to great cuisines from all around the country and those first encounters gave birth to a life-long passion for food. I love honoring these experiences by creating my own twists on things. One of my favorite cookies growing up were Fig Newtons and there is a reason they are still sold today. Figs may be an underused fruit in the current culinary world, but if you want to impress people with a dessert that is new, exciting, different, and delicious, I would suggest that you dig out this recipe for spiced figs!

## Ingredients:

- ♦ 24 dried figs, halved
- ♦ 5 cups tawny port wine
- ♦ 2 cinnamon sticks
- ♦ ½ cup white granulated sugar
- ♦ 3 tablespoons honey
- ♦ 3 tablespoons fresh lemon juice (about 1 large lemon)
- ♦ 2 teaspoons vanilla extract
- ♦ 12 strips orange rind (2 large oranges are needed)
- ♦ 4 garlic cloves
- ♦ 2 teaspoons Kosher salt
- ♦ 4 sprigs fresh thyme
- ♦ Vanilla bean ice cream

# Spiced Figs Over
# Vanilla Bean
# Ice Cream

YIELD: SERVES 8-10

## Directions:

♦ In a large saucepan or Dutch oven, over medium heat, combine the port wine, halved figs, 2 cinnamon sticks, granulated sugar, honey, lemon juice, vanilla extract, orange peels, garlic cloves, Kosher salt, and fresh thyme. Bring the mixture up to a boil. Immediately reduce the heat to a simmer. Cook the figs, uncovered, for 45 minutes, or until the liquid has started to thicken. Stir the mixture often during the cooking process.

♦ Using a slotted spoon, remove the figs from the poaching liquid. Put them into a large, deep bowl or small pot. Set aside.

♦ Strain the poaching liquid through a fine mesh sieve into another clean pot or Dutch oven. Discard any solids. Return the strained liquid to the stove and, over medium heat, simmer for another 15 minutes. Remove from the heat. After 15 minutes, return the figs to the sauce.

♦ Place a large scoop or two of vanilla bean ice cream into festive dessert bowls. Using a slotted spoon, position the warmed figs over the top of vanilla bean ice cream. Using a small ladle or spoon, pour the sauce right over the figs and ice cream. Serve immediately and enjoy!

TENNESSEE VALLEY
COALITION for the HOMELESS

Dear Reader,

Thank you for spending time with me and some of my most cherished recipes. I hope that you will make use of them time and time again.

Believe me when I say that real rewards come from sharing what makes your heart sing and from creating something that brings a smile to someone's face. Whether those smiles are on the faces of my loved ones after they have enjoyed one of my meals or complete strangers who benefitted from another act of kindness does not really matter. Why? Because all lives should matter to each and every one of us and we should strive to do what we can to make a difference!

There are so many people out there struggling with homelessness and you should know that by purchasing this cookbook, you have already helped the Tennessee Valley Coalition for the Homeless further assist some of those souls. So, thank you for spreading your own kind of joy to others and whatever you do in life, do not forget to 'Keep On Cookin'!

- Chef Cardie

# Cooking in Action!

# Index

# Index

Appetizers & Drinks ■
Salads ■
Soups ■
Side Dishes ■
Mains ■
Sweets & Savories ■

CPSIA information can be obtained
at www.ICGtesting.com
Printed in the USA
BVHW051948260620
582314BV00001B/1